FIRST CANADIAN EDITION

APPLICATIONS IN HUMAN RESOURCE MANAGEMENT

Cases, Exercises, and Skill Builders

W9-AXZ-414

FIRST CANADIAN EDITION

APPLICATIONS IN HUMAN RESOURCE MANAGEMENT

Cases, Exercises, and Skill Builders

Stella Nkomo
University of South Africa

Myron Fottler
University of Central Florida

R. Bruce McAfee
Old Dominion University

Fiona A.E. McQuarrie
University College of the Fraser Valley

THOMSON

NELSON

Australia   Canada   Mexico   Singapore   Spain   United Kingdom   United States

THOMSON

NELSON

**Applications in Human Resource Management:
Cases, Exercises, and Skill Builders
First Canadian Edition**

by Stella Nkomo, Myron Fottler, R. Bruce McAfee,
and Fiona A.E. McQuarrie

**Associate Vice President,
Editorial Director:**
Evelyn Veitch

Executive Editor:
Anthony Rezek

Senior Marketing Manager:
Charmaine Sherlock

Senior Developmental Editor:
Karina Hope

Production Editor:
Wendy Yano

**Senior Production
Coordinator:**
Kathrine Pummell

Copy Editor:
Elizabeth Phinney

Proofreader:
Theresa Crolly

Permissions Coordinator:
Cindy Howard

Design Director:
Ken Phipps

Cover Design:
Rocket Design

Cover Image:
Digital Vision/Getty Images

Interior Design Modifications:
Peter Papayanakis

Compositor:
Interactive Composition
Corporation

Printer:
Transcontinental

**Library and Archives Canada
Cataloguing in Publication**

Applications in human resource
management : cases, exercises and
skill builders / Stella Nkomo . . .
[et al.].—1st Canadian ed.

ISBN 0-17-625143-X

1. Personnel management—Case
studies.
2. Personnel management—
Problems, exercises, etc. I. Nkomo,
Stella M., 1947-

HF5549.A66 2006 658.3
C2005-907157-5

Correlation Table

TOPIC	CASES	EXERCISES	INCIDENTS	SKILL BUILDERS
AIDS	11		25	
Adverse Impact	40			
Application Blanks		44		48
Arbitration		98		
Benefits	11,64,65	35,68,69,96	75,77,78,79,88	
Bioterrorism		72		
Canada Labour Code		97		99
Career Development	50,52			
Collective Bargaining	95	96,97		
Compensation	1,62,63,66,95	67,70,71,96	76	80
Disabilities		22	24,45	
Discipline	1,81,82,83,84	23,98	47,85,86,90,91	94
Discrimination	9,16,17,40	19,20,21,22	10,14,24,26,45,85	27
Diversity Issues	9	23	10,14	
Dress Policy			85	
Employment Equity	17	23		27
Ethics	1,11,18	61,72	45,75	
Executive Perks		69		
Exit Interviews			46	
Family Issues		35		
Harassment	16	21		92
Health/Safety	11,51,65	23,72,73	25,74,75,77	92
HR Challenges		4		
HR Environment		5		
HR Forecasting				36
HR Functions	2	6,33		
HR Journals				7
HR Practices		3		15
HR Strategy	1,2,29,30	4,41		
HR Structure	2			
HR Trends		5		
HR Websites		3,5,72		7,8,15,37
Incentives	66,67		76,88	
International HR	9,11,12,13	23	10	15
Interviewing		42,43,44,97	46	
Job Analysis	40	34		49,57

(Continued)

Correlation Table (continued)

TOPIC	CASES	EXERCISES	INCIDENTS	SKILL BUILDERS
Job Descriptions		34		49,57
Labour Relations	93,94,95	98		
Layoffs/Downsizing	28		87	
Mentoring	51			
Mergers	30	4	88	
Motivation	63		87,88,90	
Nepotism			47	
Orientation	51		56	
Outsourcing		33		
Performance Appraisal	28	58,59,60,61		
Privacy Issues	82,83,84			
Promotion	1,17,50			
Quality Circles	94			
Recruiting	38,39	41		49
References		44		
Retirement			75	37
Safety/Health	11,51,65	23,72,73	25,74,75,77	92
Selection	12,13,38,39,40,81	42,43,44	10,26,45,47,85	48,49
Seniority			24	
Substance Abuse	82		86	92
Surveys of Employees	9			
Telecommuting		23		49
Temporary Employees			89	
Termination	16,81,82	23,31,97,98	89	
Testing	39,40,82	44	86	
Training	13,51,52	53,54,55	14,56,87	57
Turnover/Retention	63	6	46	
Unfair Labour Practices	93,95			
Union Organizing	93			99
Utilization Analysis				27
Violence at Work	83			
Wage Structures				80
Wage Surveys	62			
Whistle Blowing	18			
Work Schedules	32			
Wrongful Discharge	81			

Contents

PART 2

Meeting Human Resource Requirements: Job Analysis/ Design, Planning, Recruitment, and Selection 83

Job Analysis/Planning

Recruiting and Selection

PART 3

Developing Effectiveness in Human Resources: Training, Career Development, and Performance Appraisal 165

Orientation/Training/Career Development

Performance Appraisal

PART 4   Implementing Compensation and Security: Compensation, Incentives, Benefits, and Safety and Health 203

PART 5   Enhancing Employee Relations: Employee Rights and Discipline, Labour Relations, and Collective Bargaining 253

Motivation and Discipline

Labour Relations, Collective Bargaining, and Contract Administration

PART 6 Human Resource Audits/Term Assignments 305

Preface

The purpose of this book is to provide a single source of cases, exercises, incidents, and skill builders to supplement the basic text in human resource management. These materials offer a fresh approach to the management student based on dynamic, "real life" organizational events confronting both human resource managers and line managers who often implement human resource programs and policies. This book's contents are uniquely designed to increase analytical problem-solving skills and may be used in basic courses at the undergraduate and graduate level. Topics range from traditional applications of human resource management theory to the more controversial issues of AIDS, telecommuting, the financial impact of human resources, phased retirement, alcohol and drug abuse on the job, legislation addressing human rights and employment equity legislation, work and family, and the human resource aspects of merger activities. The settings cover a wide variety of organizations with an emphasis on the growing service sector.

This book offers opportunities for learning experiences in its six major sections: (1) Human Resource Management in Perspective: Environment, International, and Legal Issues; (2) Meeting Human Resource Requirements: Job Analysis/Design, Planning, Recruitment, and Selection; (3) Developing Effectiveness in Human Resources: Training, Career Development, and Performance Appraisal; (4) Implementing Compensation and Security: Compensation, Incentives, Benefits, and Safety and Health; (5) Enhancing Employee Relations: Motivation, Employee Rights and Discipline, Labour Relations, and Collective Bargaining; and (6) Human Resource Audits/Term Assignments. Each of these sections, except Part 6, contains cases, exercises, incidents, and skill builders. Suggestions for group projects and/or term assignments are offered in the final section of the book.

Most cases are based on actual events occurring in private and public sector organizations. All names have been disguised. The first two cases in the introductory section are designed to act as pre- and post-measures of the students' knowledge of human resource management. That is, the two cases in Part 1 can be used at the beginning of the course to pique interest in the material or at the end to test how much students have learned. The student becomes the decision-maker in these classroom-tested cases. The instructor may use the skill builders in Part 1 to prepare students to conduct research related to each case, or each case may be considered a class-contained learning tool. Questions are provided at the end of each case and incident to guide discussion, and/or the instructor may ask students to use the case analysis model suggested by the authors.

The exercises include opportunities for students to simulate the human resource work environment through role playing, identifying and solving human resource problems, and applying human resource management theories. The role plays require students to act just as they might in a real management situation. Virtually all of the exercises can be completed within 45 minutes and all contain a set of detailed procedures to follow.

The incidents are mini-cases composed of critical human resource management events and are designed to help students develop problem-solving skills. They are intended to raise questions around issues that don't have definitive answers and may be used to stimulate class discussions or to introduce students to human resource management topics.

Skill builders are short, individual assignments that can be completed by students outside of class. The skill builders develop the specific technical skills needed by human resource professionals and line managers to effectively manage human resources.

The final section of this book provides a set of suggestions for group projects and/or term assignments: a potpourri of field exercises, class presentations, group projects, and creative exercises to enhance the learning of human resource management. These projects are designed to be challenging and comprehensive by requiring students to draw upon material learned throughout the course.

The instructor's manual available online at www.hrm.nelson.com includes an analysis of the cases and incidents, solutions to the exercises and skill builders, and alternative approaches for using and presenting the materials in the book.

Acknowledgments

Many people have assisted in making this book possible. We are grateful to the following case contributors: American Association of Retired Persons, Joyce Beggs, J. Stewart Black, Gerald Calvasina, Susan Corriher, Diana Deadrick, J. Kline Harrison, Sam Holliday, Ed Jennigan, Ronald Karren, Margaret Foegen Karsten, Arno F. Knapper, Steve Maurer, M. Susan Taylor, and James Wimbush. Special thanks to Juanita Craig, Ralph Pederson, Jim Bavis, David Abernethy, Diane Marie Eckland, Rusty Rainey, and other friends who shared their professional knowledge and experiences in human resource management with us in developing materials for the book.

Stella Nkomo would like to thank the Graduate School of Business Leadership at the University of South Africa for its support in the revision of this edition. She appreciates the steadfast support of her husband, Mokubung, and her son, Sebenza.

Myron Fottler would like to thank his wife, Carol, for her assistance and input into the current and all previous editions of this book. Her contributions were particularly important in the development of several cases and incidents based on her own experiences and those of friends and relatives. He is also extremely grateful to Carol Cross, his assistant and friend, who has done a tremendous job preparing new materials and editing old materials for previous editions of this book.

Bruce McAfee would like to thank his wife, Chris, for proofreading, and Claire Anderson, Diana Deadrick, and Steve Maurer for their help and suggestions on improving the book. Finally, he is grateful to four graduate students who assisted in case development: Stephanie Fox, Kari Miller, Mike King, and Ben Robinette.

Fiona McQuarrie would like to thank Anthony Rezek, for taking the initiative to make the Canadian edition a reality, and Karina Hope, for her excellent editorial guidance. She is also grateful to the University College of the Fraser Valley for its support of this project. She also thanks her husband, Tom Barrett, for his research contributions and his many other demonstrations of support; her parents, Mike and Carol; and her brother, Michael.

Finally, we would like to thank our students for their invaluable suggestions for revising and clarifying the materials in this book.

Stella Nkomo
Myron D. Fottler
R. Bruce McAfee
Fiona A.E. McQuarrie

A MODEL FOR ANALYZING CASES IN HUMAN RESOURCE MANAGEMENT

Purposes of Cases

A case is a written description of events and activities that have taken place in an organization. Cases allow you to experience a different kind of learning—learning by doing. They are intended to give you an opportunity to actively experience the reality and complexity of the issues facing practising managers and human resource executives. While other disciplines like physical science allow you to test theories in a laboratory, performing a case analysis allows you to apply human resource management theories to specific organizational problems. The cases and other materials in this book will help you to develop your analytical and problem-solving skills. Cases enable you to analyze organization problems and to generate solutions based on your understanding of theories and models of effective human resource management (HRM).

Both a "decision-maker" and an "evaluator" approach are used in the cases. In the "decision-maker" approach, the primary goal is to sort the information given and to propose a viable solution to the problem(s) identified. In the "evaluator" approach, the human resource management decisions have already been implemented, and the primary goal is to evaluate outcomes and consequences and to propose alternative solutions.

Student Preparation of Written Cases

There are any number of possible approaches to analyzing a case. The most important point to remember is that case analysis involves decision-making. There is no absolutely right or wrong solution to a case problem. Your major task as a decision-maker is to present a coherent and defensible analysis of the situation based on human resource management concepts and theories. Just as managers in the "real world" must persuade their colleagues and superiors that their proposals are sound, so must you persuade your fellow students and your instructor that your analysis of the case and proposed solution are the best.

You should follow a few preliminary steps before preparing your written analysis. First, give the case a general reading to get an overall sense of the situation. Put it aside for a while, then read it a second time and make notes on the critical facts. Case facts provide information and data on attitudes and values, relative power and influence, the nature and quality of relationships, the organization's objectives and human resource management policies/functions, and other pertinent aspects of the organization. Keep two key questions in mind as you review the facts of the case: First, are there discernible patterns in the facts? Second, what can be inferred about human resource management practices in this organization from the facts presented? You should attempt to classify, sort, and evaluate the information you have identified in this preliminary step. Once you have a clear understanding of the critical facts in the case, you can prepare your written analysis using the five-step model that follows.

Written Case Analysis Model

Step 1. **Problem Identification.** The first step in your written analysis is to explicitly identify the major problem(s) in the case in one or two clear and precise sentences. For example, "The major problem in this case is a 15 percent increase in employee turnover compared to last year's rate." Herbert Simon, who received a Nobel Prize for his work on management decision-making, has defined a problem as "a deviation from a standard." In other words, one way to identify a problem is to compare some desired state or objective with the actual situation. A problem or series of problems may prevent the organization from reaching its objectives or goals. A key point here is that in order to define a problem there must be some type of standard for comparison. Possible standards include the organization's stated objectives or goals, objectives or goals of competing organizations, or standards based on normative prescriptions from human resource management theory.

Step 2. **Identify the Causes of the Problem.** Before proposing alternative solutions, the decision-maker must have a clear understanding of the underlying causes of the problem. HRM problems are usually embedded in a larger context. This means the decision-maker must examine internal and external environmental factors over time to isolate causal factors. Causes of problems tend to be historical in nature. To formulate a solid understanding of the specific causes, you should search for root causes and use relevant course concepts and theories to better define them. The "question syndrome" approach may be beneficial here: Why did the problem occur? When did it begin? Where does it occur? Where doesn't it occur? What has the organization failed to do? What else is happening as a result of the problem? Posing questions such as these will help you to probe beyond the symptoms to uncover the root causes of the problem.

The process of identifying the causes of a problem is very much like hypothesis testing. You should set forth possible causes and then test them against the facts in the case. In writing this section, it is important to present a plausible discussion of the causes so as to convince the reader that your analysis is correct.

Step 3. *Alternative Solutions.* This step involves developing alternative solutions and evaluating their contributions to resolving the problem(s) identified. The proposed alternatives should be consistent with the problem(s) and cause(s) identified. You should attempt to develop at least three possible alternatives. For many cases, you may be able to propose more than three. List each of your alternatives and the advantages and disadvantages associated with each. Keep the following criteria in mind as you evaluate your alternatives: time constraints, feasibility, cost, contribution to meeting the organization's objectives, and possible negative side effects. Developing a list of good alternatives involves creativity and avoiding preconceived attitudes and assumptions. It may be useful to brainstorm possible solutions before weighing their advantages and disadvantages.

Step 4. *Select the Best Alternative.* Indicate the alternative you have chosen to solve the problem. It is important here to justify why you chose a particular solution and why it will best resolve the problem(s).

Step 5. *Implementation Steps.* Now that you have a solution, you must develop appropriate action plans to implement it. In this section of your written analysis, you want to specify, as much as possible, what should be done, by whom, when, where, and in what sequence. For example: Who should implement the decision? To whom should it be communicated? What actions need to be taken now? What actions need to be taken later? If, for example, you recommend that the organization revise its performance appraisal process, give as much detail as possible on the content of the revisions and what impact you believe each revision will have. If you believe that there are potential difficulties associated with the implementation—even if these are outweighed by the overall benefits of the solution—you should identify these difficulties and suggest how they should be addressed in the implementation process to improve the chances of your solution successfully solving the problem. Finally, in this section you should also indicate follow-up procedures to monitor the implementation of your solution to ensure that the intended actions are taken and that the problem is corrected.

While these steps have been presented in linear fashion, case analysis does not involve linear thinking. You will probably find yourself thinking about all of the parts of the analysis simultaneously. This is perfectly normal and simply underscores the complexity of decision-making. To present a clear written analysis, however, it is important to write your report in the analytical form just described. As you gain experience with the case method, you will end the course with a better understanding of both your problem-solving ability and effective human resource management practices.

Pitfalls in Analysis

Students unfamiliar with the case analysis process often encounter the pitfall of jumping to a conclusion, which in effect bypasses analysis. For example, a student may readily observe some overt behaviour, quickly identify it as objectionable and, therefore, assume it is a basic problem. Later, with some dismay, the student may discover that the prescribed action had no effect on the "problem" and that the objectionable behaviour was only a symptom and not the actual problem.

Another common mistake is for students to reject a case because they think there is insufficient information. In real organizations, all desirable or useful information is seldom available for analyzing and resolving actual problems. Consequently, managers must do the best they can with the information available to them. Furthermore, the main issue in solving the problems of many organizations is to determine what additional and relevant information is available or can be obtained before adequate analysis can be made and appropriate action taken. If additional information is available, the manager must decide whether it is worth getting, whether it is meaningful and relevant, and whether it can be secured in time to be useful. Thus, an apparent lack of information in cases is actually a reflection of reality that students must learn to accept and overcome.

Students occasionally search for the "right" answer or solutions to cases and sometimes they ask their instructor what actually happened in a case. Although some answers or solutions are better than others, there are no "right" answers or solutions. What actually happened in a case is usually irrelevant— the focus of case study should be on the process of analysis, the diagnosis of problems, and the prescription of remedial action rather than on the discovery of answers or results. Many of the cases and incidents in this book were in the process of being studied and resolved at the time the pieces were written. Consequently, the real life outcomes were not always available. Although some of the cases do include what happened, no case is intended to illustrate either right or wrong, or effective or ineffective solutions to human resource management problems.

Human Resource Management in Perspective: Environment, International, and Legal Issues

Part 1

THE HRM FUNCTION/ENVIRONMENT

1. CASE

The New Director of Human Resources

Mount Ridge Engineering Systems designs, builds, and operates standardized, coal-fired utility plants in Atlantic Canada. These generating plants (150 megawatts to 650 megawatts) are built adjacent to industrial plants that utilize steam in their operations. Mount Ridge sells the steam to the industrial plant and electricity to the local utility. Garrett Levinson, founder of the company, firmly believed that the future of electric generation would depend upon coal as the primary fuel and standardization as a method of cost control and efficiency. This new technology, known as "cogeneration," is rapidly coming of age as many companies turn to these systems as a way to cut energy costs. Mount Ridge's very efficient plants allowed it to pursue a cost leadership business strategy.

When the firm was formed four years ago, Joyce Newcombe was hired as director of human resources. Newcombe had recently graduated with an M.B.A. degree from a large Canadian university. At the time of its establishment, the company had a total of four employees in addition to Newcombe: the president and founder, a senior vice president of operations, a vice president for administration, and a vice president of cost and estimation. From the start, Mount Ridge had both the financing and plans to build seven plants over the next five- to eight-year period. Joyce Newcombe was hired to develop all of the necessary human resource programs, plans, and policies needed to staff the plants once they became operational. She explained, "When I was hired, all we had was a dream and a plan. I had an office with a desk, chair, and telephone. I literally had to develop an entire human resource system." During the first year, Newcombe developed benefit packages for both corporate and plant personnel, an employee handbook, job descriptions, a salary program, and a supervisor's manual, and implemented other basic personnel policies. In less than three years, the company had built five plants. The size of the work force grew from 5 to 39 people at corporate headquarters and from 0 to 183 employees in the plants (see Exhibit 1.1 for the company's organizational structure). The company had been remarkably successful in a short period of time. Newcombe was promoted to vice president. In addition to having two plants currently under construction in Atlantic Canada, Mount Ridge plans to build an additional two to three plants in the Prairies. Forecasts indicate that the company will grow to a total of nine plants and approximately 650 corporate and plant employees over the next two to three years.

A major constraint faced by the company was the need not to compete for employees with its industrial hosts and the local utility. Benefits and salaries had to be competitive but not so high as to attract workers from Mount Ridge's "customers." In addition, since profits were to be re-invested into the business to finance future plant expansion, a profit-sharing plan was not feasible. Another important goal of the company was to remain non-union by offering employees a good quality of work life and attractive benefits. Balancing these two goals was often difficult. Low-cost production was critical to Mount Ridge's competitive position. The importance of these goals is reflected in the words of Levinson: "Mount Ridge places great value on its relationship with our industrial and utility clients. Our internal employee relationship has an equally important role in order to maintain an enjoyable and productive work force for the future. Management believes that companies that are good to their employees reap the benefits in terms of increased productivity and loyalty." As part of an effort to build this philosophy into its human resource programs, employee appreciation dinners are held annually at each of the five plants. The president and other corporate officers attend each of the dinners, which have been well received by employees.

Plant Operations

Most of Mount Ridge's plants are scattered throughout the region. Each plant employs approximately 45 workers. The typical plant structure is shown in Exhibit 1.2. Each plant is run by a plant superintendent who reports directly to the manager of plant operations and maintenance. While personnel operations are generally centralized at corporate headquarters, the plant superintendent and shift supervisor of each plant are largely responsible for the day-to-day administration of personnel policies. Newcombe stated, "One of our biggest problems has been getting management—especially plant management—to understand the legal and governmental regulations affecting human resource procedures." Although Newcombe had developed a detailed employee handbook and supervisor's manual, over the years there had been situations where supervisors had not followed company policy. Newcombe recounted one such incident that occurred in one of the older plants during her third year with the company.

The Termination

One of the first plants built was the Edison plant. It is located in a medium-sized rural community in eastern Nova Scotia and employs 45 workers. Bud Johnson had worked as an auxiliary operator for the plant for two years and had worked his way to that position after starting as a labourer. An auxiliary operator was responsible for assisting the control room operator and the equipment operator in the basic operations and maintenance of the plant's generating system. Over the years, Johnson had learned quickly and knew a good deal about the equipment operator's job. On many occasions, Johnson was asked to fill in when the equipment operator was absent or when there was a problem that no one else could handle. One day Johnson approached the plant superintendent, Larry Braxton, about a promotion to equipment operator:

Johnson: Larry, you know I can handle the equipment operator position, and I'd like to be considered for a promotion.

Braxton: That's not the point. We all know you are capable, but we just don't have any openings right now. Besides, the job qualifications require that you spend sufficient time as an auxiliary operator before moving up to an equipment operator. Just sit tight.

Johnson: Well, I hope some openings will come up soon. I really would like to make more money, and I know that I am qualified. You know I can learn quickly. Look at how fast I moved up from being a labourer.

After this conversation, Johnson was again called on several times to help out with the equipment operator's job and to explain the readings and gauges to Wilma Barker, one of the equipment room operators. When Johnson did not receive a pay increase or promotion after his annual evaluation, he met with Braxton and told him that he was dissatisfied with his pay and felt that, since he often performed the equipment operator's job, he ought to be paid at that rate instead of his present rate as an auxiliary operator. Braxton told him he would have to remain at the pay of an auxiliary operator and that he should be satisfied with that for the time being. Johnson became quite upset and stormed out of Braxton's office. The next day, Johnson did not report to work and did not call in to report his absence.

The company policy on absenteeism stated that when an employee is absent and fails to notify his or her supervisor, the employee may be terminated. When Johnson returned to work the following day, he told Braxton that he had decided to quit his job because he was very dissatisfied with his pay. Johnson was asked to sign a termination notice form, which was required by the company policy. He was told by Braxton that he would receive a copy of the form in the mail.

A week later, Newcombe received a phone call from Johnson. Johnson told her that the reason given on the copy of the termination form he had just received in the mail was incorrect (see Exhibit 1.3). He had not left to take another job but had left because he was dissatisfied with his pay and lack of promotion at the plant, and he had spoken with the plant superintendent about this several times. Johnson also told her that he wanted his personnel records to be corrected and that he had been asked by Braxton to sign a blank form. Johnson alleged that Braxton had added the incorrect reason after he (Johnson) had signed the form. Johnson also stated that he thought the Labour Standards Division would have something to say about this whole incident.

1. Discuss the relationship between the corporate human resources structure and the operations at the plant level. What impact, if any, did it have on the situation described by Newcombe?
2. How should Newcombe have handled this situation?
3. What, if any, disciplinary action should have been taken against the plant superintendent (Braxton) at the time of the incident?
4. If Johnson's allegations were true, what are the legal ramifications of Braxton's behaviour?
5. Describe Mount Ridge's business strategy. What is the relationship between its business strategy and its human resource practices?
6. What strategic human resource issues will Newcombe likely face as the company expands to the Prairies? How might this expansion affect the structure of the organization and its human resource department?

Exhibit 1.1 Organizational Structure

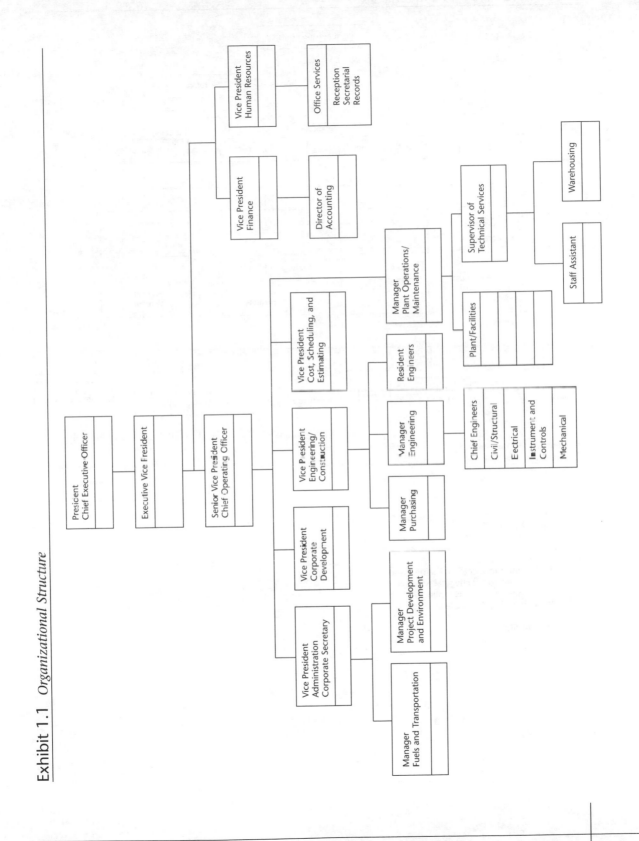

Exhibit 1.2 *Typical Plant Structure*

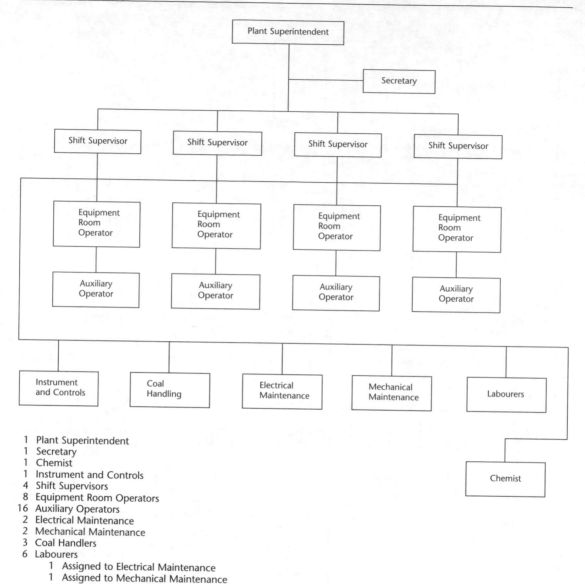

1 Plant Superintendent
1 Secretary
1 Chemist
1 Instrument and Controls
4 Shift Supervisors
8 Equipment Room Operators
16 Auxiliary Operators
2 Electrical Maintenance
2 Mechanical Maintenance
3 Coal Handlers
6 Labourers
    1 Assigned to Electrical Maintenance
    1 Assigned to Mechanical Maintenance
    2 Assigned to Coal Handling
    2 Assigned to Plant Clean Up

45 Total Plant Staff

Exhibit 1.3 *Termination Form for Bud Johnson*

NOTICE OF TERMINATION

This form MUST BE completed for EVERY termination

DEPARTMENT USE ONLY

1. SOCIAL INSURANCE NUMBER

| 1 | 2 | 3 | – | 0 | 9 | 7 | – | 6 | 2 | 5 |

Johnson   Bud   O.
2. NAME   Last   First   Middle

348 Bismark Street
3. MAILING ADDRESS   Number   Street

Enfield, Nova Scotia
City   Province   Postal Code

587-6089
4. HOME PHONE

Auxiliary Operator
5. JOB TITLE

6. Termination date	Last day worked
11/1/91	10/31/91

7. Recommended for other employment	8. Replacement Required
Yes ☐ No ☒	Yes ☒ No ☐

9. Immediate Supervisor   Phone

Larry Braxton

10. Plant Location

Edison

11. Sex   M ☒   F ☐

12. Ethnic Background

REASON FOR TERMINATION

13. LAY-OFF — No replacement required
☐

14. DISCHARGE
☐ Absenteeism (give dates)
☐ Not qualified (explain)
☐ Other (explain)

15. VOLUNTARY QUIT
☐ Leave of absence granted
   (ending . . . .)
☐ Dissatisfied pay
   (overtime, rate, etc.)
☐ Dissatisfied distance to work
   (miles . . . .)
☒ To take another job
   (employer, rate)
☐ Leaving town
☐ Dissatisfied working conditions
   (explain)
☐ Other (explain)

16. EXPLANATION (Use additional sheet if necessary)

PAYROLL DEPARTMENT

17. EMPLOYEE number   _____

18. HIRE DATE   _____

19. RATE   _____

20. HOURLY ☐   SALARIED ☐
                    Days $

Regular pay thru   _____ _____

Vacation   _____ _____

Severance   _____ _____

Pay in lieu of notice

Deductions:
   CPP   (_____)
   EI   (_____)
   Other, i.e., Insurance   (_____)
                    TOTAL $ _____

EMPLOYMENT OFFICE

Larry Braxton   *Bud Johnson*
23. Plant supervisor   24. Employee signature

_____, SIGNATURE ACKNOWLEDGES RECEIPT OF THIS NOTICE
          Date

SUPERVISOR'S REPORT OF TERMINATION

WERE WRITTEN WARNING NOTICES OR PERFORMANCE EVALUATION GIVEN?
   ☐ YES (ATTACH COPIES)   ☐ NO
WHAT WAS EMPLOYEE'S REACTION TO COUNSEL, WARNING NOTICES, OR PERFORMANCE EVALUATION?

REASON FOR TERMINATION. THE EXACT REASONS FOR TERMINATION ARE EXTREMELY IMPORTANT. THIS INFORMATION CAN BE ESSENTIAL FOR THE RESOLUTION OF SUBSEQUENT PROCEEDINGS RELATED TO THIS CASE.

_____

_____

_____

_____

_____

The Human Resource Function of Harrison Brothers Corporation

Company History

Harrison Brothers Corporation was founded in central Ontario on September 15, 1898, by Aubrey and William Harrison. Harrison Brothers is a multi-line traditional department store that deals mainly with men's, women's, and children's clothing. In recent years, the store's offerings have expanded to include household furnishings and other items for the home. The long-term goal of the company is to become a leading chain of department stores selling moderate-to better-priced merchandise to middle-class, fashion-conscious customers. Harrison Brothers is one of the largest privately owned retail stores in the country. A majority of its 20 stores are located in central Canada. Its largest store is located in a major urban centre and has 750 employees. The company is highly decentralized and maintains a very small corporate office.

Industry Challenges

Traditional department stores like Harrison Brothers are beginning to experience the effects of a number of changes in the retail industry. Not long ago, major department stores succeeded by being all things to all customers. However, today's customer is looking for both value and specialization. Superstores and giant discounters are also attracting shoppers. At the same time, the retail industry faces the challenge of keeping well-trained, highly motivated sales staff and management teams. James Harrison, who is currently CEO of Harrison Brothers, describes the company's strategic challenges for the next five years: "We can no longer continue to do the same old things that gave us a reputation for fair value. We must reposition ourselves—floor to floor—offering exciting brand names and excellent sales help, and promoting frequent sales. We need sales staff who know the merchandise and understand customer preferences. Buying expertise is also critical because fashion and consumer tastes never stay the same. We have five strategic goals:

1. Convert non-selling space into revenue-generating selling space.
2. Build up underdeveloped merchandise categories.
3. Invest aggressively in carrying well-known private brands such as Polo, Nautica, and Tommy Hilfiger.
4. Reduce costs through use of advanced computer systems to project sales and manage inventory.
5. Improve productivity of sales associates, buyers, and department heads."

James Harrison took over the business after earning an M.B.A. at a prestigious business school. Unlike previous family members involved in the business, he wanted to take a much more deliberate approach to charting Harrison

Brothers' future. To do this, he hired a consultant to assist in assessing the company's strengths and weaknesses. Harrison felt that employee quality and performance would be one of the keys to the future. As part of his analysis, the consultant sought to learn more about the human resource function within Harrison Brothers. He decided to interview a few of the human resource managers and other key managers at the store level. Both groups were also asked to complete a questionnaire of their perceptions of the responsibilities of the human resource function (see Exhibit 1.5).

The Westpark Store*

Brenda McCain has been Human Resource Manager at the Westpark store for the past four years. Prior to her employment at Harrison Brothers, Brenda had several years of retail experience, and came to Harrison Brothers after working as a buyer for one of its major competitors. She has a university degree in fashion merchandising. Currently, there are 750 employees at the Westpark store. The staff includes salespeople, sales support employees (dock, marking room, clerical, and accounting), maintenance, security, and management. The Human Resource Department consists of five people (see Exhibit 1.4). During the peak holiday season, a number of people are hired as floating sales staff. These temporary workers may number close to a hundred.

The Human Resource Manager's Job

Brenda talked about the Human Resource Department's areas of responsibility: "Our business has really grown in the last two years. We are carrying more specialty and designer clothing lines and have added items we hope will appeal to moderate- to high-income customers. When I came here four years ago, I found too many of the human resource operations being performed by the operations manager, Pat Hartlake, and one of the department heads, Rich Jenkins. Since that time, I have attempted to set up procedures and policies to assure proper staffing of the store. I spend most of my time just managing the Human Resource Department. I think it is important to keep abreast of the performance of workers, and I like to observe their work habits regularly. I also spend a good deal of time selecting applicants for the sales and support jobs. There is heavy turnover on the sales floor in our business, and the average salesperson at Harrison Brothers is either part-time, an older employee, or one who is 'inbetween jobs'—if a better job came along, they would snap it up immediately. For example, of the 119 part-time people hired in the last four months, 65 have left."

Brenda went on to explain their selection procedures: "The main sources of our applicants are newspaper ads and word-of-mouth by present or former employees. We select people based on how well they do in the interview. Right now, I conduct about 25 to 30 interviews a week and perhaps more during the holiday rush. I have enough experience in retail to know what it takes to be a good salesperson. We place a lot of weight on their motivation, personality,

*The interview at the Westpark Store reflects what the consultant heard throughout the company.

and drive. Little or no useful information is gained from high-school or university records or references. I do check their application forms for an indication of job stability, though.

"The training of new salespeople occurs every two weeks and every week during the holiday season. Now and then we get some employees who cannot effectively complete the cash register training. Our trainer, Joanne Flynn, tries to expose them to selling techniques and how to properly interact with customers. Although our trainer works full-time, I do spend a good deal of time with her and will help out if the training classes are too large.

"When I came here, discipline was a continual bone of contention between the employees and supervisors. Employees felt the present procedures were inconsistently enforced and applied. Each supervisor was administering punishment depending on his or her own interpretation of the problem. Now, I am totally responsible for all disciplinary actions. I discuss the alleged wrongful act with the employee's supervisor to assess the magnitude of the act. I then talk with the employee before deciding upon the appropriate consequences. In this way, we have better consistency in the application of disciplinary rules. Any employee who receives three disciplinary actions is eligible for dismissal.

"While we hire our salespeople at the minimum wage, we do perform an annual evaluation of their performance to determine merit increases. We use sales productivity as the major criterion. Performance is evaluated on average sales per hour. For example, say an employee works in an 8 percent department. The hourly quota would be calculated by dividing the hourly wage by the percent level. This determines how much the sales clerk would have to sell to break even. For any sales above that level, the clerk receives a commission. At evaluation time, if the clerk's sales per hour are above the break-even point, the new hourly wage is determined by multiplying the sales per hour by the percent level. For example, assume that a salesperson works in an 8 percent department and earns $8 per hour. The employee would have to sell $100 per hour to break even. Any sales above that level would receive a commission. If sales at evaluation time were actually $150 per hour, hourly pay would increase to $12 per hour (150 times .08). We have had moderate success with this system, although I'm not sure how much it helps us to retain good employees.

"For our sales support staff, we have supervisors basically evaluate the employee's quality and quantity of work. Last year, though, we incorporated a form of employee development into the evaluation process. Supervisors are required to discuss the employees' career opportunities and professional development with them. I initiated this as a form of career planning and hopefully as a way to keep good employees. Unfortunately, supervisors have been slack in doing the assessment. They seem to be more anxious to get the performance evaluation completed. Several employees came to me to say they have not received a 'professional assessment' since the program was instituted.

"There is a lot more we need to do here in human resources, but we are somewhat constrained by cost considerations and the realities of the retail industry. The work associated with the turnover in the sales areas gives me little free time to develop new programs and ideas."

Interview with the Store Manager

Jennifer Daft recently joined Harrison Brothers after being recruited from a major specialty retailer. Jennifer has a number of years of experience in management and retail. During the interview, she talked about her perceptions of the Human Resource Department in her store. "I think they are too internally focused most of the time. Brenda and the rest of her staff seem to be struggling to keep up with the day-to-day activities. I don't know if they are under-staffed or not. Our store has experienced very high turnover. With the new strategic direction of our company, however, I need human resources to be more of a key player. It's not hard to get the merchandise we want to sell, but we need people who know how to merchandise it and how to sell it to customers. There are a lot of changes going on in the company. It's not going to be a smooth ride for a while. We're all going to have to learn how to do things differently and better to stay competitive. Our human resource people are no exception."

Interview with the Operations Manager

Pat Hartlake, the operations manager, talked about interactions with the Human Resource Department: "I have a good working relationship with the Human Resource Department, but it took some time to develop that relationship. Brenda has a good understanding of the retail business, and I am impressed with her knowledge of store operations. The department has been somewhat slow in filling the vacant sales positions, and they don't always respond as quickly as they should. They seem terribly under-staffed and over-worked most of the time.

"Let me give you an example of what I mean. A few weeks ago, I was faced with an employee situation that was evolving to the point where I felt termination was necessary. I went to the Human Resource Department to discuss the case to be sure I had covered all the bases—with all of the laws today, one needs to be careful in making decisions. But the department never seems to be able to produce answers to questions without hedging. I had to wait almost two weeks before I got any help from them. In the meantime, the situation with the employee continued to deteriorate. I can understand the reluctance to terminate sales staff because of the difficulty in recruiting new people. In a way, however, the old system seemed to be a lot less complicated. Department managers knew how to handle situations that came up in their departments. Don't get me wrong! I know that as we continue to grow we're probably going to need an even larger Human Resource Department."

Questions

1. How does Brenda McCain view her role as Human Resource Manager?
2. What is Harrison Brothers' business strategy?
3. What is the structure and staffing of the Human Resource Department?
4. Analyze the data in Exhibit 1.5. What are its implications?
5. Given the organization's size and strategic goals, evaluate the development of the human resource function at Harrison Brothers. What problems do you see? How could its major human resource functions be improved?

Exhibit 1.4 *Harrison Brothers' Organization Chart*

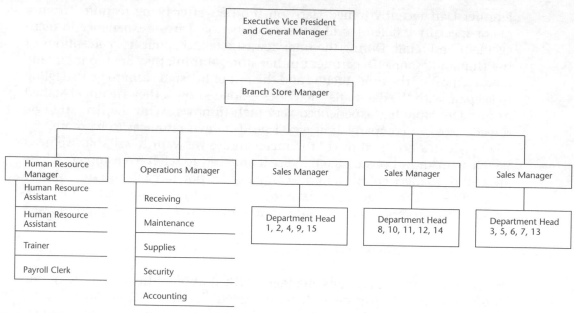

Department Identification

1. Children's (boys, girls, infants)
2. Shoes
3. Dresses
4. Men's
5. Women's coats
6. Fashion accessories
7. Intimate apparel
8. Furniture/Carpet/Bedding
9. Cosmetics
10. Domestics
11. China/etc.
12. Housewares
13. Fine jewellery
14. Sporting goods
15. Toys

(Each department head supervises several sales clerks.)

Exhibit 1.5 *Results of Questionnaire Completed by HR Managers and Non-HR Managers**

Human Resource Responsibilities	HR Managers	Store Managers
Staffing	4.5	4.5
Training	3.5	4.5
Performance Management	4.5	4.0
Compensation	3.0	3.5
Safety	2.5	2.5
Knowledge of Business	2.0	4.5
Managing Change	2.0	4.5

*Respondents were given a list of human resource responsibilities and asked to rate their importance to store performance using a scale of 1 (not very important) to 5 (very important). The responses were aggregated for all stores. The numbers in the table represent the mean ratings for each item. The questionnaire was completed by all of the human resource managers and store managers at each store.

3. EXERCISE

The Linkage between Human Resource Practices and Competitive Advantage

I. *Objectives:*
A. To familiarize students with human resource practices that may be related to competitive advantage.
B. To familiarize students with some additional human resource websites on the Internet.
C. To familiarize students with different Internet search strategies and search engines.
D. To help students to determine the relevance and validity of various human resources management practices in enhancing an organization's competitive advantage.

II. *Out-of-Class Preparation Time:* 30 minutes

III. *In-Class Time Suggested:* 20 minutes

IV. *Instructions:*
A. All students should review Pfeffer's seven human resource management practices (included here), which he believes enhance an organization's competitive advantage.
B. Students, in groups of three to five, will do an Internet search to find research, case studies, or expert opinions to support any three of these practices in enhancing any aspect of competitive advantage (e.g., profits, market share, quality, cost reduction). Each group will write a 2–3 page summary of their findings. Be sure to indicate which of the three HR practices seems to have the most and the least support. As an alternative, individual students may be given the assignment to research and write about one HR practice. In addition to generic websites and those cited elsewhere in this book, students may want to access the following human resource websites and their associated links:

http://www.bchrma.org/content/hre-sources/links/
    links_various.cfm

http://www.shrm.org/hrlinks

http://www.bubl.ac.uk/link/h/humanresourcemanagement.htm

C. Students will meet in groups of three to five during class to discuss their findings and prepare an oral report for the class (optional, at the discretion of the instructor).
D. One person from each group will report the group's assessment of their three HR practices on enhancing competitive advantage (optional).

Stanford University professor Jeffrey Pfeffer, in his book *The Human Equation: Building Profits by Putting People First* (Boston: Harvard University Press, 1998, pp. 64–65), identified seven human resource management practices that he believes enhance an organization's competitive advantage in the marketplace. These were:

1. Employment security: A guarantee of employment stating that no employee will be laid off for lack of work.

2. Selectivity in recruiting and selection: Carefully selecting the right employees in the right way.

3. Self-managed teams and decentralization: Encouraging the decentralization of decision-making, broader worker participation, and empowering workers to control their own work process.

4. High compensation: Providing compensation that is higher than that paid by competitors contingent on organizational performance.

5. Extensive training and skill development: Providing workers with the skills necessary to do their jobs.

6. Reduced status distinctions and barriers: Reducing differences in dress, language, office arrangements, and wages across levels of the organization.

7. Information sharing: Sharing financial and performance information throughout the organization.

Human Resource Challenges during Mergers

I. *Objectives:*

  A. To sensitize you to the actual and potential human resource challenges facing organizations contemplating or implementing a merger.

  B. To familiarize you with various human resource strategies and tactics for managing a successful merger process.

II. *Out-of-Class Preparation Time:* 30 minutes

III. *In-Class Time Suggested:* 50 minutes

IV. *Instructions:*

  A. In groups of three to five students, read the "Situation" below, as well as the merger challenges listed in Form 1.

  B. Each group will be assigned one or more of the merger challenges listed in Form 1. Search the websites outlined in the Internet Skill Builder in Part 1, the Internet sites listed below, or other sites to identify one or more human resource strategies and tactics to address each of your assigned merger challenges.

  C. One person from each group will present the strategies and tactics developed to address their assigned merger challenges.

  Useful websites for this research include the following:

  http://www.workforceonline.com/

  http://www.pohly.com/admin7.shtml

Situation

Katherine Montgomery is the director of human resources for a faith-based hospital in British Columbia. In addition to a B.S. degree in Nursing, she also has an M.A. in Human Resources Management and has been active in her local Human Resource Management Association chapter. Recently, Katherine has heard rumours that her hospital may be in merger discussions with the academic medical centre in the same city. The academic medical centre is larger in terms of beds (804 versus 658 beds), total revenue, staff, and external research grants. In addition, many employees of the medical centre are members of a different union from the staff at Katherine's hospital, and are covered by a collective agreement with different terms and conditions. Katherine initiated a private communication with her human resources counterpart in the academic medical centre and learned that neither of them has been involved in merger negotiations or planning.

Today, the city newspaper reported that the two institutions were into merger talks and the expectation was that a final merger agreement would be signed within three months. Katherine was saddened that her department had not been included in the initial merger negotiations, since she is well aware of the literature on merger challenges and has detailed knowledge of one health care merger failure in another city. She also strongly believes that the greater the degree to which human resources is involved in the merger process, the greater the likelihood of merger success.

As she contemplated her course of action, she listed the human resource challenges both organizations would face before, during, and after the merger. These appear in Form 1.

Until this time, she has not had to consider which human resource strategies and tactics would be most appropriate for addressing each of the challenges she has identified in Form 1. She called Professor Martin Smith in the Department of Management at the local university and asked if he or some of his graduate students could assist her in completing Form 1. With that input, she then intends to schedule an appointment to speak with her CEO in order to indicate how her department could assist in the merger process. Specifically, she plans to present him with a human resource plan for successfully integrating the two hospitals, based on the information in Form 1.

Form 1 *Potential Human Resources Challenges Facing the Merged Organization*

Potential Challenge/Problem	Appropriate Strategies/Tactics
1. Rumours, misinformation, and inadequate information	
2. Conflicting corporate cultures	
3. Different collective agreements covering different groups of unionized workers	
4. Neither organization fully aware of the skills, knowledge, and abilities of the other's management or staff	
5. Staff reconfiguration, which could include reassignments and/or layoffs	
6. Determination of which human resource practices to retain	
7. Management of staff morale and stress levels	
8. Turnover of valued employees	
9. Unclear job assignments and reporting relationships	
10. Lack of understanding of new policies and procedures	
11. Overall strategy to market the Human Resource Department's role and its potential value to the CEO	

5. EXERCISE

Scanning the Contemporary Work Environment

I. *Objective:* The purpose of this exercise is to help you understand the potential influence of trends and changes in the external environment on the design and implementation of human resource management practices.

II. *Out-of-Class Preparation Time:* None

III. *In-Class Time Suggested:* 20–30 minutes

IV. *Procedures:*

A. This exercise should be done in groups of four to five students.

B. After completion of the exercise, each group will present its ideas to the rest of the class.

C. Listed below are some of the major predictions about changes or trends in the labour/employment environment. Read each trend and list some ideas about the impact of these trends on the major human resource management functions: staffing and placement, training and development, salary administration, performance evaluation, job design, promotions, and career planning. In other words, what human resource issues will organizations face because of these changes?

Trend	Impact on HRM
1. Aging of the labour force	
2. Growth of prime-age workers (ages 25–54)	
3. Shift from a manufacturing economy to a service economy	
4. Increasing number of dual-career families	
5. Increasing number of women in the labour force	
6. Increasing number of minority workers in the labour force	
7. Increasing number of foreign-born employees	
8. Projected shortages of qualified workers in skilled trades	

Suggested Internet Resources

Human Resources and Skills Development Canada	http://www.hrsdc.ca
Conference Board of Canada	http://www.conferenceboard.ca
Canadian Centre for Occupational Health and Safety	http://www.ccohs.ca
Canadian Census Data	http://www.statcan.ca
United Nations	http://www.un.org
International Labor Office	http://www.ilo.org

Evaluating the Financial Impact of Human Resource Management Activities: Reducing Turnover Costs

I. *Objectives:*
  A. To provide you with practice in analyzing data and drawing conclusions regarding managerial implications.
  B. To make you aware of the potential costs of controllable, dysfunctional turnover and its impact on net income or profit.
  C. To make you aware of the potential benefits of human resource management activities to an organization's "bottom line."

II. *Out-of-Class Preparation Time:* 2 hours

III. *In-Class Time Suggested:* 45 minutes

IV. *Procedures:* Read the entire exercise, including the "Background" on Charlotte Manufacturing and the three exhibits. Using the data in the exhibits, do the calculations (on your own, prior to class) requested in Form 2. Then assemble groups of three to five students during the class period and discuss each of the questions. At the end of the class period, have a spokesperson for each group discuss the group's answers and rationale with the entire class.

Background

The North American garment manufacturing industry has undergone dramatic change and restructuring during the 1990s. Mergers, consolidations, and downsizing were the norm as organizations struggled to provide more cost-effective, high-quality service and products, particularly in the face of low-price competition from overseas manufacturers. The emergence of large-scale retailers has benefited the industry to some extent by increasing the number of potential sales outlets and the volume of sales for the manufacturers' products. However several of these retailers are so large and powerful that they are able to dictate to garment manufacturers exactly what products are required, what specifications the products are to meet, and at what wholesale price the products will be purchased. Manufacturers who are unable to meet these requirements may find themselves excluded from this potentially lucrative part of the retail market. This situation has created a great deal of competition among manufacturers and continual pressure to keep manufacturing costs low and production volumes high.

Charlotte Manufacturing has been in the garment manufacturing business for several decades. Originally it was a family-owned company, but in the last 20 years has been owned by a series of large corporations, most of whom also own many other businesses. Mr. Harry Majors became CEO 10 years ago; with several years' management experience at one of Charlotte's main competitors, he was hired by the corporation that purchased Charlotte at that time. Since his arrival, Majors and his executive team have managed to maintain Charlotte's relationships with most of its customers and its reputation as a reliable manufacturer. Despite this success, the company continues to be under pressure from its customers to further reduce its product costs while maintaining product quality and manufacturing cost-effectiveness.

Almost four years ago, Majors and the Board of Directors decided that the time had come to "professionalize" the human resource function because the retailers and wholesalers they were dealing with were exhibiting varying degrees of sophistication and vastly different policies and procedures. Ms. Betty Williams was recruited from another manufacturing business as the new vice president for human resources. Williams came to her job after completion of an M.A. degree in human resource management and 16 years of experience in the field. During the three years she has been at Charlotte Manufacturing, she has hired three new human resource management staff persons who are responsible for recruitment, employee benefits, and compensation.

As the board considered how to reduce the costs of production, the corporate office in general, and the Human Resource Department in particular, have come under increased scrutiny. Williams has been told she needs to justify the additional budget allocation to her department over the past three years. Exhibit 1.6 shows her department's budget for Year 1 (the year prior to Williams's arrival) as well as the three years since her arrival. The board has calculated the "extra" costs of the Human Resource Department over the past three years (using Year 1 as the base) to be $680,000. The largest percentage cost increases were in "salaries and benefits" and "equipment and supplies." Most of the latter increases were the result of upgrades in computer hardware and software.

The board has scheduled a meeting for next Monday. One of the agenda items is to examine the costs of the Human Resource Department, with the possibility of implementing a budget cut for next year. Williams has been asked to make a presentation to justify her budget and to show how expansion of her department has contributed to the system's "bottom line." She has considered a number of changes she made that she believes have improved overall system performance. Among these were the development of system career ladders to increase employee retention, in-house management training programs to improve management competence, development of "model" staffing ratios to reduce employee stress and burnout, quarterly performance reviews to increase employee feedback, absenteeism incentive programs, and initiation of an annual employee survey to identify problem areas.

After some discussion with her staff, she decided that it would be easier to "document" the benefits of increased employee retention. Exhibit 1.7 shows the decline in employee turnover for Year 1 as well as each of the three years since her arrival.

Williams and her staff have calculated the average cost of turnover per employee by personnel category and these calculations are shown in Exhibit 1.8. Most of these calculations can be documented from personnel records. The exception is the "reduced productivity during the learning period." For these calculations, the staff calculated the average monthly productivity for a small sub-sample of the individuals who left and compared it to the average monthly productivity of those who replaced them during their first three months. They then calculated the dollar cost of this lost productivity for a one-year period.

Their assumption is that the lower productivity continues at the same level for a 12-month period and then disappears. More realistically, the lower productivity probably declines over time but continues for longer than a 12-month period. However, they feel their method of calculation is a good approximation of reality since their overestimation of the productivity loss is offset by the shorter time period of their calculations.

Exhibit 1.8 shows that the total cost for each individual who leaves Charlotte Manufacturing averages $7,049, but this varies from a high of $14,484 for professional employees to a low of $3,644 for non-professional employees. These costs are divided into separation costs, replacement costs, training costs, and costs of reduced productivity (for the new employee) during the (assumed) one-year learning period.

Questions

1. Are the calculated benefits of reduced turnover sufficient to justify the $680,000 in increased costs associated with the expansion of the Human Resource Department? Would your answer be the same if "reduced productivity during the learning period" was excluded from the analysis?
2. In addition to improved employee retention, what are some other areas of potential economic benefit to the organization from having a Human Resource Department? What calculations would you do to prove such benefits?

Exhibit 1.6 *Human Resource Department Budget for Years 1 through 4*

	Department Budget per Year			
Budget Cost	**1**	**2**	**3**	**4**
Salaries and Benefits	$110,000	$233,000	$288,000	$324,000
Equipment and Supplies	24,000	39,000	48,000	57,000
Communications	41,000	62,000	73,000	81,000
Totals	$175,000	$334,000	$409,000	$462,000

Exhibit 1.7 *Annual Turnover Rate by Category for Years 1 through 4*

	Percent Turnover per Year			
Employee Categories	**1**	**2**	**3**	**4**
Executive (n = 127)[+]	12.8	11.5	9.2	8.3
Managers/Supervisors (n =167)	18.1	17.6	17.9	15.6
Other Professional (n = 315)	22.6	22.1	18.3	15.6
Nonprofessional (n = 1304)	29.0	26.3	27.1	24.3
Totals[++] (n = 1913)	23.8	22.3	21.3	18.8

[+]n is the average number of employees in each category over the four-year period
[++]the weighted average turnover rate for all four categories for each of the four years

Exhibit 1.8 *Average Costs of Turnover per Individual over the Four-Year Period by Employee Category*

Turnover Costs	All Categories[+] (n = 1913)	Executive (n = 127)	Managers/ Supervisors (n = 167)	Other Professional (n = 315)	Non- professional (n = 1304)
Separation Costs					
Exit Interviews	50.73	62.50	73.00	51.00	38.50
Administrative Costs	119.27	127.00	132.50	116.00	114.50
Separation Pay	348.01	2,254.00	1,034.00	—	—
Total Separation Costs	518.01	2,443.50	1,239.50	167.00	153.00
Replacement Costs					
Job Advertisements	1,346.49	1,805.00	2,416.50	1,127.50	953.00
Pre-Employment Administration	353.28	405.00	416.50	386.50	291.00
Entrance Interviews	324.86	486.00	724.50	284.00	148.00
Assessment Testing	271.69	382.50	695.00	214.50	105.00
Staff Time	249.00	417.50	522.00	212.00	126.00
Travel/Moving Expenses	293.68	1,215.50	1,110.50	—	—
Processing New Employees	87.50	87.50	87.50	87.50	87.50
Medical Examinations	175.00	175.00	175.00	175.00	175.00
Total Replacement Costs	3,101.50	4,974.00	6,147.50	2,487.00	1,855.50
Training Costs					
Informational Literature	80.00	80.00	80.00	80.00	80.00
Formal Training	147.53	340.00	516.50	35.00	35.00
On-the-Job Training	68.15	—	—	212.00	159.50
Total Training Costs	295.68	420.00	596.50	327.00	274.50
Reduced Productivity					
During Learning Period	3,133.37	4,000.00	6,500.00	3,452.00	1,215.50
Total Turnover Costs Per Individual	$7,048.56	$11,837.50	$14,483.50	$6,433.00	$3,528.50
Total Turnover Costs Per Individual Excluding Productivity	$3,915.19	$7,837.50	$7,983.50	$2,981.00	$2,313.00

[+]weighted average

Employee Category	Savings in Year			Total Savings
	2	3	4	
Manager/Supervisor				
Other Professional				
Non-professional				
All Categories				
	_____	_____	_____	_____

Calculation of Savings or Loss:

1. Total Incremental Savings from Higher Employee Retention
   for all Employee Categories for Years 2, 3, and 4.

2. Total Incremental Costs of the Human Resource
   Department Budget for Years 2, 3, and 4.   −$680,000

Net Savings or Loss   _____

Benefit/Cost Ratio = (1) ÷ (2)   _____

Reference Materials for Human Resource Management

I. *Objectives:*
    A. To familiarize you with practitioner journals, academic journals, and Internet sources used by human resource managers.
    B. To allow you to compare and contrast the types of information provided by each of the above sources.

II. *Time Required to Complete:* 4 to 5 hours

III. *Instructions:* You are to select one of the topics below or another topic approved by your instructor. After you have selected your topic, you should gather information on that topic from two articles taken from one of the practitioner journals and two articles from one of the academic journals. You should also find information from two Internet sources. The journals and Internet sources are listed below. Read the information gathered and prepare a short report in which you: (a) summarize what you learned about your topic from the sources, (b) analyze the differences and similarities of the information from the different sources, and (c) list the strengths and weaknesses of each source of information. Be sure to include a bibliography that cites the author, article title, journal name, date of publication, and the Internet address where the original source is located.

Suggested Human Resource Management Topics/Areas

Changing Role of the Human Resource Manager	Managing Diversity
Strategic Human Resource Management	Flexible Employee Benefits
Human Resource Planning	Performance Management Systems
Contingent Workers	Unions and Unionized Workplaces
Employment Equity	Executive Compensation
Harassment	Team-Based Compensation System
Executive and Managerial Training	Merit Pay
Dual-Career Couples	Online Recruiting
International Human Resource Management	Use of Intranets
Skill-Based Pay	Human Resource Information Systems
Gainsharing	
Telecommuting	

Information Sources

Academic Journals

Academy of Management Journal
Academy of Management Review
Administrative Science Quarterly
Human Relations
Human Resource Management
Human Resource Planning
Industrial & Labor Relations Review
Industrial Relations
International Journal of Human Resources
Journal of Applied Psychology
Relations Industrielles/Industrial Relations
Journal of Labor Research
Canadian Journal of Administrative
　　Sciences
California Management Review
Employee Relations Law Journal

Employee Rights &
　　Responsibilities
Journal of Management
Journal of Organizational
　　Behavior
Journal of Occupational
　　Psychology
Journal of Vocational
　　Behavior
Labor Law Journal
Labor Studies Journal
Organizational Behavior &
　　Human Decision Processes
Personnel Psychology
Public Personnel
　　Management

Practitioner Journals

Academy of Management Executive
Across the Board
Business Horizons
Harvard Business Review
HR Magazine
HR Focus
Management Review

Organization Dynamics
Personnel
Personnel Journal
Supervisory Management
Training
Training and Development

Internet Resources

University of Toronto Centre for Industrial Relations
　　http://www.chass.utoronto.ca/cir

Queens University Industrial Relations Centre
　　http://www.industrialrelationscentre.com

Diversity, Inc.
　　http://www.DiversityInc.com

International Foundation of Employee Benefit Plans
　　http://www.ifebp.org

Society for Human Resource Management
　　http://www.shrm.org

Human Resources and Skills Development Canada
　　http://www.hrsdc.gc.ca

8. SKILL BUILDER

Using Internet Search Engines to Conduct HR Research

I. *Objectives:*

A. To familiarize you with different Internet search strategies and search engines.

B. To acquaint you with some of the human resource websites available over the Internet.

II. *Time Required to Complete:* 1 to 2 hours

III. *Instructions:* This skill builder has two parts. Your first task is to pick a specific human resource topic and research it using the Internet. When conducting your research, select three of the following search engines:

http://www.google.com	http://www.lycos.com
http://www.altavista.com	http://www.overture.com
http://www.yahoo.com	http://www.ask.com
http://www.excite.com	http://www.webcrawler.com
http://www.alltheweb.com	http://www.northernlight.com
http://www.teoma.com	http://www.metacrawler.com
http://www.looksmart.com	

Then write a 100–200 word report that summarizes your findings. Specifically, the report should answer the following questions:

A. What *search strategy* did you follow in researching the topic using the three different search engines? Critique your strategy. Was it effective? What would you do differently next time?

B. Compare the three search engines used in terms of their ease of use and the usefulness of the information each query result provides. Overall, which search engine do you believe was most useful?

The second part of the exercise is designed to familiarize you with different human resource websites. Search each of the following sites and, in one paragraph, write down the types of information provided by each:

http://www.clc-ctc.ca	http://www.hrpao.org/hrpao
http://www.shrm.org	http://www.workopolis.ca
http://www.hrsdc.gc.ca	http://www.worldatwork.com
http://www.ccohs.ca	

9. CASE

Managing Diversity: Johnson Chemical International

Jeff Rice, vice president of corporate human resources at Johnson Chemical International, was very anxious about the meeting he was about to have with John Henderson (CEO), Gary Polaski (secretary and general counsel), Steven Hong (vice president of operations, Mississauga plant), and Matt Beale (vice president of public affairs and communications). The last two days had been quite tense in the company ever since an offensive e-mail (see Exhibit 1.9) was sent throughout the company's Mississauga plant.

Johnson Chemical International is one of the world's leading manufacturers of specialty chemical products. The company was founded in 1902 by renowned chemist Herman Johnson. Over the years, Johnson Chemical has built a reputation for producing high-quality products developed through cutting-edge technology and research. As a privately held corporation, Johnson Chemical does not report sales or earning figures. It has plants and operations in 30 countries and manufacturing facilities in 10 countries (Canada, Kenya, Indonesia, Greece, United Kingdom, Japan, Taiwan, Malaysia, Brazil, and the United States). Johnson Chemical employs more than 14,500 people worldwide. Its headquarters is located in Toronto. Employment in Canada is about one-quarter of its total work force worldwide, with a majority of those employees in the Toronto area. Because of its need for highly trained scientists and technicians, the company recruits a substantial number of employees with training in the science and engineering fields.

The Canadian manufacturing operations are conducted at the Mississauga plant near Toronto. The state-of-the-art plant is about three million square feet in size and is one of the most modern chemical manufacturing facilities in the world. The facility also has state-of-the-art laboratories and houses the company's research division. In addition to its hourly employees, the company employs a large number of research and development (R&D) employees consisting of scientists, technicians, and engineers. Because of its need for highly trained technical employees, the company conducts extensive recruiting at universities with outstanding science and engineering programs. A majority of its top management has come from the technical ranks of the company. Its current CEO, John Henderson, is a chemical engineer and the former president of international operations.

The Meeting

John Henderson: Come on in, Jeff. Good morning, folks. I want to thank you for meeting with me this morning. We have a major problem on our hands. A crude e-mail has sent a tidal wave through the company. It's already hit the press. We've had several calls from the media asking for us to comment on what has happened. Matt, how are we handling the calls?

Matt Beale: John, I have issued a press release that basically states Johnson Chemical does not tolerate any form of racist or sexist jokes and that the individual responsible will be dealt with appropriately. Our information systems folks are trying to determine the origins of the e-mail.

Gary Polaski: John, don't worry. We are on firm legal grounds if we fire the individual or individuals responsible for using the company e-mail to send racist and sexist jokes. I think we should take very strong action when we find out who is responsible.

Steven Hong: Well, we better do something fast because it is certainly affecting plant operations. People aren't working but are busy talking about the e-mail. I'm afraid that it really has taken people off track. It also seems to be unleashing some grievances that our female and minority employees have about their treatment in the company. The male employees, particularly the white ones, seem to be worried that they're going to all be blamed for the e-mail or, even worse, that everyone will think they agree with the sentiments in that e-mail. John, I'm worried about the impact of this on employee morale.

Jeffrey Rice: John, since the e-mail I have had several women and several minority employees, especially Asian employees, come to my office to talk about problems and other incidents in the company. To be honest, it has caught me off guard. We have an excellent employment equity program in place and have made some strides in hiring women and minorities in the last five years. [See Exhibit 1.10.] I am wondering if we've really done enough.

John Henderson: I'm not sure what you mean, Jeff. Our company has enjoyed a good reputation as a leader in the industry when it comes to fair employment practices. How could this happen?

Jeffrey Rice: Well, I was thinking about this last night. You know, John, in the last few years we have begun to have a more diverse group of employees after years of being a company with primarily white male employees. Perhaps it was only a matter of time before these tensions emerged.

John Henderson: Well, we're going to have to get a handle on the issues. Jeff, I want you and your staff to find out what the issues are and give me a report on your findings in 60 days. After we review your report, we'll have to determine what we need to do.

Get whatever help you need from consultants. I expect a negative media backlash on this thing, and we're going to have to show that we are a company prepared to deal with tough issues. I have prepared a company-wide message that will be sent to all employees this afternoon. [See Exhibit 1.11.]

Rice's Report

Six months after the meeting, Jeffrey Rice sent John Henderson and the rest of the executive staff a 20-page confidential report of his findings. Excerpts from his report are presented in Exhibits 1.12–1.18. With the assistance of a consulting firm, Rice organized focus groups with black employees, women employees, Asian employees, and white male employees. The participants in the focus groups were volunteers, and the group meetings were facilitated by the consultants to assure confidentiality and candidness. (See Exhibit 1.12.) The topics covered in the focus group discussions are shown in Exhibit 1.13. The views expressed by each group are summarized in Exhibits 1.14–1.17. In addition to the focus groups, an employee attitude survey was also administered to all plant employees. The results of the survey are shown in Exhibit 1.18.

Questions

1. Evaluate Johnson's actions in dealing with the e-mail.
2. Examine the data contained in Exhibits 1.10 and 1.12–1.17. What seem to be the most significant diversity issues at Johnson?
3. What is the cost to the organization of these problems? What will happen if they are not addressed?
4. Where and how do these issues need to be dealt with?
5. What support, skills, and training do managers need to deal with these issues?
6. What human resource management systems or policies need to be examined and possibly modified?

Exhibit 1.9 *The E-Mail Message*

The e-mail message

Morning Puzzle: Do you recognize these acronyms?

UFO

IBB

NAACP

Answer: UFO = Ugly ——— Orientals; IBB = Itty bitty breasts; and NAACP = ———, apes, alligators, coons and possums

Exhibit 1.10 *Employment Trends at Johnson Chemical in the Past Five Years*

- There has been a 10 percent increase in the number of employees at the Mississauga plant.
- The percentage of women employees in the plant work force has increased from 10 to 15 percent.
- The percentage of black employees in the plant work force has remained at 6 percent.
- The percentage of Asian employees in the plant work force has increased from 5 to 10 percent.
- The rate of turnover in the plant work force averages 2 percent per year, but this rate is 10 times higher for women and blacks.
- The percentage of women in management/supervisory positions in the whole company increased from 2 to 2.7 percent.
- The percentage of blacks in management/supervisory positions in the whole company increased from 1.5 to 2.0 percent.
- The percentage of Asians in management/supervisory positions in the whole company increased from 2 to 3.5 percent.
- There has been an 8 percent increase at the Mississauga plant in the number of scientists from minority groups (most of these are Asian).
- The percentage of women scientists working at the Mississauga plant has grown by 2 percent.
- The highest ranking woman in the company is Meredith Jensen, vice president and deputy counsel.
- The highest ranking black manager is Bill Jones, vice president for equal opportunity and employee relations.
- The highest ranking Asian manager is Steven Hong, vice president of operations, Mississauga plant.

Exhibit 1.11 *Letter to Employees from John Henderson, CEO*

Dear Johnson Employees:

By now, you have heard about the e-mail that was sent through the company's computer system that contained offensive comments. I want to be very clear. We will not tolerate behaviour that makes our work environment uncomfortable and hostile for others. Racist, sexist, and offensive comments are not appropriate at Johnson Chemical. These comments are disrespectful of fellow employees. Using company e-mail to perpetuate offensive views of others violates company policy. Rest assured that we will see that those responsible for sending the e-mail are duly disciplined.

I am counting on you to respect your fellow employees and to commit to ensuring a working climate that is tolerant of our diversity.

John Henderson

John Henderson

Exhibit 1.12 *Letter of Invitation to Participate in Focus Group Discussions*

As you know, we continue to be committed to having an equal opportunity work climate at Johnson. In an effort to achieve this goal, we invite you to participate in a focus group to help us collect data around issues of diversity. The focus groups will be organized so that we bring together different categories of employee groups over the next two months.

To assure confidentiality and anonymity, the actual discussion sessions will be facilitated by an outside consultant group we have contracted to assist us in our efforts. Discussion will focus on your experiences and thoughts on topics related to our human resource policies and systems, and our work climate.

I hope you will be willing to participate in one of the focus groups. Thank you in advance for your help. If you have any questions, please call my office. I'll be happy to provide additional information.

Sincerely,

Jeffrey Rice

Jeffrey Rice, Vice President
Corporate Human Resources

Exhibit 1.13 *Focus Group Discussion Guidelines*

1. Comment on your experience and view of the following areas of the company:
   A. Recruitment and hiring: Sources of recruits; selection criteria; orientation of new employees
   B. Promotion: Fairness of rating system; adequacy of opportunity
   C. Training and career development: Access to training; selection of trainees; adequacy of and availability of career development counselling
   D. Performance management: Pros and cons of the performance appraisal process; supervisor feedback
   E. Benefits: Adequacy; administration of benefits
   F. Employment equity program: Effectiveness of efforts to equalize opportunities for hiring, training, or promotion; attitudes toward those who benefit from the implementation of this program
   G. Treatment: Personal experiences of bias or barriers because of one's race, ethnicity or gender, or other areas

Exhibit 1.14 *Statements Made by Participants in Black Employee Focus Group*

- Recruitment of black scientists and engineers is inadequate.
- Blacks have to be "more qualified" than other groups to get a job in the company.
- Black students participate in summer intern programs but are rarely hired as full-time employees.
- Blacks do not have access to the same training and development opportunities as white employees. The selection for training and development is made by supervisors. This allows supervisors with negative views of the potential of black employees to control who gets access to training.
- The promotion system is driven by potential ratings given by supervisors, and blacks are disproportionately given low potential ratings for promotability.
- White supervisors are not comfortable working with black employees, and many supervisors do not know how to give helpful performance feedback.
- Most of the black employees are pigeonholed into staff positions in management.
- Blacks can't break into the "informal network," and are excluded from many social activities.
- Because there are so few blacks in higher level positions, there are no mentors and role models for lower-level black employees.
- Blacks are stereotyped as being non-technical, lazy, and not suitable for management.
- Racial slurs and jokes are often heard on the plant floor.
- There is the "rule of three"—no three black employees should be seen together in the cafeteria or other places. If so, majority group employees assume something is going on or ask, "Why are the black employees all eating together?"

Exhibit 1.15 *Statements Made by Participants in Female Employee Focus Groups*

- Women are not treated as individuals but as sex-role stereotypes. They are seen as emotional, non-technical, and subordinate. Women who display non-stereotypical behaviours (e.g., being assertive, having good technical skills) are characterized as "pushy" or "macho."
- A myth persists that many of the women in the company don't need to work because they have husbands or partners with full-time jobs who could support them.
- Many male supervisors don't know how to work with women as peers, and therefore treat female subordinates in condescending ways.
- Women are often made to feel that their ideas are inconsequential. They are cut off in meetings, especially when a woman is the only female in a group meeting.
- There are too few women in management and supervisory positions.
- None of the top women in the company are in line positions.
- There are no women in senior management.
- Women receive lower ratings for promotion potential than the men in the company.
- Women are excluded from the "old boys" network.
- Women are always being tested with offensive sexual jokes or comments.
- Employment equity programs stigmatize women and make them look like victims rather than leaders.
- Company benefits do not include programs to help women balance work and family.

Exhibit 1.16 *Statements Made by Participants in Asian Employee Focus Groups*

- Asian employees are stereotyped as having excellent technical skills but not having the skills needed for management positions.
- Asian employees are not promoted because supervisors tend to give them low ratings on communication skills.
- Asian employees are stigmatized by the employment equity program and shouldn't be lumped with other minority groups in the company.
- There are a very small number of Asian managers in the company relative to the number of Asian employees in the company's total work force.
- Most employees are ignorant of the diversity among Asian employees with different cultural backgrounds (e.g., Chinese, Korean, Japanese).

Exhibit 1.17 *Statements Made by Participants in White Male Employee Focus Groups*

- White men are stereotyped as racist and sexist.
- The company's employment equity program has taken opportunities away from white employees.
- White supervisors have to be careful when managing minority employees.
- Black employees are hostile toward white supervisors.
- The company's focus on employment equity doesn't include white men.
- Women employees are overly sensitive; plant environments are tough.

Exhibit 1.18 *Results of Employee Survey: Percentage of Employees with Favourable Responses*

Question	All Employees	Black	Asian	Women
My department is effectively managed.	75	57	74	60
People in my department have the skills and abilities to be an effective team.	85	79	82	78
I feel proud to work at Johnson.	75	60	70	61
I am satisfied with my opportunity to get a better job.	79	39	65	44
I like the work I do.	85	75	84	74
My manager gives me feedback that helps improve my performance.	52	38	51	35
My department has a climate that respects employee diversity.	65	49	60	48
My manager is sensitive to the relationship between my work life and my personal life.	61	58	59	49
My supervisor applies company policies and rules regardless of the individual's personal characteristics (e.g., race, gender).	77	54	65	55

Too Much Diversity?

Bill Baldwin, president and founder of Baldwin Scientific Instruments, had just finished meeting with Tran, a Baldwin assembler of Vietnamese descent. Tran was very upset about the treatment that he and his Vietnamese coworkers had been receiving from their first-line supervisors, a brother and sister who were originally from Peru. Tran had reported that the two supervisors did not respect any of the 10 Vietnamese assemblers, that they were intentionally mean and rude to them, and that they spoke negatively about them in Spanish behind their backs. Tran pointed out that the assemblers were the key to the firm's success, and asked the president to take immediate action to restore the respect they deserved.

Bill was aware that distrust and friction existed between the Latino and Vietnamese employees. Fortunately, there had never been any fights or even loud arguments. However, he noticed that during lunch both groups sat apart and spoke in their native languages. At the annual company summer picnic and Christmas party, both groups also sat separately, and, while cordial, were never very friendly toward one another. Bill realized that part of the problem might be that Latinos were often in supervisory positions whereas the Vietnamese were mostly assemblers. This structure reflected the fact that the Latino supervisors had far more experience and length of service than the new employees of Vietnamese descent. Bill also realized that another part of the problem might be that the head of the assembly department, a Canadian-born Latino who was responsible for the first-line supervisors, was an ineffective leader who refused to address employee relations problems. He knew a lot about assembling instruments, but allowed problems to fester between different parts of the work force rather than solving them.

As Bill was pondering what should be done, the sales manager walked into the office and gleefully announced that another large order had just come in. Bill knew this would necessitate the hiring of five more skilled assemblers, and that advertisements in the area newspapers would result in mostly Latino and Vietnamese applicants. He wondered what the firm's hiring policy should be, given that he did not want to create more problems.

Questions

1. If you were Bill, what actions would you take in response to Tran's request?
2. What hiring policy should the firm follow?
3. Does the firm have too diverse a work force?

African Gold, Inc.—Ethics and AIDS in the Workplace

Harry Goldstone, head of human resources for African Gold, Inc., in South Africa, examined the stack of newspaper and business magazine clippings on his desk. In the last few weeks, there had been numerous stories about the company's decision not to continue paying transport, coffin, and funeral costs for employees who die from non-mining-related causes. The decision was linked to the depletion of the funding source normally used to cover these costs. In the last two years, the fund had decreased rapidly because of the increasing number of HIV/AIDS deaths among miners working for African Gold, Inc., in South Africa. The company planned to continue its education program on HIV/AIDS for employees.

Although African Gold did not have exact figures of the prevalence of HIV/AIDS among its present labour force, recent company data indicated that, countrywide, there was an average of 20 funerals a month for workers who had succumbed to the disease. The average cost of a funeral is 10,000 rands (about $1,800). Additionally, the costs of the company's medical aid and disability programs were also skyrocketing because of the costs of treatment for HIV/AIDS-related diseases (e.g., tuberculosis, pneumonia). Goldstone also realized that these amounts would be even higher if the cost of absenteeism, productivity losses, recruitment, and training were calculated. The increased costs were coming at a time when the profits of many gold mining companies were falling because of the growing strength of South African currency (i.e., the rand). The price of gold in rand terms had fallen 6 percent over the last few quarters. Decreasing profits hit smaller mining companies like African Gold, Inc., greater than the largest producers.

The number of HIV/AIDS-related deaths as a proportion of total deaths in South Africa virtually doubled from 4.6 percent to 8.7 percent between 1997 and 2001. South Africa has one of the fastest growing HIV epidemics in the world with an estimated 1,700 new infections diagnosed daily. Additionally, the mining industry in South Africa has the highest prevalence of HIV/AIDS infections compared to other industries. It is estimated that 24 percent of underground miners have HIV, compared to 19.9 percent of the remainder of the South African working population.

The change in company policy holds potentially devastating financial implications for families of mine workers, many of whom live hundreds of miles away from African Gold, Inc.'s mining operations. The mining industry in South Africa has always relied heavily upon migrant labour from neighbouring countries such as Lesotho, Botswana, Malawi, Zimbabwe, Swaziland, and Mozambique. Because of the industry's reliance on inexpensive migrant labour, many of the workers live in housing at the mine site and spend months away from their families. Some health experts believe that this may contribute to the higher incidence of HIV/AIDS among mine workers. Most families cannot afford to pay for the funerals since the average mine worker earns about 2,000 rands per month (about $350).

In addition to the negative media coverage, Goldstone was also faced with challenges from the National Union of Mine Workers. In a memorandum sent to Goldstone, the union accused the company of hiding behind excuses to avoid dealing with the problem of HIV/AIDS in the workplace. They argued that the company's decision was unethical and that African Gold, Inc. could well afford to continue the funeral benefits for its work force. In the memorandum, the union threatened further action if the company did not reinstate the benefits.

Questions

1. Did African Gold, Inc. make the right decision? Should an organization be expected to go beyond legally mandated benefits to help workers with a devastating illness like HIV/AIDS?
2. What responsibility, if any, does African Gold have to its workers?

12. CASE

Selecting a Manager for a Nigerian Facility

Victoria Oilfield Equipment is a supplier of drilling equipment for oil and gas exploration. Its headquarters is located near Calgary, Alberta. The company has seven offices and warehousing facilities near potential markets for its equipment. Only 30 percent of Victoria's profits come from selling equipment; the rest comes from leasing. Within its leasing operations, half the profit comes from supplying operators for the equipment. Victoria has over 25 years of experience in the Canadian oilfields, and 10 years of experience in several Latin American countries. Most of its customers are large multinational oil companies. However, approximately 20 percent of its contracts are with small, independent exploration companies.

Victoria has just completed construction of a new facility near Port Harcout, Nigeria—its first venture into Africa. The machinery, trucks, and equipment to operate this facility are to arrive within the next three months. You are the assistant staffing officer for Victoria, and you have been instructed to review the records of the three leading candidates for manager of this new facility. You must recommend one of the three to your boss, the human resources director.

Before you examine the records, you make a list of factors that you believe should be taken into consideration:

1. The general criteria for selection will be education, experience, job knowledge, desire, and stability.

2. The Nigerian facility will be in the start-up phase.

3. Victoria wants to develop the skills of some of its current managers in international operations.

4. Few Nigerians have experience in the technical aspects of drilling for oil, yet Victoria has built its reputation on the expertise of its managers and customer acceptance of its managers as knowledgeable professionals.

5. Although some of Victoria's managers have had experience in Latin America, none have had experience in Africa.

6. Political power within the Nigerian government shifts periodically, and many of those with whom Victoria negotiated its move into Nigeria are no longer in the government.

7. The supply of trained oil-drilling equipment operators in Nigeria is much less than the demand.

The three candidates are:

Henry Smith: Age 34, Canadian citizen, graduate of University of Waterloo, served three years in the Canadian Armed Forces and then joined Victoria. In his 10 years with Victoria, his record has been outstanding, and it is often said that he will be president of Victoria someday. He has never been outside of North America for an extended period.

Juan Lopez: Age 46, Venezuelan citizen, has been with Victoria for 21 years and worked his way up through positions in several offices in Latin America. He spent two years in company headquarters planning operations in Latin America and is well respected throughout the company. He currently manages Victoria's facility in Ecuador.

Matthew Ohwueme: Age 52, Nigerian citizen, educated in England, member of the Ibo ethnic group. He is the owner/manager of the largest Honda dealership in Lagos but has had no experience with oilfield equipment.

Questions

1. Would it be best for Victoria to select a manager who is a local (citizen of Nigeria), a home-country national (citizen of Canada), or a third-country national (citizen of some country other than Nigeria or Canada)?
2. Which of the factors to be considered would favour the selection of Henry Smith? Juan Lopez? Matthew Ohwueme?
3. Which candidate would you recommend? Why?

Original case contributed by Sam C. Holliday, formerly with the University of Southern California.

Fred Bailey: An Innocent Abroad

Fred gazed out the window of his 24th floor office at the tranquil beauty of the Imperial Palace amid the hustle and bustle of downtown Tokyo. Only six months ago, Fred had arrived with his wife and two children for a three-year assignment as the director of Kline & Associates' Tokyo office. Kline & Associates is a large, multinational consulting firm with offices in 19 countries worldwide. Fred was now trying to decide if he should simply pack up and tell the home office that he was coming home, or whether he should somehow try to convince his wife and himself that they should stay and finish the assignment. Given how excited Fred thought they all were about the assignment to begin with, it was a mystery to Fred as to how things had gotten to this point. As he watched the swans glide across the water in the moat that surrounds the Imperial Palace, Fred reflected on the past seven months.

Seven months ago, the managing partner of the main office in Ottawa, Dave Steiner, asked Fred to lunch to discuss "business." To Fred's surprise, the "business" was not the major project that he and his team had just finished but was instead a very big promotion and career move. Fred was offered the position of managing director of the firm's relatively new Tokyo office that had a staff of 40, including 7 North Americans. Most of the North Americans in the Tokyo office were either associate consultants or research analysts. Fred would be in charge of the whole office and would report to a senior partner who was in charge of operations in the Asian region. It was implied to Fred that if this assignment went as well as his past ones, it would be the last step before becoming a partner in the firm.

When Fred told his wife about the unbelievable opportunity, he was shocked at her less than enthusiastic response. His wife, Jenny, thought that it would be rather difficult to have the children live and go to school in a foreign country for three years, especially when Christine, the oldest, would be starting middle school next year. Besides, now that the kids were in school, Jenny was thinking about going back to work—at least part-time. Jenny had a degree in fashion merchandising from a well-known university and had worked as an assistant buyer for a large women's clothing store before she and Fred had started their family.

Fred explained to Jenny that the career opportunity was just too good to pass up and that the company's overseas package would make living overseas terrific. The company would pay all the expenses to move whatever the Baileys wanted to take with them. The company had a very nice house in an expensive district of Tokyo that would be provided to them rent-free, and the company would take care of subletting their house in Ottawa during their absence. Also, the firm would provide a car and driver, would pay tuition fees for the children to attend private schools, and would pay a cost-of-living adjustment and overseas compensation that would nearly triple Fred's gross annual salary. After two days of consideration and discussion, Fred told Dave Steiner he would accept the assignment.

The previous Tokyo office managing director was a partner in the firm but had only been in the new Tokyo office for less than a year when he was transferred to head up a long-established office in England. Because the transfer to England was taking place "right away," Fred and his family had about three weeks to prepare for the move. Between getting things at the office transferred to Bob Newcome, who was being promoted to Fred's position, and the logistical hassles of getting furniture and the like ready to be moved, neither Fred nor his family had much time to really find out much about Japan, other than what was in the encyclopedia.

When the Baileys arrived, they were greeted at the airport by one of the young Japanese associate consultants and the senior North American expatriate. Fred and his family were tired from the long trip, and the two-hour ride to Tokyo was a quiet one. After a few days of settling in, Fred spent his first day at the office.

Fred's first order of business was to have a general meeting with all the employees of associate consultant rank and higher. Although Fred didn't really notice it at the time, all the Japanese staff sat together and all the North Americans sat together. After Fred introduced himself and his general idea about the potential and future direction of the Tokyo office, he called on a few individuals for their ideas about how their responsibilities would likely fit into his overall plan. From the North Americans, Fred got a mixture of opinions with specific reasons about why certain things might or might not fit well. From the Japanese, he got very vague answers. When Fred pushed to get more specific information, he was surprised to find that a couple of the Japanese simply made a sucking sound as they breathed and said that it was "difficult to say." Fred sensed the meeting was not fulfilling his objectives, so he thanked everyone for coming and said he looked forward to their all working together to make the Tokyo office the fastest growing office in the company.

After they had been in Japan for about a month, Fred's wife complained to him about the difficulty she had getting everyday products like maple syrup, peanut butter, and quality beef. She said that when she could get products like these at one of the specialty stores they cost three to four times what they would cost in Canada. She also complained that the washer and dryer were much too small, and she had to spend extra money by sending things out to be dry-cleaned. On top of all that, unless she went to the Canadian embassy in downtown Tokyo, she never had anyone to talk to. After all, Fred was gone from 10 to 16 hours a day. Unfortunately, at the time, Fred was preoccupied, thinking about a big upcoming meeting between his firm and a significant prospective client—a top 100 Japanese multinational company.

The next day, Fred, along with the lead consultant for the potential contract, Ralph Webster, and one of the Japanese associate consultants, Kenichi Kurokawa, who spoke perfect English, met with a team from the Japanese firm. The Japanese team consisted of four members—the vice president of administration, the director of international personnel, and two staff specialists. After shaking hands and making a few awkward bows, Fred said that he knew the Japanese gentlemen were busy and he didn't want to waste their time so he would get right to the point. Fred then had Webster lay out the proposal for the project and what the project would cost. After the presentation, Fred asked the Japanese team what their reaction to the proposal was. They did not respond immediately and so Fred launched into his summary version of the proposal, thinking that the translation might have been insufficient. But, again, the Japanese team members had only the vaguest of responses to his direct questions.

The recollection of the frustration of that meeting was enough to shake Fred back to reality. The reality was that, in the five months since the first meeting, little progress had been made and the contract between the firms had yet to be signed. "I can never seem to get a direct response from the Japanese," he thought to himself. This feeling of frustration led him to remember a related incident that had happened about a month after his first meeting with the client.

Fred reasoned that not much progress was being made with the client because Fred and his group just didn't know enough about the client to package the proposal in a way that was appealing to the client. Consequently, he called in Ralph Webster, the senior consultant associated with the proposal, and asked him to develop a report on the client so the proposal could be re-evaluated and changed where necessary. Jointly, they decided that one of the more promising Japanese research associates, Tashiro Watanabe, would be the best person to take the lead on this report. To impress upon Tashiro the importance of this task and the great potential they saw in him, they decided to have the young Japanese associate meet with both Fred and Ralph. In the meeting, Fred and Ralph laid out the nature and importance of the task. Fred then leaned forward in his chair and said, "You can see that this is an important assignment and that we are placing a lot of confidence in you by giving you this assignment. We need the report this time next week so that we can revise and re-present our proposal. Can you do it?" After a somewhat pregnant pause, the Japanese responded hesitantly, "I'm not sure what to say." At that point, Fred smiled, got up from his chair, walked over to the young Japanese associate, extended his hand, and said, "Hey, there's nothing to say. We're just giving you the opportunity you deserve."

The day before the report was due, Fred asked Ralph how the report was coming. Ralph said that since he had heard nothing from Tashiro, he assumed that everything was under control, but that he would double-check. Ralph later ran into one of the North American research associates, John Maynard. Ralph knew that John had been hired for the Tokyo office because of his language ability in Japanese and that, unlike any of the other North Americans, John often went out after work with some of the Japanese research associates, including Tashiro. So Ralph asked John if he knew how Tashiro was coming along with the report. John then recounted that, last night at the office, Tashiro had asked if Canadians sometimes fired employees for being late with reports. John had sensed that this was more than a hypothetical question and asked Tashiro why he wanted to know. Tashiro did not respond immediately and, since it was 8:30 in the evening, John suggested they go out for a drink. At first Tashiro resisted, but then John assured him that they would grab a drink at a nearby bar and come right back. At the bar, John got Tashiro to open up.

Tashiro explained the nature of the report that he had been requested to produce. Tashiro continued to explain that even though he had worked long into the night every night to complete the report, it was just impossible; he had doubted from the beginning whether he could complete the report in a week.

At this point, Ralph asked John, "Why the hell didn't he say something in the first place?" Ralph didn't wait to hear whether John had an answer to his question or not. He headed straight to Tashiro's desk.

The situation just got worse from that point. Ralph chewed Tashiro out and then went to Fred to tell him that the report would not be ready and that Tashiro didn't think it could have been from the start. "Then why didn't he say something?" Fred asked. No one had any answers, and the whole thing just left everyone more suspect and uncomfortable with one another.

There were other incidents, big and small, that had made the last two months especially frustrating, but Fred was too tired to remember them all. To Fred, it seemed that working with Japanese persons both inside and outside the firm was like working with people from another planet. Fred felt he just couldn't communicate with them, and he could never figure out what they were thinking. It drove him crazy.

Then, on top of all this, Jenny had laid a bombshell on him yesterday. She wanted to go home, and yesterday was not soon enough. Even though the kids seemed to be doing okay, Jenny was tired of Japan—tired of being stared at, of not understanding anybody or being understood, of not being able to find what she wanted at the store, of not being able to drive and read the road signs, of not having anything to watch on TV, of not being involved in anything. She wanted to go home and could not think of any reason why they shouldn't. After all, she reasoned, they owed nothing to the company because the company had led them to believe this was just another assignment, like the two years they had spent in San Francisco, and it was anything but that!

Fred looked out the window once more, wishing that somehow everything could be fixed, or turned back, or something. Down below, the traffic was backed up. Though the traffic lights changed, the cars and trucks didn't seem to be moving. Fortunately, in the ground below, one of the world's most advanced, efficient, and clean subway systems moved hundreds of thousands of people around the city and to their homes.

Questions

1. What factors (individual, work, and organizational) contributed to Fred and Jenny's lack of adjustment to Japan?
2. What mistakes did Fred make because of his lack of understanding of Japan?
3. What criteria would be important in selecting employees for overseas assignments?
4. What special training and development programs might have been beneficial to Fred and his family prior to his assignment in Japan?
5. Assume you are Dave Steiner and you receive a call from Fred about his difficulties in Japan. How would you respond? What should be done now?

Original case contributed by J. Stewart Black, Amos Tuck School of Business Administration, Dartmouth College.

The Cultural Diversity Training Program

Dr. Jennifer Barnes is an assistant professor of organizational behaviour and human resource management at a major university. Her university is located in a large city, in which 30 percent of the population is of Asian descent. In recent years, the university has aggressively recruited Asian faculty and graduate students. Specifically, the university has funded new faculty positions and graduate fellowships for minorities.

Recently, Dr. Barnes read about a new university-sponsored cultural diversity training program that was required for all academic administrators/supervisors and offered to faculty and staff. Since Dr. Barnes teaches two human resource management courses, she decided to enroll in the one-day seminar in anticipation of utilizing the material in her own courses. She expected the program would cover the full range of work force diversity including age, race, gender, ethnicity, physical abilities, and sexual orientation. She also thought there might be some discussion of the impact of parental status, religious beliefs, and dual-career couples. Finally, she expected to experience a high level of involvement in the process through the use of case studies, sensitivity training, incidents, and role playing.

When Dr. Barnes attended the program, she was quite disappointed. There were lectures by seven different speakers, including one external consultant on cultural diversity and several university administrators. While the seminar coordinator told the participants she wanted their input and involvement, the speakers were scheduled for one-hour blocks and used most or all of their allotted time for their formal presentations. Throughout the day, only seven comments or questions were asked by participants. In addition, the only concept of diversity discussed by the presenters was racial diversity.

Other types of work force diversity were mentioned in passing by one presenter, but otherwise were ignored. The emphasis in most of the presentations was on the changing work force demographics and the consequent necessity for the university to be more open, accommodative, and responsive to Asian students, employees, or potential employees. One of the speakers noted that, while Asians constituted 30 percent of the city's population, only 15 percent of the students and 4 percent of the faculty are Asian. The unspoken assumption was that the program participants (most of whom were white) harboured racial animosity toward Asians. Therefore, they needed to modify their attitudes and behaviour in order to better recruit, retain, and relate to Asian employees or students.

Dr. Barnes felt that both the content and process of the seminar left much to be desired. After the seminar, she discussed her experience with her department chair. The chair agreed to discuss it with the Dean of the School of Business. After doing so, he reported that it had been decided at the highest levels of the university that "in our environment, diversity means Asian."

Questions

1. What is cultural diversity?
2. Why is cultural diversity an important issue for all organizations? What are the potential disadvantages of ignoring it as an issue? What steps should a proactive organization take to respond to this challenge?
3. Evaluate the content and training method used by the university in this training program. Do you have any suggestions for improvement?

Going International

I. *Objective:* To give you an understanding of the human resource issues that emerge when a company establishes foreign operations.

II. *Time Required to Complete Assignment:* 5 to 6 hours

III. *Instructions:* Your instructor will divide the class into teams and assign each team one of the countries listed in the scenario described below. Your team is to conduct research on another country and prepare a report addressing the two questions listed in the scenario. Each team should be prepared to make an oral presentation of its research findings and recommendations.

There are a number of excellent sources of information on foreign countries. In addition to the sources your team may locate, you might try the following:

A. Consulate offices in Canada for each country

B. The World Factbook

C. Asia Pacific Management Forum (http://www.apmforum.com)

D. The Society for Human Resource Management's Global Forum (http://www.shrm.org/global)

E. Canadian Department of Foreign Trade and International Affairs (http://www.dfait-maeci.gc.ca)

Scenario

Piedmont Electronics produces paging devices. The demand for the company's products has grown rapidly in the last few years. The company's new strategy includes a direct investment initiative to establish assembly and manufacturing plants. The long-term objective is to establish operations in key markets throughout the world. Piedmont is considering the following host countries:

Malaysia

China

India

Brazil

Mexico

Malawi

Philippines

United Kingdom

The company's president has asked a human resource team to prepare a research report on each country. The report should:

1. Describe:

   a. labour and employment laws;

   b. wage rates and worker benefits;

   c. average education and literacy levels of the labour force;

d. labour availability;

e. living standards; and

f. cultural norms and values of the country.

2. Discuss the implications of the research findings in terms of what Piedmont should consider when setting up human resource management practices in the host country.

16. CASE

The Storage Room Massage: A Case of Harassment?

Background

Wheatfields Savings has 10 branches in both rural and urban locations throughout the Prairies. Each branch employs approximately 25 workers. Since banking is a federally regulated industry in Canada, the company's operations fall under the jurisdiction of federal law. Wheatfields' human resource operations are generally centralized at corporate headquarters located in Saskatoon, Saskatchewan. However, each branch manager is largely responsible for the day-to-day administration of human resource policies.

The Incident

Bill Winthrop, a teller supervisor at the Moose Jaw branch, had been employed with the company for about six years. On June 11, 2003, Winthrop was terminated by the branch manager, Jim Hudson, for harassment of a female employee, Mary Harper Jones, on June 9 (see Exhibit 1.19). Jones was employed as a teller in the Moose Jaw branch and accused Winthrop of unwanted sexual advances (see Exhibit 1.20).

A few months after Winthrop was terminated, the company received a notice from the Canadian Human Rights Commission (CHRC) that a complaint had been filed by Winthrop, alleging that he had been harassed by Jones on three occasions and that her actions unreasonably interfered with his work performance and created a negative work atmosphere. He further alleged that the company failed to take action on his complaints about Jones and that he had been unduly discharged (see Exhibit 1.21).

The Company's Position

In its reply to the CHRC, the company maintained that Winthrop had been terminated for harassment and not on the basis of his race, sex, or any other manner of retaliation. The company also pointed out that, after his termination on June 11, Winthrop had applied for unemployment benefits and the Employment Insurance office, after reviewing his application, agreed that Winthrop was terminated for just cause. Consequently, Winthrop was disqualified from receiving unemployment benefits for a period of nine weeks. The report on Winthrop's application stated: "Winthrop displayed poor judgment in requesting the 'massage,' and the employer's discharge of the claimant was for good business reasons to avoid instances of like nature in the future." The company argued that his harassment charges were unsubstantiated and should be dismissed (see Exhibit 1.22). Two weeks after forwarding his letter (see Exhibit 1.22) to the CHRC, the human resource director, Jacob Bevins, received a reply from the CHRC (see Exhibit 1.23) requesting additional information about the charges.

Questions

1. Evaluate the company's handling of Winthrop's termination. Was he terminated for just cause?
2. Under federal human rights legislation, what are the legal ramifications of a supervisor accusing an employee of harassment?
3. What alternative actions could Jones have taken in dealing with Winthrop?
4. What is the definition of "harassment" in the human rights legislation of your province or territory? Would your decisions be any different if this definition were used to evaluate the complaint?

Exhibit 1.19 *Memo from Branch Manager to the Human Resource Director Regarding Winthrop's Termination*

Memorandum

To: Jacob Bevins, Human Resource Director, Wheatfields Savings
From: Jim Hudson, Branch Manager, Moose Jaw
Date: June 11, 2003
Subject: Termination of Bill Winthrop (Teller Supervisor)

Based on allegations substantiated by others (allegations of Miss Mary Harper Jones, First Nations female, who is employed as a teller at the above-named branch), a personal interview was conducted at approximately 11:00 a.m. this date, and, as a result of the interview, Mr. Bill Winthrop was relieved of his duties and terminated effective this date.

Mr. Winthrop admitted he allowed Miss Jones to physically rub his back and allowed such action to take place at the workplace on or about noon on Monday, June 9, and was witnessed by another employee (Mr. Jim Joyner, accountant). Mr. Winthrop disavowed other allegations made by Miss Jones. By his admission of the above contact, Mr. Winthrop was informed that a possible sex discrimination and/or harassment suit could result. Mr. Winthrop stated it was all in jest. I informed Mr. Winthrop of the dire consequences of his actions and the fact that Miss Jones had in fact made it serious as she called his actions to the attention of the branch manager and others. A copy of Miss Jones's statement is attached for your information.

Respectfully submitted,

Jim Hudson

Jim Hudson

Exhibit 1.20 *Statement from Mary Harper Jones Concerning the Events of June 9, 2003*

To Whom it May Concern

I was balancing my cash at the start of my shift and Bill (Winthrop) came up to me and asked how much I would charge for a massage. I said a professional would charge $35 an hour. I said I was not a professional. He asked me if I would meet him in the storage room. I thought he was joking. I smiled and he walked away. He had asked in general if the storage room was locked.

Later, I was walking down the hall during my break and saw Bill outside the coffee room motioning for me to come in. I went in and he said, "Sit down and rest; you've been standing all morning." I sat in J.P.'s chair. Jim Joyner came in at that point. Bill said to me, "Don't sit in that chair; that's where J.P. Garnett [assistant branch manager] sits." I said it was okay because he is my friend. Bill asked Jim to listen to what I was saying. Jim asked me why I liked J.P., and I told Jim that J.P. has been the same person since the day I met him. Bill then said to me, "I'm going to give you a piece of advice, Mary. Stay away from J.P. because he will get you in trouble." Bill asked Jim what he had done over the weekend. Jim was talking about his weekend, and Bill cut him off, saying, "Mary, give me $5 worth." Jim looked at me funny, and I had forgotten about the massage. Bill looked at Jim and smiled. Jim left. Bill said, "Mary, come on and stand behind me and massage my shoulders." And then I said, "You told me to come in here and rest and now you are putting me to work." Mr. Hudson (branch manager) walked in at that point and Bill told me to get over by J.P.'s chair, and I stepped over to it. Mr. Hudson came to where we were, and Bill started talking to him about how the day was going. Mr. Hudson and Bill were talking for a while. Eventually, Mr. Hudson left and went back to his office.

Bill told me to go to the storage room and to go one way while he went another way. When I got there he was already there. I walked in and asked him, "What's up?" He sat down on a box and asked if there was any way to lock the door. I told him there was no way to lock the door. I told him that no one ever came up there except the office staff and they only came in when they ran out of something. Then he told me to come on and finish massaging his shoulders. Before I started, I asked him if his wife ever did this and he said she was too puny and did not have the grip that I did. I felt funny because he asked me to do it now and had asked me to stop earlier when Mr. Hudson had walked into the coffee room. After I massaged him three or four times, I patted him on the shoulder and said, "Okay, Bill, time is up. I am finished." I asked him if something was wrong. He said it was all of the pressure here and his son had gotten hurt over the weekend. He said, "Thanks a lot, Mary," and then stood there for a few minutes. I started to leave and he grabbed my arm and pulled me to him and hugged me. I left. When I got downstairs I saw Donald (a loans officer) and told him I needed to talk to him. I told him the story and he suggested I go to J.P. Garnett (assistant branch manager) and talk to him. Garnett suggested I talk to Joan (executive assistant). I then went and told the story to Joan.

Mary Harper Jones

Mary Harper Jones

Exhibit 1.21 *Statement Provided by Bill Winthrop to the Canadian Human Rights Commission*

I was initially hired at Wheatfields Savings in November 1985 and have been employed as a teller supervisor since that time. Wheatfields Savings employs approximately 225 persons. There are 23 employees at the Moose Jaw branch, of whom 13 are males.

On or around April 8, 2003, on or around April 18, 2003, and on June 9, 2003, I was harassed. On or around April 8, 2003, I reported to Jim Hudson (male), branch manager, that I had been harassed by Mary Harper Jones (female), teller. I am not aware of the company's policies regarding harassment.

I believe that I have been discriminated against because of my sex. On or around April 8, 2003, Mary Harper Jones (female), teller, propositioned me. On or around April 18, 2003, Ms. Jones made a sexually derogatory statement. On or around June 9, 2003, Ms. Jones propositioned me again. Ms. Jones's sexual advances unreasonably interfered with my work performance and created a negative work atmosphere. On or around April 8, 2003, when I informed Jim Hudson (male), branch manager, about Ms. Jones's sexual advances, he stated that Ms. Jones had propositioned him too. However, no action was taken regarding my complaint.

On June 11, 2003, I was discharged from my position as teller supervisor. Jim Hudson (male), branch manager, stated I was being discharged because of a complaint of harassment. According to the Wheatfields employee handbook, I can be discharged due to the following reasons: (1) decrease in business, (2) accepting employment with another company, (3) leaving work without properly being relieved, (4) reporting to work in a condition not suitable for normal performance, (5) gross insubordination, (6) bringing drugs or alcohol on site, (7) fighting, (8) bringing any type of weapon on site, (9) failure for any reason to perform assigned duties, (10) excessive tardiness or absenteeism, and (11) conduct not in the best interest of the company.

I believe I was fired in retaliation for my complaints about being harassed. Ms. Jones alleged that I harassed her on June 9, 2003. Actually, Ms. Jones harassed me on that date. I am not aware of any management employee who received a complaint of harassment against me.

Exhibit 1.22 *Letter from Company Vice President of Human Resources to the Canadian Human Rights Commission*

October 5, 2003
Canadian Human Rights Commission
344 Slater St., 8th Floor
Ottawa, ON K1A 1E1
Attention: Ms. Harriet Burton
RE: Complaint of Bill Winthrop

Dear Ms. Burton:

This letter is to advise your office of our company's position with regard to the above referenced complaint. Mr. Bill Winthrop was terminated from employment with our organization on June 11, 2003, for harassment. He was not terminated on the basis of his sex, or for any manner of retaliation.

We emphatically deny the harassment charge against our employee. Several unusual circumstances surround this incident. For your information, Mr. Winthrop has applied for unemployment benefits, and the office hearing his appeal agreed that Mr. Winthrop was terminated for just cause; thus, he was denied unemployment benefits for the appropriate number of weeks. We have interrogated Mr. Jim Hudson, branch manager, over the phone, and he has emphatically denied that Mr. Winthrop had at any time told him he was harassed; and, had Mr. Winthrop raised this complaint, Mr. Hudson would have conducted an investigation immediately. It is interesting that the reason for Mr. Winthrop's termination is the same as his charge against his employer.

The superintendent, Mr. Hudson, in our telephone conversation of October 3, 2003, stated that during the last part of March, Ms. Mary Harper Jones did come to him and inquire if the bank gave employee loans since she needed a down payment for a car. Mr. Hudson told Ms. Jones that the bank had a conflict of interest policy preventing it from giving loans to its own employees. She made the comment, "Geez, I would do almost anything for a down payment for a car." Mr. Hudson remarked he was sorry he could not help her out. Mr. Hudson did not interpret this as a proposition and neither does our company.

We have reviewed our company records and the dates mentioned in the charge are not documented so we cannot establish the exact date of Mr. Winthrop's allegations. We therefore assume he is not being factual.

Because of Mr. Winthrop's position as teller supervisor, we in no way can see how Ms. Jones, a subordinate, could influence Mr. Winthrop's receiving advances, promotions, pay increases, etc. Due to the fact that Mr. Winthrop's allegations were not known by anyone at the plant, we find these charges to be made without fact and suggest that they should be dismissed.

Very truly yours,

Jacob Bevins, Human Resource Director
JB:tf
cc: Jim Hudson, Moose Jaw
Bill Winthrop File

Exhibit 1.23 *Request for Additional Information from the Canadian Human Rights Commission to Wheatfields Savings*

1. Please provide a signed statement from Jim Hudson concerning what Winthrop told him about being harassed. Also include whether or not Hudson told Winthrop that Mary Harper Jones had propositioned him.
2. If Winthrop reported being harassed to management, to whom did he report this and what were the specifics?
3. Please provide a copy of your company's policy on harassment.
4. Please provide the personnel files of Winthrop and Jones.
5. Please provide a copy of your company's policy on discipline and discharge.
6. Please explain in detail the reasons for Winthrop's discharge.
7. Please provide a list of employees that were discharged during the last year, indicating their name, race, sex, date of hire, position held, reason for discharge, date of discharge, and prior disciplinary history. Provide the personnel file of a First Nations female employee that was discharged.
8. Please provide a signed statement from Jones concerning whether or not Winthrop harassed her on June 9, 2003.
9. Please provide signed statements from witnesses concerning whether or not Winthrop was harassed or Jones was harassed.
10. Please provide a position statement on every point raised in the complaint.

Analyzing Promotion Data: Applying the 80 Percent Rule

Thomas L. Rutherford, Human Resource Director of Food Chain Supermarkets, Inc., was jolted by the conversation he just had with Walter Jackson, an employee in the company's distribution warehouse. Jackson had complained that minority employees were being passed over for promotions in favour of white employees who had less experience and seniority. Jackson had gone on to explain that he had resigned from his position in the meat department of the warehouse because, despite his experience and job performance, he felt he would not get promoted. He explained that he had been passed over for promotion three times since he had started work with Food Chain.

After Jackson left his office, Rutherford immediately began to investigate his claims. He called in Mark Walters, his personnel assistant, and explained his conversation with Jackson to him. "The last thing I want on my hands is a discrimination suit," Rutherford told Mark. "I want you to get some data on promotions that have occurred in the last couple of years in our warehouse operations. Also, while you're at it, get the same information for our stores. Also, here are the names of three minority employees given to me by Jackson. Pull their files and try to get any facts on what happened with their promotion requests." Mark replied, "I don't think it will be too difficult to pull together the information, Tom, now that we have finally gotten our personnel records centralized. But I'll probably have to talk with some of the department managers and supervisors also." Rutherford suggested that he also interview the three minority employees. As Mark left his office, Rutherford began to think about the company's human resource practices and Jackson's allegations.

Background

Food Chain Supermarkets, Inc., is a regional chain of supermarkets located in central Canada. Additionally, the company operates a central warehouse, bakery, and its own transportation system. Its main office, distribution centre (warehouse), and a dozen stores are located near Montreal. Presently, the company employs over 1,600 people in this area. According to recent census data, about 22 percent of the workers in the area's labour force are from minority groups. The company has plans to refurbish its stores and to open four additional stores over the next two years. Rutherford was hired in anticipation of this growth to help better manage the company's personnel needs.

The distribution centre has five departments: grocery, meat, frozen food, produce, and transportation. Each department has two shifts. The starting times of various employees on the same shifts are staggered. Both receiving and shipping functions are carried out at the warehouse. Order puller, order selector, order picker, and picker are synonymous terms for the same position. A warehouse crew leader is a working supervisor who assigns duties but also performs the same duties as subordinates. Management positions in the stores consist of assistant produce manager, produce manager, grocery manager trainee, relief grocery manager, deli manager, relief assistant manager, assistant manager, head cashier, and assistant head cashier.

Human Resource Practices

When Rutherford was hired four months ago, the president had explained that, because of the physical dispersion of the stores, human resource policies were decentralized with a great deal of responsibility placed on the district managers. Promotion recommendations and decisions were made by supervisors of the different departments in the warehouse. In order to be promoted to a warehouse crew leader, an employee had to be on the same shift and in the same department as the opening. The factors utilized in promotion decisions at the warehouse were character, integrity, good sound morals, correct attitude, and initiative. The company felt that the supervisor was in the best position to judge whether or not an employee was promotable. There was no formal system for employees to apply for promotions. Written performance evaluations were limited to office employees, merchandisers, and store managers. At the retail stores, store supervisors made promotion recommendations to the district manager. Promotions were limited to persons recommended by the store managers. The district managers agreed with the store managers 90 to 95 percent of the time. The district manager decided who would be promoted, transferred, demoted, hired, or terminated for all positions up to the department head. Job vacancies were not routinely posted. Employees could be transferred from store to store as needed.

Rutherford recalled a conversation he had recently with one of the district managers, Joe Perkins: "We really don't need to post jobs since each district manager is usually aware of openings in his or her district and which employees are ready for promotion. Also, an employee doesn't have to ask in order to be considered for a promotion. Although we don't have a written evaluation system, the job performance of an employee is conveyed by word of mouth from one level of supervision to another."

Two Weeks Later

Rutherford had received the reports and data prepared by Mark on promotions within the warehouse and stores for the past two years (see Exhibit 1.24). Mark had also prepared summaries of what had happened to Jackson and the other three minority employees mentioned by Jackson. As Rutherford began reading through the report, he wondered what changes would be needed at Food Chain. He certainly did not want to have another conversation like the one he had had with Jackson two weeks earlier.

Questions

1. Analyze the table in Exhibit 1.24. What conclusions do you reach? Is there evidence of discrimination in promotion decisions?
2. Do you believe that Gemson, Thompson, LeBlanc, and Jackson were discriminated against?
3. What are some of the potential disadvantages of a "word of mouth" promotion system?
4. What should Rutherford do now?
5. What kinds of policies can the company design to better integrate minorities into management positions?

Exhibit 1.24 *Report on Promotion Rates*

TO: T. L. Rutherford, Director of Human Resources
FROM: Mark Walters, Human Resource Assistant
RE: Promotions

I have collected the data you requested on promotion rates at our warehouse and stores for the last two years (see table). I have also summarized what I could learn about the Jackson situation and the other three promotion cases he mentioned.

Promotion Rates

Unit	Year	Total Employees		Total Promotions		Promotion Rates	
		White	Minority	White	Minority	White Rate	Minority Rate
Warehouse/ stores	1998	1,603	284	171	21	10.66%	7.39%
Warehouse/ stores	1997	1,414	291	122	27	8.62	9.27
Warehouse	1998	411	173	42	13	10.21	7.50
Warehouse	1997	223	192	18	21	8.07	10.90
Stores	1998	1,192	111	129	8	10.80	7.20
Stores	1997	1,191	99	104	6	8.73	6.10

Note: In 1998, minorities represented 5.8 percent of 137 store promotions and 9 percent of the work force.
      In 1997, 94.6 percent of the managers were white; in 1998, 94.7 percent of managers were white.

Clifford Gemson: Clifford Gemson was hired as a produce clerk in June 1997. He had originally applied for a management position. He had three years of grocery store management experience including six months in produce management with another company. Gemson worked in two stores between June 1997 and April 1998. On several occasions, Gemson asked his district manager (J. Perkins) and his store manager (C. Fagen) about promotion to vacant produce manager positions. The first vacancy was filled on October 8, 1997, by Bob Watkins, a white employee. Watkins, a produce clerk, had 18 months of experience with us. Watkins, who had no management experience, was replaced by another white employee, Sheila Wilson, on November 8, 1997. Wilson was selected on the basis of her Food Chain experience as a produce clerk and as assistant produce manager for six months. Gemson was not considered for either vacancy.

Roy Thompson: Roy Thompson was hired by Food Chain at our warehouse on September 18, 1996 as a maintenance (sanitation) employee. His duties included forklift driving, sorting damaged food, and rebuilding pallets. His prior work experience included supervisory duties and self-employment. Thompson trained a white employee of Food Chain (Neal Marcy, hired May 12, 1997) who was promoted to crew leader of the maintenance (sanitation) department on June 16, 1997. Before Marcy was hired, Thompson asked his supervisor (E. Jones) for the crew leader job to which Marcy was promoted. Jones told Thompson that he would never be a crew leader as long as he was supervisor. Jones denies saying this. According to Thompson, his supervisors had repeatedly told him that he had both excellent attendance and performance. On August 15, 1998, a junior white employee, Earl Hanes (with less company experience than Thompson), was promoted to sanitation crew leader for the same shift and in the same department that Thompson worked in. According to Jones, Hanes was better qualified because of his previous work experience.

Leslie LeBlanc: Leslie LeBlanc was hired by Food Chain on July 8, 1996 as a frozen food picker. Her next position was frozen food loader. LeBlanc was trained to act as a "fill-in" crew leader, and in fact did fill in as a crew leader until Ricky Anderson (white) was hired. LeBlanc trained Anderson in the duties of a "fill-in" crew leader. Anderson then assumed LeBlanc's place as "fill-in" crew leader. Anderson was offered a full-time crew leader's position, which he refused. LeBlanc was never offered this job. LeBlanc had previously informed Food Chain management of her prior experience as a shift leader at a textile mill.

Walter Jackson: Walter Jackson was employed by Food Chain on April 14, 1996 at the warehouse in the meat department. Milk, dairy products, and meat are in the same department. Jackson's job duties prior to April 1998 included milk picking, unloading, and forklift driving. In the spring of 1998, a crew leader told Jackson that he was up for promotion to crew leader in the department. Terry Gibson (a white employee) received the job on June 7, 1998. Gibson was initially hired on January 11, 1996, resigned February 5, 1996, and was re-hired November 3, 1996. Jackson had more company and departmental experience than Gibson. However, he was never considered for the position. Gibson's prior duties were solely picking meat, and Jackson had supervised Gibson when Jackson served as "fill-in" crew leader prior to Gibson's promotion. The supervisor asserted that Gibson had broader departmental experience than Jackson. Since that time, two other employees in the meat department with less seniority and experience have been promoted over Jackson.

Blowing the Whistle: Accounting Practices at Glenfair Electronics

Bob Schein, vice president of human resources at Glenfair Electronics, sat at his desk thinking about the meeting he had just had with Anwar Patel, an accountant in the Finance Department. He had listened intently to Anwar Patel describing what had transpired in the Finance Department during the last few weeks. Anwar joined Glenfair after completing his degree in accounting five years ago. For the past three years, Anwar had been preparing Glenfair's sales revenue reports. As a publicly traded company, Glenfair was required to issue public sales and profit forecasts. Glenfair Electronics had over 2,000 employees and a reputation for producing high-quality electronic components used in a number of manufacturing applications. The company had begun to experience a slowdown in product demand, and its share price had declined as well in the last year and a half.

Anwar had told Bob he had been instructed to use a different and more aggressive accounting method for forecasting and calculating projected sales revenue for the coming year. Anwar believed that such an approach could mislead shareholders about Glenfair's likely future sales performance. The previous chief financial officer (CFO) had taken a rather conservative approach and did not stretch the boundaries of acceptable practices. Since the beginning of the year, however, Anwar was working under a new CFO, John Beatty. John had joined Glenfair earlier in the year after not obtaining a promotion to CFO at his previous company. Everyone perceived John to be smart and ambitious. It was clear that he was determined to make his mark at Glenfair. When Anwar pointed out that the proposed accounting methods were very different from Glenfair's traditional practices for reporting sales revenue, he told Bob that John had said, "Well, I am the new CFO, and I have a different view and approach." It was his next remark that disturbed Anwar the most. According to Anwar, John went on to say, "Sales should turn around next quarter, and we are justified in reporting higher expected sales revenue in the coming months. Besides, Anwar, don't you want your Glenfair stock to do well?" Projected higher sales revenue could indeed burnish Glenfair's earnings outlook and probably help its stock price. When Anwar persisted in questioning the accounting methods, John allegedly told him to do his job as instructed. Since that conversation, Anwar felt that John had become hostile toward him, and they no longer had a friendly relationship. Despite his fears, Anwar felt he had to come to Bob for advice. Bob could see that Anwar was worried about John finding out about their meeting.

Bob was disturbed by what he had heard from Anwar and sat at his desk thinking about what he should do as vice president of human resources.

Questions

1. If you were Bob, what would you do, if anything? Explain.
2. What should Bob do about Anwar's claim that John has become hostile toward him?
3. What rights and protections do whistle blowers have in the Canadian workplace today?

The Older Worker

I. *Objectives:*
    A. To familiarize you with typical stereotypes toward older workers and the managerial implications of these stereotypes.
    B. To provide you with factual information regarding older workers.

II. *Out-of-Class Preparation Time:* 15 minutes to complete the Older Worker Questionnaire shown in Exhibit 1.25

III. *In-Class Time Suggested:* 45 minutes for group and class discussion of all items on the Older Worker Questionnaire

IV. *Procedures:* Prior to the class meeting in which this exercise will be discussed, you should read any material on older workers assigned by your instructor and complete the Older Worker Questionnaire.

    At the start of the exercise, the class will be divided into groups of three to five by your instructor. Your group's task is to discuss each item on the questionnaire and arrive at a consensus regarding the correct answer (20-minute time limit). After all groups have finished, the instructor will present the correct answers along with an explanation. Each group should record these answers alongside the group's own and then compare the two to determine the number of right and wrong answers.

Exhibit 1.25 *The Older Worker Questionnaire*

Mark the statements "T" for true or "F" for false.

_____ 1. Younger workers tend to have higher job satisfaction than older ones.

_____ 2. A worker's creativity peaks between the ages of 55 and 65.

_____ 3. The life expectancy of the average Canadian citizen has been increasing.

_____ 4. The proportion of people age 65 and over in the Canadian population is expected to decline between now and 2030.

_____ 5. Few individuals (less than 1 percent) work after age 65.

_____ 6. The percentage of people over age 65 is lower in Canada than it is in Japan, Italy, Germany, and Great Britain.

_____ 7. The average retired worker receives over $20,000 a year in Canada Pension Plan benefits.

_____ 8. Older workers generally require less light for performing a task than do younger workers.

_____ 9. The majority of older employees are set in their ways and are unable to adapt to changing conditions.

_____ 10. In general, older workers are less healthy than younger ones.

_____ 11. Most individuals over age 65 who are employed work part-time.

_____ 12. Older employees usually take a longer period of time to learn something new than do younger employees.

_____ 13. Over 40 percent of Canadians over age 65 live below the poverty level.

_____ 14. Younger workers have higher injury frequency rates than do older workers.

_____ 15. Ninety percent of workers over age 50 say they learn best by watching and listening.

_____ 16. More Canadians over age 65 live in British Columbia than in any other province.

_____ 17. Older employees tend to react more slowly than younger employees.

_____ 18. Loyalty to a firm among workers over the age of 45 is strong.

_____ 19. One's ability to taste and smell tends to improve with age.

Is This Discrimination?

I. *Objectives:*

    A. To help you understand the application of the major laws that regulate equal rights in employment. These laws are the *Canadian Charter of Rights and Freedoms*, the federal and provincial human rights codes, the federal and provincial employment equity acts, the federal and provincial employment/labour standards acts, and the federal and provincial pay equity acts.

    B. To help you understand the interpretation and application of these laws.

    C. To help you understand the legal definition of discrimination and the burden of proof placed on defendants and plaintiffs.

II. *Out-of-Class Preparation Time:* 60 minutes

III. *In-Class Time Suggested:* 45 minutes

IV. *Procedures:*

    A. Read the exercise and review the major laws before class.

    B. The class should be divided into groups of four.

    C. Each group should read each of the incidents that follow and answer these questions:

        1. Does this case fall under federal or provincial/territorial jurisdiction?

        2. What legal statute(s) apply in this case?

        3. What issue(s) must be decided in this case?

        4. If you were deciding this case, how would you rule? Did the employer discriminate unlawfully? Why or why not?

1. Elaine Mobley worked as a social worker with a federally funded child abuse prevention program for two years. Mobley was a member of the non-sectarian Unitarian Universalist Church. During her first six months on the job, she divorced her husband of 10 years. Her supervisor, a devout Baptist, encouraged her to discuss her marital problems with a Christian psychotherapist. On a number of occasions, the supervisor encouraged other employees in the department who were also Baptists to convert Mobley. Some employees held prayer meetings at her desk while others gave her the silent treatment. Their attempts to convert Mobley did not stop. At one point, the supervisor made her participate in a Christian puppet show. Another time she found a handwritten note on her desk from Jesus that read, "How can you speak of God and reject me? I love you and know all about you." Her attendance at work declined because there were days she didn't want to face the stress in her work environment. Mobley filed a complaint with the director of the program stating that she was being constantly bombarded with efforts to convert her to a Baptist. Shortly thereafter, Mobley was fired from her job. Mobley filed a complaint claiming that she had been fired because of religious discrimination.

2. Edward Roberts, a black truck driver, applied in person for a tractor-trailer truck driver position at a trucking company on March 31, 1998, in response to a newspaper ad. Roberts' application listed 22 months of prior experience as a road driver. He had an additional 10 years of experience that he did not list on the application due to a lack of space on the form. Roberts was neither interviewed nor contacted by the company about the status of his application. In June 1998, Roberts saw an identical advertisement for tractor-trailer truck drivers. Upon inquiry, Roberts learned that eight persons (all white) had been hired as truck drivers between April and June 1998. All of the hirees had less than 22 months of driving experience. The company contended that Roberts was not hired because no opening existed when he applied. Roberts filed a complaint of discrimination on the basis of ethnic origin.

3. Thelma Jones had worked at a large public accounting firm for five years when the partners proposed her as a candidate for partnership. Of the 662 partners in the firm, 7 were women. Of the 88 persons proposed that year, Jones was the only woman. Forty-seven were admitted to partnership, 21 were rejected, and 20, including Jones, were held for "reconsideration." Thirteen of the 32 partners who submitted comments on Jones's performance supported her candidacy, 3 recommended holding her application, 8 stated that they had insufficient knowledge to comment, and 8 recommended denial. While the partners praised her outstanding performance, both supporters and opponents of her candidacy indicated that she was sometimes overly aggressive, unduly harsh, difficult to work with, and impatient with staff. One partner described her as "macho." In a meeting with a senior partner about her candidacy, she was told that, to improve her chances for partnership, she should "walk more femininely, talk more femininely, dress more femininely, wear makeup, style her hair, and wear jewellery." When the partners refused to re-propose her candidacy the following year, she filed a gender discrimination complaint.

4. James McFadden was a transsexual who, while still biologically male, announced to his employer, a regional airline, that he intended to dress and act as a woman in preparation for "surgical sex reassignment." Mr. McFadden was subsequently fired from his pilot's job for refusing to comply with its requirement that he continue to dress and act as a man. McFadden filed a complaint alleging that the employer had conspired to discriminate against him on the basis of sex (now to be female) and that he was treated differently from other women employed by the airline.

5. Andrew Johnson, a black maintenance worker, was constantly referred to as "Chicken Little," "Chicken George," "Sparerib Kid," "Boy," and "Watermelon Man" by his white supervisor. These names were used not just during private conversations but in the presence of other workers. Despite several complaints to senior management, the name calling persisted for several months. When management finally investigated Johnson's claims, the supervisor admitted that he had made the comments but argued that he was only kidding. The supervisor was instructed to stop both the name calling and kidding. A fellow employee warned Johnson that his days were probably numbered because he had gone over the head of his supervisor. Shortly thereafter, Johnson was injured on the job. While he was at home recuperating, his supervisor called to say that he accepted

his resignation. Johnson denied resigning and wrote asking for his job back. His request was denied. Johnson filed a complaint alleging that he had been a victim of harassment because of his race.

6. Paul Sherman had worked 12 years for the provincial Department of Transportation when he applied for a promotion to dispatcher. Sherman scored 75 on an interview test. Betty Palmer, another candidate, scored 73 and got the job. Sherman filed a complaint of discrimination. The department said that both Sherman and Palmer were qualified and that Palmer had gotten the job as part of an employment equity plan designed to achieve a work force that reflected the race and gender composition of the provincial work force. The department pointed out that none of 238 skilled craft worker jobs in the Department of Transportation were held by women.

7. Sandra Williams, an Asian female teacher with 10 years of classroom experience and partial completion of her doctoral degree in education, applied for several vacant middle and secondary school principalships in a regional school district. Each time she applied, she was told by the superintendent that "the school district believed that a 'male image' is necessary for a middle or secondary school principal." No females had ever occupied a principal position in the school district. Williams subsequently filed a complaint accusing the school system of discrimination.

8. Frank Poole had been teaching hearing-impaired students in several high schools in a regional school district for six years when he was hospitalized with pneumocystis carinii pneumonia and, subsequently, was diagnosed as having AIDS. Despite the district's medical director's report that Poole's condition did not place his students or others in the school at any risk, the district reassigned Poole to an administrative position and barred him from teaching in the classroom. Poole filed a complaint alleging that the district discriminated against him on the basis of his handicap (AIDS).

9. After working as a title clerk for a car dealership for five years, Donna Skeen resigned. At 62 years of age, Donna had decided that she did not want to put up with the treatment she had received at the dealership. She had demanded an end to the teasing she experienced, but to no avail. In a complaint she filed against the dealership, Donna alleged that the managers in the dealership referred to her as the "old lady with the sagging boobs." When she forgot something or made an error on a title, she was asked if she had Alzheimer's disease. If she complained about the temperature in the dealership, she was asked if she was suffering from hot flashes. The dealership owner, Frank Harrison, said that there was lots of informal teasing in the dealership among employees and that Skeen often referred to herself as the "grandma" of the staff.

10. Officials of a civic government charged with discrimination signed an agreement for an employment equity plan with specific promotion and hiring goals for increasing the number of minority firefighters in the city's fire department. Four years later, when faced with severe budget problems, the city implemented a layoff plan aimed at protecting minority employees who had been recently hired. Jerome Atwood, a white firefighter, was laid off even though he had greater seniority than many of the minority firefighters who retained their jobs. Atwood filed a complaint charging the city with discrimination.

Is This Discrimination? **Exercise 20**

11. Herbert Fox worked as an office furniture salesman for 25 years with the same company. In his 25th year with the company, he went on leave for clinical depression. When it was time for him to return from leave, he told the company he could not return to work as scheduled. Subsequently, Fox and the company agreed upon a new date for return. However, Fox also requested that he be allowed to miss the first couple of morning sales meetings (a request prompted by the side effects of his antidepressant medicine) or to work on a part-time basis. His request was denied by the company, and they also told Fox that, because of increasing financial pressures, the company would be expecting "110 percent" from him on his return to work. Fox did not report to work on the agreed-upon date and filed for disability benefits. The company subsequently terminated him. Fox filed a complaint against the company alleging that the requirements attached to his return to work caused a relapse of his depression.

12. Lia Lee, a Canadian citizen born in Laos, worked for a credit union for over three years as a teller. She had always received outstanding performance reviews from her supervisors. Consequently, when a position became available at the customer service desk that handled customer inquiries and problems, Lia applied for the position. She did not get the promotion. The credit union argued that she was not promoted because she did not have sufficient English skills to calm irate customers. Lia Lee filed a complaint alleging that the credit union had overlooked her for a promotion because of her accent.

13. Margaret Reynolds, 178 cm (5 ft. 10 in.) tall, and weighing 86 kg (190 lbs.), applied for a job as a fitness instructor teaching aerobics at Slendercise, Inc. She had always been very healthy and fit. She ate healthy foods, worked out five days a week, and could do all of the complicated aerobics steps and exercises. Slendercise, Inc., rejected Margaret's application to teach aerobics because of her size. Reynolds did not look anything like the svelte women on the company's website and promotional brochures. The company further argued that an aerobics instructor had to look leaner than the public and that people must believe Slendercise, Inc., would help them improve their shape, not just maintain it. Margaret filed a complaint with the provincial human rights commission alleging discrimination.

14. Abdul Mohammed, an Arab-Canadian, was employed as a steelworker. As a devout Muslim, Mohammed was obligated to engage in daily prayer. Abdul, along with five other Muslims working at the plant, asked management to provide a room where they could hold their daily prayers during lunch hour. The plant was located miles from the nearest mosque. Management told the employees that it did not have a room that could be used for such purposes. Consequently, Abdul and his fellow Muslims were forced to recite their prayers in full view of other employees. Other employees ridiculed the Muslims during their daily prayers and called them derogatory names like "camel jockey" and "raghead." After being humiliated on several occasions by taunts from other employees, Abdul and his fellow Muslims once again asked management to provide them with a private space in which to pray. Management again denied their request. Shortly thereafter, Abdul filed a case with the provincial human rights commission alleging religious harassment and ethnic discrimination.

What Is Harassment?

I. *Objectives:*
    A. To familiarize you with the Canadian federal harassment guidelines.
    B. To teach you the meaning of these guidelines as they relate to the workplace.
    C. To teach you the manager's and organization's role in preventing harassment.
    D. To show you the complexities involved in identifying harassment in the workplace and in interpreting these guidelines.

II. *Out-of-Class Preparation Time:* 20 minutes to read the guidelines and complete the harassment questionnaire

III. *In-Class Time Suggested:* 45 minutes for group and class discussion of all items on the harassment questionnaire

IV. *Procedures:* Prior to the class meeting in which this exercise will be discussed, you should read the Canadian Human Rights Commission's definition of harassment in Exhibit 1.26 and any other material related to harassment assigned by your instructor. You also need to complete the 20-item harassment questionnaire in Exhibit 1.27.

    At the start of the exercise, the class will be divided into groups of three to five students by the instructor. Your group's task is to discuss each item on the questionnaire and arrive at a consensus regarding whether the situation described in each item constitutes harassment. More importantly, you need to develop a rationale for your answer (20-minute time limit). After all groups have finished, the class as a whole will discuss the questionnaire items. To facilitate discussion, groups will take turns presenting their analysis, i.e., one group will present its analysis regarding Item 1, another group will present Item 2, another Item 3, and so on.

Exhibit 1.26 *Excerpts from the Canadian Human Rights Commission's Definition of Harassment*

Harassment is any unwanted physical or verbal conduct that offends or humiliates you. Such conduct can interfere with your ability to do a job or obtain a service.

    Harassment is a type of discrimination. It can take many forms, such as:

- threats, intimidation, or verbal abuse;
- unwelcome remarks or jokes about subjects like your race, religion, disability or age;
- displaying sexist, racist or other offensive pictures or posters;
- sexually suggestive remarks or gestures;
- inappropriate physical contact, such as touching, patting, pinching or punching;
- physical assault, including sexual assault.

Harassment can consist of a single incident or several incidents over a period of time.

Harassment can create a negative or hostile work environment which can interfere with your job performance and result in your being refused a job, a promotion or a training opportunity.

The harasser, who could be of the same or opposite sex as the person harassed, may be a supervisor, a coworker, or someone providing you with a service, such as a bank officer or a clerk in a government department.

Harassment will be considered to have taken place if a reasonable person ought to have known that the behaviour was unwelcome.

Source: "Harassment, What Is It?" Canadian Human Rights Commission. http://www.chrc-ccdp.ca/discrimination/what_is_it-en.asp. Reproduced with the permission of the Ministry of Public Works and Government Services, 2005.

Exhibit 1.27 *Harassment Questionnaire*

Instructions: Read each situation and circle your answer.

Situation	Would It Be Harassment?		
1. Mr. (Ms.) X (Supervisor) posts cartoons on the bulletin board containing sexually related materials.	Yes	No	Uncertain
2. Mr. (Ms.) X (Supervisor) constantly tells sexually related jokes to female (male) subordinates.	Yes	No	Uncertain
3. Mr. (Ms.) X (Supervisor) asks a female (male) subordinate for a date and she (he) willingly accepts.	Yes	No	Uncertain
4. Mr. (Ms.) X (Supervisor) pats or pinches a female (male) subordinate.	Yes	No	Uncertain
5. Mr. (Ms.) X (Supervisor) terminates a female (male) subordinate for not complying with his (her) request for sexual favours. He (she) has recently given the subordinate a positive performance appraisal.	Yes	No	Uncertain
6. Mr. (Ms.) X (Supervisor) sexually assaults a female (male) subordinate.	Yes	No	Uncertain
7. Mr. (Ms.) X (Supervisor) denies a raise to a female (male) subordinate for failing to go out on a date with him (her).	Yes	No	Uncertain
8. Mr. X (Supervisor) habitually calls all female employees "sweetie" or "honey."	Yes	No	Uncertain
9. Mr. (Ms.) X (Supervisor) asks a female (male) employee how she (he) feels about sex education in schools.	Yes	No	Uncertain
10. Mr. X (Supervisor) recommends that a female subordinate wear revealing attire at work.	Yes	No	Uncertain
11. Mr. (Ms.) X (Supervisor) fails to promote a female (male) subordinate for not granting sexual favours.	Yes	No	Uncertain
12. Mr. (Ms.) X (Supervisor) invites a female (male) subordinate to accompany him (her) to a two-day meeting in another city.	Yes	No	Uncertain
13. Mr. X (Supervisor) leans and peers over the back of a female employee when she wears a low-cut dress.	Yes	No	Uncertain
14. Mr. (Ms.) X (Supervisor) tells a female (male) job applicant that she (he) won't be hired unless she (he) agrees to grant sexual favours.	Yes	No	Uncertain
15. Mr. (Ms.) X (Supervisor) invites a female (male) subordinate to meet him (her) at a bar that features female (male) exotic dancers.	Yes	No	Uncertain
16. Mr. (Ms.) X (Supervisor) invites a female (male) subordinate to come over to his (her) apartment for a hot tub party.	Yes	No	Uncertain

17. Male (female) workers whistle every time female (male) employees walk by their work area.   Yes   No   Uncertain

18. A married female employee and a married male employee are having an affair.   Yes   No   Uncertain

19. Male (female) employees repeatedly use vulgar language when talking to each other. Two female (male) employees often overhear what is said and find it offensive.   Yes   No   Uncertain

20. A male (female) repair technician who works for another firm asks female (male) employees for dates whenever he (she) comes to repair equipment.   Yes   No   Uncertain

22. EXERCISE

Understanding Human Rights Legislation and Disability

I. *Objectives:*
   A. To help you understand the application of the provisions relating to disability in federal and provincial human rights legislation.
   B. To help you understand the interpretation of these provisions.
   C. To help you understand the meaning of the terms "disability" and "reasonable accommodation."

II. *Out-of-Class Preparation Time:* 45 minutes

III. *In-Class Time Suggested:* 45 minutes

IV. *Procedures:*
   A. Read the exercise and review the definitions of "disability" and "reasonable accommodation" in the federal human rights legislation and the human rights legislation of your own province or territory.
   B. The class should be divided into groups of four.
   C. Each group should read each of the case incidents that follow and answer these questions:
      1. What issue(s) must be decided in this case?
      2. What would you decide? Did the employer discriminate unlawfully? Why or why not?

1. The Overweight Hospital Attendant

Betty Thomas applied for a position as an attendant for the mentally challenged in a residential facility operated by Entwell Group Homes. She had previously worked for the organization in an identical position. She had an excellent work record and left employment with Entwell on good terms. When Thomas re-applied for the position she previously held, she stood 157 cm (5 feet 2 inches) tall and weighed 145 kg (320 pounds). During her pre-employment physical, it was determined that, although Thomas was morbidly obese, there were no limitations that affected her ability to do the job. Entwell refused to hire Thomas because of her obesity, claiming that her weight compromised her ability to evacuate patients in the event of an emergency and put Thomas at greater risk of developing serious ailments that might lead to higher absenteeism, as well as increasing Entwell's exposure to workers' compensation claims. Thomas filed a human rights complaint alleging that she was being discriminated against on the basis of her weight.

2. The Asthmatic's Nightmare

June Deil was promoted to blood bank administrator for a large metropolitan hospital in 1999. Her education and experience were primarily in the general field of administration. Her work area was in a windowless basement of one of the hospital's facilities, where the blood bank fumes and poor ventilation aggravated her asthma. Deil complained to the hospital, and informed the director of safety programs and the medical director about her health problems.

Three months into her new job, Deil's doctor advised her that she should stay away from the blood bank because the location was "an asthmatic's nightmare." Once Deil informed her immediate supervisor of the doctor's conclusion, Deil was allowed to administer the blood bank from an office in another part of the hospital complex. Her health improved rapidly over the next several months.

In 2002, the appointment of a new medical director led to a change in Deil's work routine. The new director requested to meet with Deil on a regular basis at the blood bank facility. When she refused to go to the facility, Deil was discharged. Deil's supervisor had offered to help her find another job either within the hospital or outside of it. Deil filed a complaint with the human rights commission alleging discrimination on the basis of her disability.

3. The Ultimatum

Joan Garlock, a warehouse worker, was diagnosed with carpal tunnel syndrome. She was subsequently assigned to reduced duties. However, the duties were later multiplied, increasing her arm and wrist pain. When Joan presented her employer with a doctor's note advising her to take a six-week leave of absence, the employer gave her an ultimatum—show up for work or lose her job. Joan decided to file a complaint with the provincial human rights commission, claiming that carpal tunnel syndrome was a disability worthy of accommodation.

4. The Fainting Technician

Jane O'Neill was fired after she fainted on the job, because the company believed she was suffering from an unknown disability. After the fainting episode, she had been sent to a physician for an examination and testing. The physician's initial diagnosis was that Jane suffered from syncope, a loss of consciousness caused by a temporary deficiency of blood supply to the brain. Later, the physician determined that Jane's test results were within normal limits (in other words, the test results did not fall within the range that would usually indicate the condition was present), and that there was no explanation for the fainting. The company discharged Jane without any further medical examination, concluding that she was a safety risk because she was likely to faint again. Jane filed a human rights complaint alleging that the employer should accommodate her condition.

5. The Gunslinger

John Sheppard was fired when he was caught carrying a gun into work. He was hospitalized following the incident and was diagnosed with a mental disorder. His attorney informed the company of his mental status and asked that they delay any decision about his employment status. The company fired John for his clear violation of company rules. On his attorney's advice, John then filed a human rights complaint alleging that the company discriminated against him because of his mental disorder.

Original case contributed by Gerald E. Calvasina, Southern Utah University.

23. EXERCISE

Group Debate Project

I. *Objectives:*
   A. To help you understand both sides of controversial human resource management issues.
   B. To allow you to apply human resource management concepts in understanding the policy implications of the issues.
II. *Out-of-Class Preparation Time:* equivalent to time required for students to complete a major term paper assignment
III. *In-Class Time Suggested:* 45 minutes
IV. *Procedures:*
   A. Each debate will consist of two teams: an affirmative team who upholds the proposition and a negative team who opposes it. Debates can be scheduled throughout the semester to coincide with course content. For example, the comparable worth debate could be held after compensation is covered in the course. Alternatively, all debates could be held at the end of the term.
   B. Students should be divided into groups of three or four depending on the number of debate topics to be covered during the semester. The number of debaters on each side should be equal and the time allowed for each side is the same.
   C. Each group should be assigned to either the affirmative or negative side of a topic.
   D. Each team conducts research on its topic. Because of the current nature of the debate topics, you are encouraged to consult current periodicals in addition to academic journals and books. You may want to review the lists of journals and sources in the Skill Builders in Part 1.
   E. Each team prepares a written paper (8–10 pages) analyzing both sides of the topic in addition to presenting its arguments. The paper should be divided into three major parts: Introduction, Discussion, and Conclusion. (See additional instructions that follow.)
   F. The debate is held in class; the two sides present their arguments with the affirmative side opening and closing the debate.
   G. A chairperson presides over the debate and keeps time.
   H. The debating teams' presentations are evaluated by the rest of the class and the instructor (see Form 3).

Additional Instructions for Debate Teams

Structure of Classroom Debates

First Affirmative	6 minutes
First Negative	6 minutes
Second Affirmative	6 minutes
Second Negative	6 minutes
Rebuttals: Negative	5 minutes
Affirmative	5 minutes
Audience Cross-Examination	10 minutes

Tips on Oral Presentation

1. All of the speeches in the debate, *except* the first affirmative speech, should be given extemporaneously by the debaters. They should not be read. Essentially, the debaters' comments must reflect what was presented in the previous speech.

2. The first affirmative speech should be used to build the affirmative case. It is a good idea to give an overview of the major arguments you will use to uphold the proposition.

3. The first negative speech must be presented with the content of the first affirmative speech in mind. The aim of the negative speech is to cast doubt on the affirmative's arguments. The second speeches on both sides attempt to elaborate and build arguments as needed.

4. The rebuttal should directly address the arguments made by the other side.

5. Two excellent sources of information on debating are: Arthur N. Kruger, *Modern Debate: Its Logic and Strategy* (New York: McGraw-Hill, 1960) and Thomas K. Hanley, *An Introduction to Debate* (Boston: Ginn & Company, 1965).

Suggested Debate Propositions

1. Resolved: That employment equity is a fair method of achieving equal opportunity in the workplace.

2. Resolved: That employee diversity enhances organizational performance.

3. Resolved: That telecommuting enhances employee productivity and morale while reducing turnover.

4. Resolved: That employers should develop and enforce policies prohibiting dating between coworkers.

5. Resolved: That family-friendly policies which benefit only employees with dependent children are unfair to other employees.

6. Resolved: That Canadian immigration laws should be changed to allow more immigration by technical specialists from emerging/developing countries.

7. Resolved: That Canadian professional bodies (e.g., colleges of physicians, dentists, engineers, veterinarians, nurses) should not require professionals whose qualifications were achieved in other countries to re-train and/or pass qualifying examinations before being able to practise in Canada.

8. Resolved: That the use of contingent workers is an effective and efficient means of staffing.

9. Resolved: That stock options and bonuses for high-level executives should be provided irrespective of the company's performance or the stock's performance in order to attract and retain high-level executives.

Your written paper will follow a form known as a "full brief"—a comprehensive analysis of both sides of a given proposition, outlined logically, from which the debater can develop his or her case. Each team should have a minimum of 10 references (in most cases you will have many more). The paper will consist of three parts: Introduction, Discussion, and Conclusion.

Introduction:

a. Statement of the proposition and your group's position.

b. Explanation of why the issue is important.

c. Origin and history of the issue—keep it brief.

d. Outline the conflicting arguments—why is there a controversy?

Discussion: (This is the major section of your analysis.)

a. Present arguments to support your position.

b. Back up your arguments with sound reasoning and evidence.

Conclusion:

a. Summarize the main points of the discussion—recapitulate your major points.

b. End with an affirmation or denial of the proposition (depending on whether you have the affirmative or negative position).

Debate:

Use the following scale to write in a rating on each item below for each team.

1	2	3	4
POOR	**FAIR**	**GOOD**	**SUPERIOR**

	Affirmative Team	*Negative Team*
I. Analysis (Was the analysis reasonable, complete, and clear?)		
II. Reasoning and evidence (Were the arguments structured soundly, based on research facts and examples? Were arguments logical?)		
III. Organization (Was each speech clearly and cogently organized so that you could follow the structure of the debate?)		
IV. Rebuttal (Were unsupported points and assertions challenged by the opposing team?)		
V. Delivery (Was each speech effectively presented? Consider voice inflection, eye contact, and tone.)		
VI. Questions (Did the team adequately answer audience questions?)		
VII. Overall team rating		

In my opinion, the better debating was done by the _____ team.

(Affirmative or Negative)

Comments for Affirmative Team:

Comments for Negative Team:

Giving Up Seniority to Accommodate a Disabled Colleague

Jim Martin had been loading and unloading cargo for East Coast Airlines for five years. His job performance ratings had always been above average. One day, Martin injured his back on the job. Because of his injury, he could no longer perform his job as a cargo handler.

The human resource manager, Angela Fisher, suggested that he apply for a transfer to another job appropriate to his skills and qualifications that did not involve physical strain. Transfer requests were governed by East Coast Airlines' seniority policy. Everything being equal, employees with greater seniority were given preference for transfers. Martin requested a transfer to a vacant mailroom position. At the same, Bryan Beckwith, an employee with greater seniority than Jim, also applied for the vacant position. A position in the mailroom was viewed by many employees as an attractive alternative to some of the other blue-collar positions like cargo and baggage handling.

After reviewing the transfer requests of the two employees, Angela Fisher awarded the position to Bryan Beckwith, who had greater seniority at East Coast Airlines than Martin. Her decision was based on East Coast Airlines' seniority policy. In desperation, Martin went to Beckwith and asked him to please withdraw his transfer bid, explaining that he had requested the transfer because of an injury. Martin was hoping that his colleague would understand his plight. Beckwith refused to withdraw his request. Martin went to Fisher and requested an exception to the seniority policy that would allow him to work in the mailroom instead of Beckwith. Martin argued that since he was disabled because of his work as a cargo handler, he should be given preference over Beckwith. Fisher said that company policy did not allow her to make any exceptions. Martin lost his job at East Coast Airlines because there were no other vacancies for which he qualified.

Questions

1. If you were Beckwith, would you have dropped your transfer request to help Martin?
2. Should Fisher have given Martin preference over Beckwith because of Martin's disability? Does seniority override the "reasonable accommodation" as specified in human rights legislation?

The Employee with AIDS

It was another hectic day for Mary Landschulz, cafeteria manager for a department store located in Winnipeg. She had just received a call from one of her employees, Cathy, stating that she would not be able to come to work that day. When she asked Cathy why, Cathy reluctantly stated that yesterday her doctor had informed her that she had AIDS (Acquired Immune Deficiency Syndrome). She did not know when she would return to work but knew that it wouldn't be soon. She said she would call next week.

Hanging up the telephone, Mary sat motionless in her office. She was stunned by what she had just heard. Cathy was an excellent employee and had served food on the cafeteria line for five years. Cathy had been sick recently for several days, but Mary had thought Cathy just had the flu or a cold. Now she knew the truth, and it was not a pretty picture. "Oh, my gosh!" she exclaimed to herself. "What am I going to do?"

As Mary pondered this question, the alarm on her watch "beeped," reminding her that she had to attend a meeting with her employees. Slowly, she got out of her chair and walked down the hall to the meeting room. When she entered the room she found it buzzing with talk about Cathy. Mary headed for the nearest seat, hoping that the topic of discussion would change. As she and the others sat down around the large oval table, one of the cafeteria workers turned to her and asked, "What's wrong with Cathy? She told Frank she might not ever be back to work." A hush fell over the room as everyone awaited Mary's reply.

Questions

1. How should Mary respond to the question?
2. Would it be an invasion of Cathy's privacy if Mary told the employees that Cathy has AIDS?
3. Assuming that the employees ultimately learn that Cathy has AIDS, how should Mary deal with their fears? What should she do if the employees refuse to work with Cathy when she returns?
4. As a result of the incident, should the company develop a specific AIDS policy?

"Beautyism" in the Workplace

Harold Hughes is a professor of management and chair of the department of management in a School of Business Administration at a major Canadian university. Professor Hughes is 52 years old and has been divorced for the past eight years. During that time, he has dated several women for varying periods of time, but is not currently dating or in a relationship.

Recently, Professor Hughes's long-time administrative assistant (Helen Schully) retired from the university at age 60 after 25 years of service. Professor Hughes put together a committee of three departmental members to assist him in selecting a new administrative assistant. These three committee members were Professor Don Hall, Professor Mike Meyers, and Pauline Nelson, the department's financial officer. The position was advertised internally within the university as well as externally in the local newspaper.

The committee met, developed a list of selection criteria with appropriate weights, reviewed 13 applications, and selected four female applicants for interviews. These four were Melissa (a 47-year-old administrative assistant in a local insurance company), Sally (a 38-year-old secretary at the university), Carol (a 52-year-old administrative assistant at the university), and Diane (a 27-year-old secretary at a local bank). Melissa and Carol have B.S. degrees while Sally is studying for her B.A. degree at the university. Diane is a high-school graduate with no post-secondary education. A bachelor's degree (in hand or in process) and/or previous experience as an administrative assistant were two of the selection criteria the committee had developed prior to the interviews.

Originally, the committee had selected only Melissa, Sally, and Carol for final interviews. However, Diane had personally brought her application to the office, met briefly with Harold to express her interest in the position, and had received his assurance that she would be among those interviewed. He then informed the other committee members that he had added Diane to the group to be interviewed. During the interview process, the other three committee members noticed that Howard seemed quite "taken" with Diane, even though (on paper) she seemed to have the least impressive credentials for the position. She was extremely attractive and recently divorced with a four-year-old son. The three other committee members all agreed that Carol seemed to have the education and all the skills, knowledge, and abilities the committee had previously identified (including knowledge of the university bureaucracy).

Despite their consensus, Harold said the person would be working for him, and that he "felt more comfortable with Diane." After the decision was made and Diane was offered and accepted the position, Professor Hall remarked to Professor Meyers, "Harold must have been thinking with his ____!" Professor Meyers agreed but added that Diane was "hot" and would definitely "enhance the scenery around here." Pauline Nelson was upset because she felt Harold was sexist and had made the selection decision "based purely on physical attraction."

Questions

1. What is "beautyism"?
2. To what degree was "beautyism" a factor in this decision? How do you know?
3. Why do more attractive male and female job applicants have an advantage in the interview process?
4. Should the "beautyism" bias be eliminated from the selection process? If so, how?

27. SKILL BUILDER

Data Analysis for Employment Equity Plans

    I. *Objectives:*
- **A.** To enhance your understanding of how to prepare a representation analysis for employment equity plans.
- **B.** To teach you how to collect and analyze the data required under federal employment equity guidelines.

  II. *Time Required to Complete:* 2 to 3 hours

 III. *Instructions:* You work for a local manufacturing firm, and your company has just been awarded its first federal contract of $250,000. This contract is to supply one of your major products over a two-year period to the Department of National Defence. You have been asked by your boss, the plant manager, to perform the analyses required under the federal *Employment Equity Act*.

    You have reviewed the federal government's guidelines for conducting work force analyses (see Exhibit 1.28). You have also pulled together labour market data in addition to compiling a detailed breakdown of the company's work force by job category and designated group status (see Exhibits 1.29, 1.30, 1.31, and 1.32).

Required

Using the relevant data, complete Form 4. You may need to generate additional forms for your use. It is easier to set this up in a spreadsheet format. This is the first step toward developing an employment equity plan. Be sure to list any assumptions you make about the relevant labour market for each job category. Also be sure to indicate the job categories where women, members of visible minorities, Aboriginal persons, and persons with disabilities are underrepresented. Make any other recommendations you deem necessary to the plant manager.

Exhibit 1.28 *Federal Employment Equity Act Guidelines*

Definition

The *Employment Equity Act* requires employers to develop and implement an employment equity program, in consultation and collaboration with employee representatives, to remove barriers for women, members of visible minorities, Aboriginal persons, and persons with disabilities, in order to achieve a representative work force.

Analysis

The employer must analyze work force data in order to determine the degree of underrepresentation of members of designated groups in each occupational group or category.

    The employer must calculate the external representation of designated group members in each occupational group or category. External representation from each designated group must be based on the labour pool from which the employer may reasonably be expected to recruit, taking into account qualifications, eligibility, and geographic recruitment area for each occupational group or category. The employer must compare external representation with work force data to determine the degree of underrepresentation, if any, for each designated group in each occupational group or category.

The employer must review its employment systems, as well as policies and practices, to identify barriers to members of designated groups for occupational groups or categories in which underrepresentation has been found. The results of the systems review must be documented, and must provide probable explanations for the underrepresentation found in each occupational group. The explanations for the underrepresentation must provide a reasonable basis for the employer to take corrective action.

Plan

The employment equity plan must specify the short-term measures the employer will implement to eliminate barriers identified through its employment systems review. The plan should include measures to remove each of the barriers identified in the course of the systems review that cannot be justified on the grounds that (a) they are a bona fide or validated occupational requirement; (b) they are protected by legislated provisions relating to seniority, priorities, or work force adjustment measures; or (c) they are authorized by law related to employer obligations. The plan should also include a timetable for the implementation of each of these measures within a reasonable period of time, taking into account (a) the significance of the measure, (b) internal and external resources and constraints, (c) alternatives available, and (d) the complexity and costs of implementation. At least some significant measures to address each barrier must be undertaken within three years. The employment equity plan must also include provisions for the accommodation of the needs of applicants and employees from the four designated groups.

Source: Adapted from http://www.chrc-ccdp.ca/employment_equity/part2-en.asp?pm=1 and http://www.chrc-ccdp.ca/employment_equity/part1-en.asp?pm=1.

Exhibit 1.29 *Work Force Analysis*

Job Categories	Overall Totals (Sums of Columns B–I)	White Male	Aboriginal Male	Minority Male	Disabled Male	White Female	Aboriginal Female	Minority Female	Disabled Female
	A	B	C	D	E	F	G	H	I
Officials and managers*	154	138	2	0	0	13	1	0	0
Professionals	137	126	1	0	0	10	0	0	0
Technicians	76	61	2	1	1	6	2	0	3
Sales workers	77	65	4	0	0	7	1	0	0
Office and clerical	188	21	3	0	1	144	2	17	0
Craft workers (skilled)	150	120	15	1	2	9	0	3	0
Operatives (semiskilled)	294	200	2	60	10	16	0	4	2
Labourers (unskilled)	652	504	6	82	10	38	0	10	2
Service workers	89	17	7	49	1	2	2	11	0
TOTALS	1,817	1,252	42	193	25	245	8	45	7

*Includes supervisors

Data Analysis for Employment Equity Plans **Skill Builder 27**

Exhibit 1.30 *Regional Labour Force by Sex and Race*

Sex and Race	Civilian Labour Force	Employed	Unemployed
Both Sexes			
TOTAL	514,796	489,574	25,222
White	417,540	400,260	17,280
Minority	90,270	82,710	7,560
Aboriginal	1,093	1,048	45
Disabled	5,893	5,556	437
Female			
TOTAL	233,298	220,545	12,753
White	184,190	175,420	8,770
Minority	45,970	42,150	3,820
Aboriginal	495	467	28
Disabled	2,643	2,508	135

Exhibit 1.31 *Occupations of the Male Regional Labour Force by Sex and Designated Group Status*

Occupation	Total[1]	White	Minority	Aboriginal	Disabled
TOTAL: All industries	447,254	364,832	78,955	1,348	1,837
Managerial and professional specialty	87,018	77,673	8,482	119	689
Technicians	10,077	8,557	1,415	20	80
Sales occupations	45,837	42,341	3,241	84	141
Administrative support including clerical	72,927	62,762	9,857	115	173
Service workers	47,097	29,970	16,627	225	249
Farming, forestry, and fishing	5,483	4,301	1,103	53	19
Precision production and craft	59,987	51,716	7,830	282	130
Operators and fabricators	92,707	69,331	22,678	344	251
Handlers, equipment cleaners, helpers, and labourers	26,121	18,181	7,722	106	105

[1] "Designated group" columns may not be additive to total due to "not classified" or missing responses in census data.

Exhibit 1.32 *Occupations of the Female Regional Labour Force by Sex and Designated Group Status*

Occupation	Total[1]	White	Minority	Aboriginal	Disabled
TOTAL: All industries	202,039	160,509	40,184	524	702
Managerial and professional specialty	36,447	30,864	5,346	48	167
Technicians	4,667	3,716	923	7	16
Sales occupations	20,006	17,652	2,211	53	71
Administrative support including clerical	55,628	48,504	6,928	86	95
Service workers	28,122	17,269	10,557	134	143
Farming, forestry, and fishing	1,166	877	278	6	5
Precision production and craft	5,778	4,488	1,256	13	14
Operators and fabricators	43,556	32,601	10,588	169	165
Handlers, equipment cleaners, helpers, and labourers	6,669	4,538	2,097	9	26

[1] "Designated group" columns may not be additive to total due to "not classified" or missing responses in census data.

Form 4 *Representation Analysis*

Job Category	Male	Female	White	Minority	Aboriginal	Disabled	Total
Number of employees							
Percentage of employees							
Percent available in external labour force							
Represen- tation rate							

Note: A table will be needed for each job category.

Meeting Human Resource Requirements: Job Analysis/ Design, Planning, Recruitment, and Selection

Part 2

JOB ANALYSIS/PLANNING

28. CASE

Employee Layoffs at St. Mary's Hospital

St. Mary's Hospital is a medium-sized, 400-bed hospital. It was established in 1908 by the Sisters of the Sacred Heart, an order of Catholic sisters. The facility has grown gradually over the years and is now the third-largest hospital in the city where it is located. The hospital has never experienced an employee layoff since its inception.

Sister Mary Josephine has been the chief executive officer of the hospital for 11 years. Eight years ago, she hired Sharon Osgood as director of personnel. Osgood has an M.A. in Human Resource Management and has been instrumental in formalizing the institution's human resource policies and procedures.

Patient occupancy rates in the hospital had run between 76 and 82 percent from 1970 to 1982. However, since then, occupancy has fallen to an average of 57 percent. Such declines have not been unusual in health care during this time as a result of changes to medical coverage, emphasis on out-patient services, and changes in population densities. However, the declining occupancy rate has affected this hospital's financial status to such an extent that it ran a deficit for the first time last year. The only response to these changes thus far has been a tightening of requirements for equipment or supply purchases.

At the most recent quarterly meeting of the Board of Directors, Sister Mary Josephine presented the rather bleak financial picture. The projected deficit for the coming year was $3,865,000 unless some additional revenue sources were identified or some additional savings were found. The board's recommendation, based on the immediate crisis and need to generate short-term savings, was that employee layoffs were the only realistic alternative. They recommended that Sister Mary Josephine consider laying off up to 10 percent of the hospital's employees, with an emphasis on those in "non-essential" areas.

Sister Mary Josephine responded that the hospital had never laid off employees in the history of the institution. Moreover, she viewed the employees as part of the "family" and would have great difficulty in implementing such a layoff. Nevertheless, since she had no realistic short-term alternative, she reluctantly agreed to implement a layoff policy that would be as fair as possible to all employees, with a guarantee of re-employment for those laid off, and to find additional sources of funds so that layoffs would be unnecessary in the future.

Sister Mary Josephine called Sharon Osgood into her office the next morning, shared her concerns, and asked her to prepare both a short-term plan to save $3 million over the next year through employee layoffs as well as a long-term plan to avoid layoffs in the future. Her concerns were that the layoffs themselves might be costly in terms of lost investment in some of the laid-off employees, lost efficiency, potential lawsuits, and lower morale. She was concerned that the criteria for the layoffs not only be equitable, but also appear to be equitable to the employees. She also wanted to make sure that those being laid off received "adequate" notice so they could make alternative plans or so that the hospital could assist them with finding alternative employment. Since the hospital had no previous experience with employee layoffs, her feeling was that both seniority and job performance should be considered in determining who would be laid off.

Sharon knew the hospital's performance appraisal system was inadequate and needed to be revamped. While this task was high on her "to do" list, she also knew she had to move ahead with her recommendations on layoffs immediately. The present performance appraisal system uses a traditional checklist rating scale with a summary rating. Since there is no forced distribution, the average ratings of employees in different departments vary widely.

Exhibit 2.1 shows the summary ratings of employees in each department. Most supervisors in all departments rate many of their subordinates as either "satisfactory" or "outstanding." Sharon has done a quick review of those employees whose overall ratings were "unsatisfactory" or "questionable." Most are employees with less than three years of seniority, whereas the average "satisfactory" employee has worked for St. Mary's approximately seven years. Sharon is preparing to submit her recommendations to Sister Mary Josephine and has come to you for advice. Exhibit 2.2 provides a summary of the distribution of employees and payroll expense by department for the most recent year.

Questions

1. Identify the major problem or problems, and the causes.
2. What are some alternatives for dealing with these problems? For example, is it possible to avoid layoffs through the use of attrition?
3. Develop a plan for implementing employee layoffs over the next year that will generate $3 million in savings. Give specific details concerning departments affected, the use of seniority versus merit to determine candidates for layoffs, the amount of notice the laid-off employees will receive, and outplacement activities. What additional information (if any) will you need? Provide a rationale for each recommendation, together with reasons why other alternatives were not chosen.
4. What might be the effects of a layoff plan on "survivors" in terms of morale, job security, organizational commitment, productivity, and career planning? How could you avoid or minimize any potential problems in these areas?
5. What long-term solutions do you see for the hospital once it gets its financial problems under control and eliminates its deficit? What can it do to improve its financial status so that future layoffs will not be necessary?
6. What difficulties exist in using "performance" as a criterion for layoffs? How can such difficulties be overcome?

Exhibit 2.1 *Percentage Distribution of Performance Appraisal Ratings by Department*

Summary Ratings by Department at St. Mary's Hospital

Department	Unsatisfactory: Needs to Improve Substantially	Questionable: Needs Some Improvement	Satisfactory: Meets Normal Expectations	Outstanding: Substantially Exceeds Norms
Nursing	6.4	6.4	54.2	33.0
Allied Health	5.7	6.2	47.8	40.3
Central Administration	2.7	3.1	67.5	26.7
Dietetics/Nutrition	2.1	6.2	68.3	23.4
Housekeeping/ Maintenance	7.8	12.4	54.6	25.2
Medical Staff	1.1	6.2	63.8	28.9

Exhibit 2.2 *Payroll Expenditures and Turnover Rates at St. Mary's Hospital by Department*

Department	Number of Employees	Payroll ($)	Annual Turnover Rates (%)
Nursing	602	$30,100,000	12.2
Allied Health	261	10,440,000	8.7
Central Administration	154	6,160,000	3.5
Dietetics/Nutrition	65	1,950,000	7.3
Housekeeping/Maintenance	36	1,080,000	8.4
Medical Staff	32	2,560,000	2.1
TOTAL	1,150	$52,290,000	9.5*

*Represents weighted average turnover for all employees.

Strategic Human Resource Management

The School of Business Administration at Riverside University is one of eight degree-granting business schools in its province. It is located in a city with a population of 400,000 and a diversified industrial base. One small community college in the same area provides competition to the university's School of Business Administration.

Recently, the school has experienced a leadership transition. Dr. George Barnes, Dean of the School of Business Administration since 1978, retired. During his administration, the enrollment had increased from 1,202 undergraduates and 76 M.B.A. students in the 1978–79 academic year to 2,089 undergraduates and 218 M.B.A. students in the most recent academic year.

Dean Barnes was well liked by students, faculty, and the central administration of Riverside. However, he had not led the School of Business Administration in any new directions and had basically concentrated on "doing the same things better." The "same things" meant an emphasis on traditional programs (e.g., accounting, marketing, finance), teaching undergraduate students in the age range of 18–22 in daytime programs, and teaching a small number of full-time M.B.A. students. The latter have been mostly graduates of the school's undergraduate program who decided they were willing to spend two more years on campus to obtain the second degree.

Dean Barnes had also been successful in upgrading the proportion of faculty with Ph.D. degrees from 56 percent in 1978 to 85 percent in the most recent year. Exhibit 2.3 provides faculty and student enrollment data for the school for selected years during Barnes's tenure.

During the most recent academic year, the Dean's Search Committee (consisting of faculty, students, alumni, central administration, and local business representatives) met frequently, screened over 100 applicants, and personally interviewed 6. While the committee arrived at no consensus, the majority supported Mr. Jack Blake for the Deanship. An offer was made and, after several weeks of negotiation, Blake accepted the position of Dean. His background consisted of an M.B.A. from a prestigious business school, and executive leadership positions in a variety of Canadian corporations in marketing. He left the position of vice president of marketing at a large Canadian industrial company to accept the Deanship.

During the screening interviews with the Search Committee, Blake had made it clear that, if he were selected, the School of Business Administration would be "moving in new directions and exploring new markets." It was very clear Blake did not want to be a "paper pusher," but did want to be an innovator and an entrepreneur. When pressed for specifics, he had indicated he "would have to study the situation in more detail."

When the new Dean arrived on campus in the fall, he immediately convened a Strategic Planning Committee to (1) evaluate the school's external environment, opportunities, constraints, competitive advantages, and internal environment; and (2) recommend a new set of long-term missions, goals, objectives, and programs. The committee consisted of two senior professors, the university's vice president for academic affairs, one graduate student, one undergraduate student, two prominent alumni, and two local business leaders.

The committee recommended that the school focus on the adult learner, since demographic analysis suggested the number of Canadians aged 18–22 was shrinking and would be a declining market over the next decade. Specific recommendations included (1) offering more evening courses for both under-graduate and graduate students; (2) structuring the schedule so that both degrees could be earned entirely in the evening; (3) offering credit courses in some suburban locations; (4) offering requested non-credit practitioner courses at the school, at the employer's work site, and in various under-served small cities around the province; (5) exploring the possibility of offering degree pro-grams at these locations; (6) offering new M.B.A. degree concentrations in such areas as management of the arts, health care management, and public sector management; and (7) offering a new "executive" M.B.A.

The new Dean enthusiastically endorsed the report and distributed copies at the last faculty meeting of the fall semester. Several questions were raised, but it didn't appear that serious opposition existed. However, at a subsequent meeting of department chairs, the Dean indicated that his top priority for the next academic year was to fill the five vacant positions with new faculty who would be supportive of the new directions in which the school was moving. Specifically, he asked the chairs to keep several criteria in mind while recruiting and selecting new faculty. These included previous managerial work experi-ence, a willingness to teach night courses, a willingness to travel to other cities to teach courses, an ability to work with management practitioners on special projects, and previous experience in teaching executives.

The Dean also suggested that the chairs consider those criteria when evaluating the performance of existing faculty and recommending salary increases. Finally, he indicated that one of the vacant faculty positions would be used to recruit a new assistant dean for external affairs, who would become the school's link to the practitioner community. The new assistant dean would be involved with helping practising managers identify their needs, working with faculty to meet these needs, and negotiating contracts for these services.

When word of the Dean's faculty recommendations spread through the "rumour mill," the reaction was swift and negative. Many of the "old guard" faculty felt they had been hired primarily to teach full-time students on campus during the day. Consequently, they were threatened by the new evaluation criteria. They were also concerned that the Dean was interjecting non-academic criteria into their departmental faculty recruitment processes and diverting the school's resources to non-academic activities. These faculty felt the inevitable result would be a declining quality of education in the school.

A group of these faculty have asked to meet with the Dean to discuss his proposals. The Dean is preparing a justification for both his strategy and his human resource management (faculty) recommendations.

Questions

1. How and why do strategic decisions affect human resource management policies? Can human resource policies or constraints ever affect strategy? Why or why not?
2. Identify the problem and causes of the problem in this case.
3. Evaluate Dean Blake's strategy and human resource policies. Does the strategy make sense in terms of the internal and external environment of the school? Do the human resource strategies support and reinforce the organizational strategy? Why or why not?
4. Evaluate the process by which Dean Blake implemented the strategic and human resource changes. Can you suggest any improvements?
5. How can resistance to his plans and strategies be overcome?

Exhibit 2.3 *Faculty and Student Enrollment Data for the School of Business Administration in Selected Years, 1978–2003*

Academic Year	Faculty	Faculty with Ph.D.	Student Enrollment		
			B.S.	M.B.A.	Total
1978–79	54	30	1,202	76	1,278
1980–81	58	36	1,289	98	1,387
1985–86	66	46	1,654	134	1,788
1990–91	74	57	1,913	154	2,067
1995–96	78	66	2,065	221	2,286
2002–03	80	68	2,089	218	2,307

The Bank Merger

Jack Duncan Ramsey, senior vice president of human resources at Central Bank, re-read the memo calling a meeting of top management to discuss the merger agreement signed with Sinclair Bank. Sinclair Bank was one of the largest banks in the country (see Exhibit 2.4), and this would be one of the largest mergers they had ever undertaken. Sinclair Bank enjoyed a strong market position, and over the years had exhibited above-average profitability. Sinclair Bank was a heavy personal and real estate lender. About 45 percent of its earning assets represented personal and real estate loans, while about 10 percent were commercial and industrial loans.

In contrast, Central is a big commercial lender, offering a diversified range of financial services, with about 35 percent of its earning assets in corporate loans. Although Central Bank had been basically put together through mergers, usually the mergers were with much smaller banks, and most involved converting the acquired bank's operational procedures for loans and deposits to their system. Most of the banks that were purchased did not have centralized operating or administrative functions. The major personnel actions involved putting employees of the acquired bank on the payroll and conducting a short orientation program to inform them about benefits and bank policies and procedures. Typically, no employees lost jobs because of the merger, and any needed adjustments to the size of the work force were handled through normal turnover and attrition.

Ramsey felt that this merger would be quite different and would require a more complex process to implement. Sinclair Bank had over 80 branches in 38 cities and more than 1,800 employees. As is often the case in banks of this size, Sinclair Bank had centralized support functions such as operations, personnel, audit, and accounting. Ramsey knew that consolidating the support functions and, in some cases, the line functions would be a major challenge in this merger.

The Planning Meeting

Larry McDonald, chairman and chief executive officer of Central Bank, opened the meeting with the top officers: Jack Ramsey, Pat Stevenson (senior vice president of operations), and Thomas "Buddy" Kent (president).

McDonald: Our merger with Sinclair Bank is a natural fit. We are located in regions with very similar social, cultural, and political heritages. We already have a large corporate customer base and our advertising has covered many of its markets for years. I called this meeting today because we want this to be one of the smoothest mergers in our history. We need to come up with a plan to complete and implement the merger. I think we need to start now even though the merger is still pending board and shareholder approval.

Ramsey: Larry, from the personnel side, I can already anticipate some concern from Sinclair Bank about protecting their employees. There are probably already all kinds of rumours circulating and a lot of anxiety about what this merger is going to mean in terms of job security for their employees. We may have very few changes in personnel on the line side of the bank, but some problems may crop up if there are major changes on the staff side.

Stevenson: I also think we're going to have to make some decisions about consolidating computer systems and getting their people up to speed on using our equipment and technology. The economies of scale here are a real plus and we should definitely keep that in the forefront of our thinking and planning.

Kent: We also probably need to come up with a combined business plan that should help us in getting Sinclair management committed to our goals. We need to capitalize on our geographical proximity and similar cultures in developing a business plan.

McDonald: We must remain true to our own corporate philosophy. We have recognized for years that our customers will be treated well if our employees are treated well. This strategy has worked for us and we want to carry it over to all our bank employees. We can't guarantee them a job because we are going to take advantage of the economies of scale and consolidate many positions, but we should at least try to do everything possible to absorb and maintain as many good people as possible.

Ramsey: I agree with you, Larry. I think our hardest task is going to be managing the people side of this merger, especially the communication part. We've done the operations part many times before and have had good results. I really believe a successful merger is 10 percent planning and 90 percent communication.

The Steering Committees

Shortly after the meeting, three steering committees were formed to guide the merger process over the next 12 to 18 months. The Business Planning Committee consisted of the president of Central Bank, the president of Sinclair Bank, and the top managers from the operations, human resources, and line functions of each bank. The committee compared bank products, made pricing decisions, and decided how to handle the transition period and how to phase in the merger. The committee developed a one-year profit plan and a three-year business plan for the combined banks. The business plan spelled out the bank's objectives for each of its major activities as well as an overall market strategy. The planned strategy was around the theme "Your Hometown Bank." A major outcome of this planning was a decision to consolidate most of the bank's support functions at the headquarters of Central Bank in Toronto. These and other projected consolidations would save about $16 to $18 million a year. Once the overall business plans were formulated, the post-merger organization structure was developed for each major division of Sinclair Bank to reflect which jobs would remain. For example, the pre- and post-merger organization chart developed for the Toronto Trust Centre is shown in Exhibit 2.5. A profile of the employees in that division is given in Exhibit 2.6.

The Operations Committee developed detailed work plans to operationally merge the banks. These plans included procedures for the conversion of loans, deposits, cheque processing, and other operational activities. The committee included managers from every major unit in the Operations Group of each bank, as well as managers from support functions throughout both banks.

The Human Resource Steering Committee, headed by Jack Ramsey, consisted of human resource staff from both banks. The committee was charged with developing a strategy for implementing human resource policies, practices, and procedures for finding other positions for employees whose jobs might be eliminated. During initial meetings, differences in philosophy emerged. Sinclair Bank traditionally had taken a more conservative, by-the-book approach to applying human resource policies. Central Bank tended to be more flexible and would often consider the particular employee's circumstances and situation before making personnel decisions. At the time of the merger, Sinclair Bank did not have formal job descriptions and, because of its smaller size, did not have the same level of employee benefits as Central. The turnover rate at Sinclair Bank was around 10 percent annually, somewhat higher than Central's. One of the first things done by the committee was to draw up a list of major human resource issues to be managed over the next year or so. The list contained these issues:

1. Managing staff reductions and transfers.
2. Maintaining employee productivity during the merger transition period.
3. Ensuring communication flow to employees to minimize unwarranted rumours.
4. Socializing employees to Central's "culture and philosophy."
5. Designing appropriate training programs.

Two months after the merger announcement, Ramsey received a memorandum (see Exhibit 2.7) from the Business Planning Committee requesting that a plan of action be developed to deal with expected staff displacement. Ramsey was somewhat alarmed at the number of employees who were being displaced—almost 20 percent of Sinclair Bank's work force. He also learned that there were a number of officer positions included in that total.

Two days after receiving the memo, Ramsey's assistant, Ed Flanders, burst into his office with the news that he had received several phone calls from employees of Sinclair Bank. The callers had heard that a big layoff was about to occur, and they wanted to know how they could keep their jobs. Flanders wanted to know how he should respond to the employees. Ramsey simply said, "I knew this one would be different."

Questions

1. Evaluate the bank's approach to implementing the merger.
2. Are there human resource issues other than those listed by the Human Resource Steering Committee that emerge when two companies merge?
3. Do you agree with Ramsey's comment that "a successful merger is 10 percent planning and 90 percent communication"? Why or why not?

4. Develop a plan of action for handling the projected labour surplus. What factors need to be considered?
5. How should the Human Resource Steering Committee handle the needed staff reduction in the Trust Centre?

Exhibit 2.4 *Profiles of Central Bank and Sinclair Bank*

	Central	Sinclair
Net income	$101.3 million	$18.7 million
Return on assets	0.71%	1.08%
Return on equity	13.92%	15.09%
Total assets	$13.5 billion	$1.6 billion
Total deposits	$9.6 billion	$1.2 billion
Number of employees	7,560	1,857
Number of branches	201	83

Exhibit 2.5 *Trust Centre, Sinclair Bank, Pre- and Post-Merger Organization Chart*

Pre-Merger Organization Chart

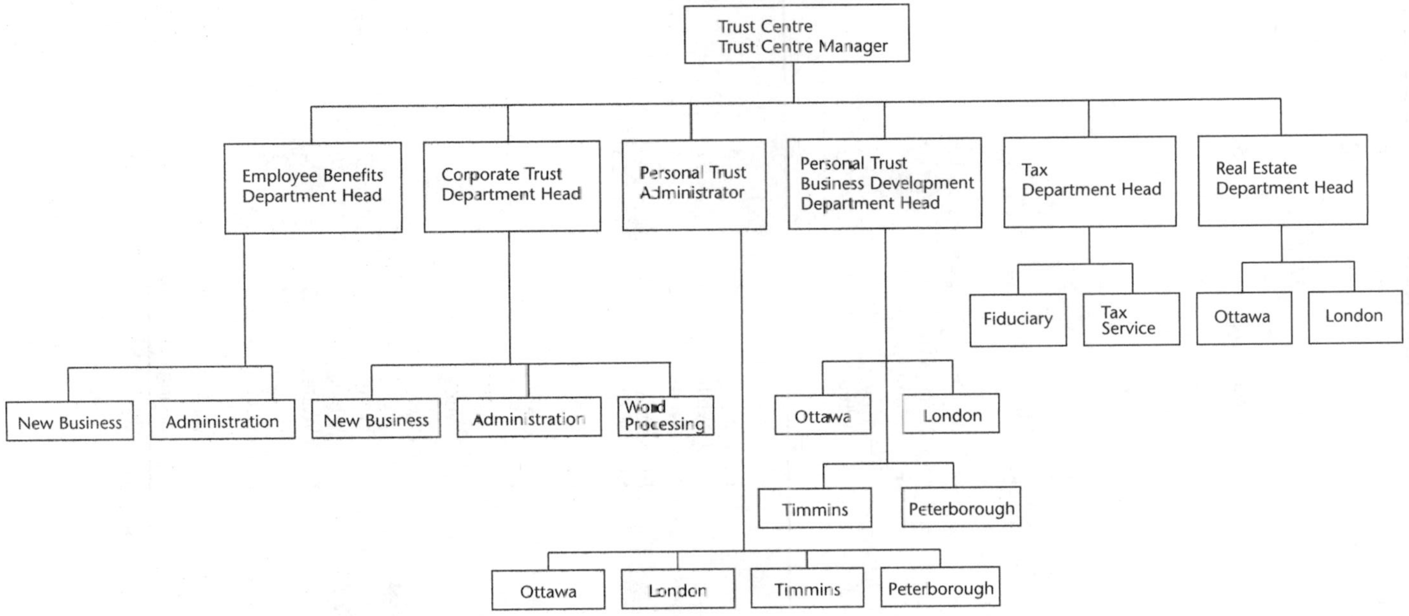

Expected Post-Merger Organization Chart

The Bank Merger **Case 30**   95

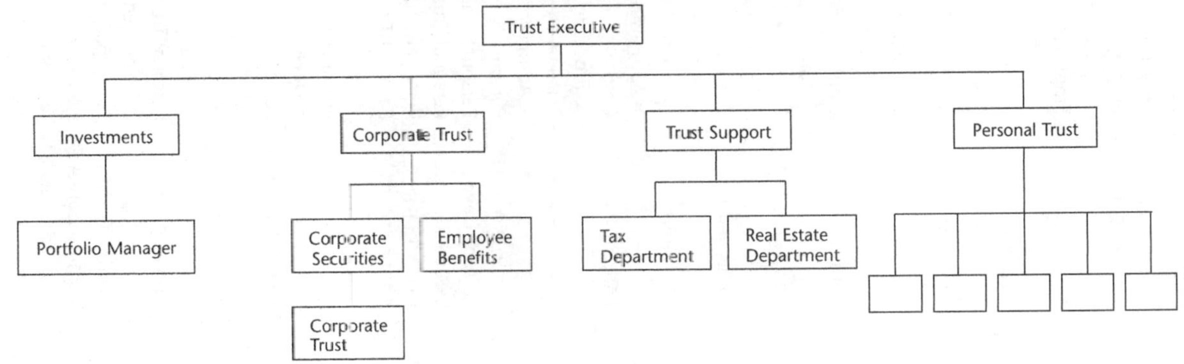

Exhibit 2.6 *Sinclair Bank, Employee Profile (Trust Centre)*

Name	Position	Sex	Ethnicity	Age	Employment	Last Years of Performance Rating*
Douglas Reid	Trust Centre Manager	M	White	52	20	5
Harriet Jones	Employee Benefits Department Head	F	White	40	18	4
Bryan Dinkins	Employee Benefits New Business	M	White	37	8	4
Diva Brown	Employee Benefits Administration	F	Black	32	5	3
Carol Cheong	Employee Benefits Administration	F	Asian	28	4	4
Diane Reeves	Employee Benefits Administration	F	White	41	7	3
Kathy Neel	Employee Benefits Administration	F	White	50	17	3
Bob Watson	Corporate Trust Department Head	M	White	54	19	5
Henry Jeffrey	Corporate Trust New Business	M	White	44	10	4
Margaret Neale	Corporate Trust Administration	F	White	29	3	4
Barbara Westin	Corporate Trust Word Processing	F	White	31	2	3
Vivian Hawkins	Personal Trust Administrator	F	Black	37	10	4
Victor Dale	Personal Trust Ottawa	M	Black	49	12	4
William Devoe	Personal Trust London	M	White	39	7	5
Leslie Hill	Personal Trust Timmins	F	White	33	4	4
Donald Phillips	Personal Trust Peterborough	M	White	59	23	4
Arthur Barnett	Personal Trust Business Development Head	M	White	62	25	5
Albert Lee	Personal Trust Business Development Ottawa	M	Asian	35	8	4
Kendrith Hanks	Personal Trust Business Development London	M	White	27	4	3
Robert Davidson	Personal Trust Business Development Timmins	M	White	28	5	5
Jennifer Degen	Personal Trust Business Development Peterborough	F	White	47	9	5
Cynthia Fuchs	Tax Department Head	F	White	38	10	5
Michael Gridley	Fiduciary	M	White	34	4	3
Rosalind Lopez	Tax Services	F	Hispanic	26	3	4
Leonard Clay	Real Estate Department Head	M	White	57	15	4
Katherine Stern	Real Estate Ottawa	F	White	27	2	3
Betty Henderson	Real Estate London	F	Aboriginal	40	9	5

*The company uses a rating scale of 1 (poor) to 5 (outstanding).

Exhibit 2.7 *Memorandum on Post-Merger Staffing*

Memorandum

Date: September 15, 2004
To: Jack Duncan Ramsey, Chair
             Human Resource Steering Committee
From: Buddy Kent
             Business Planning Committee
Re: Post-Merger Staffing

Approximately 375 individuals will be displaced in the next 6 to 12 months—almost all of these in Toronto. We will be unable to deal with this total number via reassignments and normal turnover. A plan of action must be developed to handle this situation. One such reduction needs to occur in the Trust Centre where we must cut that staff from 27 to 19. In addition to a general plan of action, we would also like to see a run-through on a proposal for handling the situation in the Trust Centre. I believe your committee has the necessary data.

31. EXERCISE

Which Employee Should Be Terminated?

I. *Objectives*:
   A. To make you aware of the difficulties involved in making termination decisions.
   B. To familiarize you with possible criteria a manager can use in making termination decisions.
   C. To give you practice in conducting termination interviews.
II. *Out-of-Class Preparation Time:* 10 minutes to read the exercise and decide which employee should be terminated
III. *In-Class Time Suggested:* 40–50 minutes
IV. *Procedures:* Either at the beginning of or before class, you should read the exercise and determine which title examiner should be fired.

To start the exercise, the instructor will ask five students to play the role of title examiners. One of you will play the role of Rick Feinberg, another the role of Jeff Simon, and so on. These individuals will be asked to leave the classroom and prepare to play their role. They should study carefully the material contained in this exercise and determine how to respond if, in fact, they are the one chosen to be terminated.

The instructor will divide the remaining students into groups of four to six. Each group should develop a list of criteria for layoffs, and rank the title examiners from first to go to last to go. After the group has reached a consensus, it should select one spokesperson to communicate the decision to the title examiner who is to be terminated.

After all groups have finished performing the preceding tasks, the role play begins. One at a time, each group's spokesperson announces to the class which title examiner his or her group believes should be terminated. The instructor then brings that person into the room and asks him or her to sit down in the front. The spokesperson sits down opposite the title examiner, tells that person that he or she is terminated, and gives the rationale behind the decision. The title examiner then responds in any realistic way that he or she deems appropriate. This process continues until all groups' spokespersons have had an opportunity to present their decision. A critique of the role plays and a discussion of the difficulties involved in terminating an employee should then follow.

Situation

The Stanton Title Insurance Company was founded in 1964 by Harvey Stanton to sell title insurance policies to buyers of real estate. The company works closely with a group of about 35 lawyers who, although they do not actually buy the title insurance policies, encourage their clients (the property purchasers) to do so. When the company was originally established, Stanton was its only employee. As company sales increased, new employees were hired, and now 23 individuals are working in various capacities for the firm. Stanton has always followed the policy of making all major decisions himself. This includes all personnel decisions, such as determining who should be hired and how much they should be paid.

Five of the employees work primarily on examining titles at local government offices. In recent weeks, Stanton has noticed that the workload of these five employees has declined considerably. In part, this is due to the recent election of three "no-growth" candidates to the city council. In addition, a competing firm has recently opened an office in town and is successfully taking business away. Stanton has reluctantly decided that he must terminate the employment of one of the title examiners. He simply cannot transfer one of them to a new position. His only question is, which one?

A summary of Harvey's evaluation of each title examiner is in Exhibit 2.8; a profile of each of the five title examiners appears below.

Rick Feinberg: Forty-five years old; white; married with three children; 20 years with the company; graduated from a community college; knows how to resolve difficult title policies due to his extensive experience; is difficult to get along with; antagonizes other employees at main office; hates to fill out company reports not related to title examination and refuses to do so on occasion; will not work overtime under any condition, which puts a burden on others.

Jeff Simon: Twenty-three years old; black; married; attending community college; one year with the company; wife works at main office as a computer programmer; works very hard and is eager to learn; well liked by all employees and is highly dependable; is never absent and will gladly work overtime to meet emergencies; with more experience, he should be an outstanding title examiner; is highly loyal and dedicated; moved recently to a new apartment across the street from the government office where he works.

Kathy Wong: Twenty-four years old; single; college degree; Asian; working on M.B.A. at night; three years with company; well liked by employees; very active in community affairs; capable of moving up to a top management position with the company; often misses work due to school and community activities.

Doris Matthews: Thirty-six years old; married; white; attended community college but did not graduate; 10 years with company; niece of Harvey Stanton; has had eye problems and headaches, which affected work quality this year, and may continue to have these problems; has been very helpful in getting new business for the company; is well-known and highly respected by law firms.

Anthony Pope: Sixty-three years old; white; 15 years with company; no post-secondary education; hard working and well-liked by employees; three children in university; a solid, stable employee who is able to remain calm and solve problems in crisis situations; excellent at resolving conflicts between employees; well-known to local government officials; very slow but highly accurate worker.

Exhibit 2.8 *Harvey's Evaluation of Individual Job Performance for Title Examiners for Last Year*

Title Examiner	Current Salary	Work Quality	Work Quantity	Knowledge of Job	Depend-ability	Coopera-tiveness
Rick Feinberg	$40,000	Excellent	Good	Excellent	Good	Poor
Jeff Simon	$32,000	Good	Good	Fair	Excellent	Excellent
Kathy Wong	$38,500	Good	Fair	Good	Fair	Excellent
Doris Matthews	$34,000	Poor	Good	Excellent	Good	Good
Anthony Pope	$35,500	Good	Poor	Excellent	Excellent	Excellent

The Alternative Work Schedule

March 13 marked an important day in the history of Building Products, Inc. The Planning Committee was meeting to determine the work schedule for all of the production workers at its new plant. The Human Resource Director, the plant manager, and the production manager were all attending the meeting. The plant was scheduled to open in a few months, and it was time to begin hiring new employees.

The committee knew that the new work schedule needed to meet specific parameters. First, the plant's production process requires that chemicals and materials be heated to high temperatures so the plant must operate 24 hours a day, seven days a week, 363 days a year. On Christmas Day and the day before Christmas, the plant would be shut down with only two employees needed—a production operator and a maintenance technician. Second, workers would not be able to take breaks all at one time. Rather, they would need to stagger the breaks and cover for each other. Third, having the standard 8–to–5 work schedule would be out of the question, given the need for 24-hour coverage. Likewise, a work schedule that entails three shifts, each working eight-hour days, would not work, because coverage is needed seven days a week, and employees need time off to rest.

After much discussion, the Human Resource Director suggested that the firm try a schedule that she had heard about at another firm. The schedule entailed dividing workers into four crews and having each work 12 hours at a time for either three or four straight days or nights, with time off in between. It also meant that employees would switch between day shifts and night shifts. More specifically, the schedule of rotation for one crew would be as follows:

> *4 night shifts—12 hours per night (7 p.m. to 7 a.m.)*
>
> *2 days/nights off*
>
> *3 day shifts—12 hours per day (7 a.m. to 7 p.m.)*
>
> *2 days/nights off*
>
> *3 night shifts—12 hours per night (7 p.m. to 7 a.m.)*
>
> *2 days/nights off*
>
> *4 day shifts—12 hours per day (7 a.m. to 7 p.m.)*
>
> *8 days/nights off*
>
> *Repeat sequence throughout this and future years*

A typical schedule over a 28-day period for each of the four crews would be:

Crew	Week 1 S M T W T F S	Week 2 S M T W T F S	Week 3 S M T W T F S	Week 4 S M T W T F S
A	O N N N O O D	D D D O O O O	O O O O N N N	N O O D D D O
B	N O O D D D O	O N N N O O D	D D D O O O O	O O O O N N N
C	O O O O N N N	N O O D D D O	O N N N O O D	D D D O O O O
D	D D D O O O O	O O O O N N N	N O O D D D O	O N N N O O D

Key: N – night shift; O = off work; D = day shift

The Human Resource Director noted that, by dividing all of the workers into four crews, the schedules for the crews could be integrated in such a way that only one crew would be working, yet all hours could be covered (see schedule above). Each crew would consist of 17 production operators, two warehouse/forklift truck workers to take product off the line, and one production supervisor. Also, she suggested that overtime pay be granted to employees when they work more than 40 hours per week. An employee who works a 48-hour week would receive straight pay for 40 hours and time and a half for 8 more hours. This equates to 52 hours of straight pay. Thus, in the course of a 28-day period, employees would work shifts totalling 168 hours, but be paid for 176 hours. In addition, she recommended that employees who work over a holiday receive double pay for those hours, but that no additional overtime pay be provided for working Saturday or Sunday.

After hearing the Human Resource Director's recommendations, the plant manager and the production manager sat quietly, trying to digest the plan. The schedule was completely unlike anything they had ever experienced, and it struck them as being really bizarre. They couldn't help but question whether the plan would actually work. They also wondered if there might not be a better production schedule.

Questions

1. What do you see as the strengths and weaknesses of the Human Resource Director's work schedule from (a) the employees' perspective, and (b) the firm's perspective?
2. Would you recommend the firm use the new work schedule? Why?
3. What alternative work schedules could be used?

33. EXERCISE

Outsourcing of Human Resource Management Functions

I. *Objectives:*
   A. To familiarize you with the potential costs and benefits of human resource management outsourcing.
   B. To familiarize you with the degree to which various human resource management functions are being successfully outsourced.
II. *Out-of-Class Preparation Time:* 50 minutes
III. *In-Class Time Suggested:* 30 minutes
IV. *Instructions:*
   A. In groups of three to five students, read the "Situation" below, as well as Forms 1 and 2.
   B. Each group will complete Forms 1 and 2, as well as Question 1. List as many outsourcing benefits and costs for both employers and employees as you can on Form 1. Put an X beside your group's assessment of the corporate benefits (Form 2) of outsourcing each human resource management function.
   C. One person in each team will report the group's assessment and recommendations (Question 1) to the class.

Situation

Sharon Osmond is the vice president of human resources for Silicon Electronics, a small electronics company. She has been concerned that their patched-together human resource information system uses a software program so outdated that PeopleSoft won't support it anymore. This morning she met Edward Cutter, the CEO of her company, in the parking lot as they were both coming in to work.

Cutter told her of a conversation he had with a consultant from Hewitt Associates, Inc., a human resource management consulting company. The consultant said that when the entire human resource management function was outsourced to Hewitt, they had saved a company similar to his almost $400,000 in human resource management costs last year. The consultant also told Cutter that a number of reputable companies have joined the outsourcing bandwagon, including AT&T, Motorola, American Express, and Prudential. Based on that conversation, Cutter then asked Sharon to do some research and let him know whether it made sense to consider outsourcing some or all of the current human resource management functions at Silicon Electronics to Hewitt or a similar firm.

Sharon was quite upset after the conversation because she knew her own position, as well the positions of her subordinates, might be in jeopardy. However, after recovering from her initial shock, she called Mary Gannon, her old professor of Human Resources Management at Moosehead University, to solicit her input. Professor Gannon told Sharon she would get back to her in a week after giving this assignment to one of the student groups in her human resources management class.

Your group has been given this assignment. Professor Gannon has asked your group to do the research necessary to complete Forms 1 and 2 and then answer the questions below.

Questions

1. Complete Forms 1 and 2 using information gathered from the various human resource websites listed throughout this book. Identify as many benefits and costs from both the employer and employee perspective as you can (Form 1). Also consider which human resource functions have the greatest potential to be outsourced based on what other companies are doing and why (Form 2). On the basis of these assessments, which of the three strategies should Sharon Osmond recommend to Cutter and why? Circle either a, b, or c and be prepared to explain your reasons based on the information you list on Forms 1 and 2.
   a) Do not outsource any of the human resource functions.
   b) Outsource only the following human resource functions.
   c) Outsource all of the human resource functions.

Form 1 *Benefits and Costs Associated with Outsourcing of Human Resources Functions*

Employer
Benefits
Costs

Employee
Benefits
Costs

Form 2 The Potential Expected Benefits Associated with Outsourcing of Specific Human Resource Functions

HR Functions	Potential Expected Benefits			
	Uncertain	Very Low	Moderate	Very High
1. Payroll and Benefits				
2. Recruitment				
3. Selection				
4. Information Technology				
5. Training				
6. Performance Management				
7. All HR functions				

Writing Job Descriptions

I. *Objectives:*
  A. To familiarize you with the job analysis process and with job descriptions.
  B. To give you practice in writing job descriptions.
II. *Out-of-Class Preparation Time:* 30 minutes
III. *In-Class Time Suggested:* 45 minutes
IV. *Procedures:*
  A. Before beginning this exercise, you should (a) review carefully, if you have not already done so, the different methods organizations use to conduct job analyses; and (b) review the Job Analysis Questionnaire (Exhibit 2.9).
  B. Students should be divided into pairs. Each person should then interview his or her partner with reference to a job that the partner is very familiar with (preferably a job that he or she has actually held). Use the Job Analysis Questionnaire for the interview. The questionnaire can be used to help determine the major responsibilities and tasks of the job and the required knowledge, skills, abilities, and personal characteristics needed to perform the job.
  C. After each student has interviewed his or her partner, write a job description covering your partner's job. Remember to use action verbs when describing the employee's tasks, duties, and responsibilities. It is also important that specific duties be grouped and arranged in descending order of importance. The completed job description should follow the format shown in Exhibit 2.10. The completed job description should be shown to the partner to determine whether additional information is required or whether changes should be made. Your instructor may require that you turn in a final copy of the completed job description for the next class.
  D. If time permits, the entire class discusses the various uses of job descriptions and the effectiveness of the interview as a method of job analysis.

Exhibit 2.9 *Job Analysis Questionnaire*

A. Job Responsibilities and Duties
1. Job title
2. Department title and/or division title
3. Title of immediate supervisor
4. Description of duties (Describe the duties in enough detail to provide a complete and accurate description of the work.)
   a. Provide a general overall summary of the purpose of your job.
   b. What are the major results or outputs of your job?
   c. Describe the duties and tasks you perform daily; weekly; monthly.
   d. Describe duties you perform irregularly.
5. List any machines, instruments, tools, equipment, materials, and work aids used in your job. Indicate percentage of time used.
6. Describe the nature of your responsibility for non-human resources (e.g., money, machinery, equipment). What monetary loss can occur through an error?
7. What reports and records do you prepare as part of your job? When are they prepared?
8. What is the source of instructions for performing your job (e.g., oral or written specifications)?
9. Describe the nature and frequency of supervision received.
10. How is your work reviewed, checked, or verified?

B. Reporting Relationships
11. How many employees are directly under your supervision? What are their job titles?
12. Do you have authority to hire, terminate, evaluate, and transfer employees under your supervision? Explain.
13. What contacts are required with other departments or persons other than your immediate department in performing your job? Describe the nature and extent of these contacts.

C. Working Conditions
14. Describe the working conditions present in the location and environment of your work such as cold/heat, noise, fumes, dust, and so forth. Indicate frequency and degree of exposure.
15. Describe any dangers or hazards present in your job.

D. Job Qualifications (Be certain not to list the incumbent's qualifications, but what is required for performance by a new employee.)
16. Describe the kind of previous work experience necessary for satisfactory performance of this job.
17. What is the amount of experience required?
18. What kinds of knowledge, skills, abilities, and other qualities (KSAOs) are needed to perform the job?
19. What is the minimal level of education (e.g., elementary/middle school graduation, high school graduation, two-year college diploma or certificate, university degree) required to perform the job satisfactorily?
20. Are any special physical skills and/or manual dexterity skills required to perform the job?
21. Are there any special certification, registration, licensing, or training requirements?

Exhibit 2.10 *Sample Job Description*

Job Title: Shift Supervisor

Position Purpose: The purpose of this position is to maintain a safe and efficient plant operation through directing the activities of the operation's staff and providing a management support function for the plant superintendent.

Typical Job Duties:
1. Directs the activities of the operation's staff and coordinates the activities of the maintenance staff.
2. Issues written communication to employees concerning personnel policies and operational concerns.
3. Administers maintenance request program through collecting requests, scheduling, and recording maintenance activities.
4. Administers the plant tagging procedure.
5. Conducts the training and safety programs for shift employees.
6. Schedules shift assignments to reflect workload and vacation schedules.
7. Performs administrative tasks such as recording workers' time, maintaining records concerning operational activities, and updating written procedures.
8. Prepares annual budget for assigned plant area and maintains the inventory level on these items.
9. Appraises performance of shift employees annually.
10. Counsels employees on disciplinary problems and job-related performance.
11. Assumes plant superintendent's duties when assigned.

Physical Requirements: Walking and climbing stairs

Working Conditions: Good, some noise

Equipment and Machines Used: CRT, spectrometer, PH meter, conductivity meter

Reporting Relationships: The shift supervisor reports directly to the plant superintendent. The shift supervisor directs the control room operator, two or more utility operators, trainees, and other assigned staff, and coordinates the activities of the maintenance staff present on shift.

Qualifications:
Education: Completion of two-year program at a college or institute, or equivalent training (e.g., management training classes) OR five (5) years of management experience.

Related Experience: Minimum of three (3) years as a control room operator for a coal-fired boiler operation.

Job Knowledge/Skills Required:
1. Comprehensive understanding of plant systems.
2. Fundamental understanding of electrical systems and motor control centres.
3. Thorough knowledge of boiler chemistry.
4. Comprehension of flow, logic, and electrical prints.
5. Ability to perform elementary mathematical and algebraic calculations.
6. Communication and human relations skills.
7. Ability to operate CRT, spectrometer, PH meter, and conductivity meter.
8. Managerial skills.

35. EXERCISE

Work and Family Issues

I. *Objectives:*
   - **A.** To understand the conflicts that sometimes arise between the individual's work and family responsibilities.
   - **B.** To analyze the advantages and disadvantages of alternative policies and programs that attempt to reconcile the sometimes conflicting demands of work and family.

II. *Out-of-Class Preparation Time:* 2 hours

III. *In-Class Time Suggested:* 45 minutes

IV. *Procedures:*
   - **A.** Read the entire exercise before class. Students may want to conduct research on the topic prior to class.
   - **B.** Develop a list of possible policies and programs for this company to better reconcile work and family life.
   - **C.** Form groups of two to five students and either choose one of the three options below, or follow the option assigned to you by the instructor.
       1. Option 1—Use Form 3
          Prepare specific recommendations for the Task Force regarding policies and programs they should consider to help their employees better reconcile their work and family responsibilities. List these recommendations on Form 3 together with your estimate of how much time will be required for each recommendation to be implemented. The time frame for implementation will depend upon how high a priority the group assigns to a particular recommendation and how much time will be required to work out the details of the proposal. In preparing your recommendations, consider the pros and cons of responding to the needs of workers with small children.
       2. Option 2—Use Form 4
          Develop new policy statements for the employee handbook in the areas of absence, employee benefits, leave without pay, and sick leave. These new policy statements should modify the present policy statements shown in Exhibit 2.12. The revised policies are then written on Form 4.
       3. Option 3—Use Form 5
          Examine the four daycare service options recommended by the Task Force. For each option, list their expected advantages or benefits and their expected disadvantages or costs on Form 5. Circle your recommended option on Form 5.
   - **D.** Share your group's recommendations with the rest of the class.

Background

Anderson's Department Stores is a regional retail chain based in Halifax. Over the past 10 years, Anderson's Department Stores has been very successful in providing high-quality merchandise to upper-middle-class customers primarily in Atlantic Canada. It currently has 10 stores employing 1,300 employees, as well as a corporate headquarters with 24 employees. (See Exhibit 2.11 for a demographic profile of the current work force.) Anderson's Department Stores' rate of return on sales and growth rate in sales have been the highest in the retail industry in its region over the past decade. While shares of company stock are publicly traded, the Anderson family currently controls about 40 percent of this stock.

Anderson's Department Stores built its reputation and success on customer service. It has a high ratio of salespersons to customers, and each salesperson is highly trained in products and customer service. In addition, the sales commissions are among the highest in the overall retail industry. Company publications indicate that the company views its employees as "family members." This is reinforced by company-sponsored events such as dinners, picnics, and other social occasions. These approaches to customers and employees seem to have worked well. Not only are the financial results excellent, but there are 7.5 applications for each position in the company. This allows the company to be very selective in its hiring policies.

The company also has taken the position that the individual's family and work life are, and should be, separate. Both require time and effort, but should never interfere with each other. The company's philosophy has been that each individual has a responsibility to hire or otherwise provide child-care service or whatever other services are necessary for the proper functioning of the family. The company's responsibility has been only to provide jobs for employees while serving customer needs.

Recently, that philosophy has been challenged by several employees who claim the company is "insensitive" to employees who have family responsibilities. In particular, they cite the lack of any child-care facilities and family leave policies. They argue that uniform personnel policies applied rigidly to all employees (irrespective of their family situation) are inherently unfair. They have stated that if the company really viewed their employees as "family members," it would be more flexible in accommodating employees' family responsibilities. Exhibit 2.12 provides excerpts from the Anderson's Department Stores Policy Manual. The sick leave policy, for example, indicates that the company does not provide any sick leave to care for a sick child or family member or to care for elderly relatives.

Anderson's Board of Directors consists of the major stockholders in the Anderson family, several non-family top executives, and outside directors from other companies. At its most recent meeting, the board discussed its current philosophy regarding the work/family life separation, the charge of "insensitivity," and possible modifications. The major concern expressed was that the company's image as "a good place to work" was being threatened, and that, in turn, could adversely affect the company's ability to recruit and retain the highest quality staff. If the quality of staff (particularly salespersons) were to decline, this would jeopardize the business strategy of differentiating their product based on excellent customer service.

In addition, Mr. Peter Anderson, the company CEO, recently read an article in *Business Week* identifying the "best companies for women." This article identified a number of family-oriented policies and programs used by 24 leading companies. Among the most significant of these were modifications in the company culture, executive development to enhance "sensitivity," child care, sick-child care, women on the board, career development policies, family leave policies, maternity leave with partial pay, modified work and family benefits, flexible benefits, hiring a "pluralistic" work force, job sharing, mentoring programs, and part-time professional and/or executive positions. Some of the 24 corporations identified in the *Business Week* article were in retail trade.

The Task Force

In response to employee criticism and the potential for negative publicity, the board of trustees made a decision to establish a "Task Force on the Work/Family Interface." The mission of the Task Force was to make recommendations on possible additions and modifications to company policies and programs that would better accommodate the family responsibilities of its employees. Members of the Task Force included company executives, exempt and non-exempt employees, and members of the board of trustees. Members of the Task Force reviewed newspaper, magazine, and journal articles, and discussed options with others in the community prior to making their recommendations.

The Task Force made recommendations in a large number of areas, including health insurance coverage, absence with pay, leave without pay, sick leave, promotion criteria and policies, training programs, family leave, job sharing, flextime, and child care. The latter recommendation on child care provided several options from which the company could choose. These are listed in Exhibit 2.13.

The Task Force recognized that each of the four daycare options has advantages and disadvantages. The benefits will be both economic and non-economic, but the non-economic benefits may be translated into economic terms by estimating the expected reductions in employee turnover and then calculating the expected savings in recruitment and training costs. The present annual turnover rate for female employees is 18.6 percent compared to 15.8 percent for male employees. However, the female turnover rate is higher for non-managerial positions, for married females, for those under 35, for those with children, and for those with children under six years of age. All of these subgroups have turnover rates of 20 to 30 percent. The Human Resource Department has calculated that the recruitment/training cost of replacing an "average" employee is $1,750. These costs are higher for managerial positions and full-time positions (these positions average a turnover cost of $2,000–$2,500 for each employee replaced). Even these costs may be understated, since the average employee leaving Anderson's Department Stores is estimated to be more productive than the average employee retained.

The disadvantages or costs may also be economic or non-economic. The economic costs can be estimated by gathering data on the direct costs of providing each particular program or service. For example, the Human Resource Department has determined that the average daily cost of child care per child is $23.84 in the cities where their department stores are located. Since the typical employee works 240 days per year, the yearly cost per child would be $5,722 ($23.84 × 240 days). The total yearly cost of the service would be that figure times the estimated number of individuals using the service.

Exhibit 2.11 *Percentage Distribution of Anderson's Department Stores Work Force by Demographic Category*

	Demographic Category	
	Managerial % (n = 335)	Non-Managerial % (n = 965)
Sex		
Male	45.9	20.5
Female	54.1	79.5
Job Status		
Part-time	0	38.3
Full-time	100	61.7
Marital Status		
Single	32.1	33.1
Married	52.2	54.9
Divorced	15.7	12.0
Age		
18 and under	0	.3
19–25	10.1	27.8
25–35	15.2	43.2
36–50	47.1	19.6
51–59	18.6	5.1
60 and over	90.0	4.0
Number of Children		
None	10.1	8.1
1–2	60.9	58.3
3–4	18.0	23.7
5–6	5.0	7.5
6 or more	6.0	2.4
Age of Children		
0–2 years	3.1	15.1
3–5 years	4.9	31.9
6–12 years	15.0	25.0
13–18 years	57.0	18.0
Over 18	20.0	10.0
Ethnic Status		
White	89.1	70.1
Black	4.0	13.2
Aboriginal	1.0	2.0
Visible Minority	5.9	14.7
Spouse Employed	43.7	79.6

Exhibit 2.12 *Excerpts from Anderson's Department Stores' Policy Manual*

Authorized Absence with Pay

You will be excused with pay at the discretion of your department supervisor as follows: (1) in the case of death in your immediate family; (2) to serve on jury duty; and (3) leave required for active duty in the armed forces or for annual training as a member of the military reserves.

Employee Benefits

The company offers several forms of benefits for you and your dependants.

Medical Coverage: You may purchase individual, spousal, and dependant extended medical coverage. For any purchase of extended coverage, the company will pay 50% of the costs and make deductions from your paycheque for the other half.

Dental Coverage: Coverage for yourself and/or for your spouse and dependants may be purchased from an inexpensive group plan that emphasizes diagnostic and preventive care. The employee will pay 100% of this cost.

Life Insurance: The employee's life insurance is paid for by the company. You may purchase insurance for your qualified dependants. The employee will pay 100% of the cost for dependant coverage.

Leave without Pay

Each employee is eligible for up to five days of unpaid leave per year with the written permission of your immediate supervisor.

Sick Leave

You are eligible to take sick leave with pay in case of personal illness or disability.

Full-time employees accrue sick leave at the rate of one working day of sick leave for each full month of service.

Permanent part-time employees accrue sick leave as follows: 20 hours but less than 30 hours per week—6 days annually; 30 hours but less than 40 hours per week—9 days annually.

Sick leave may be used if the absence is caused by: (1) personal illness or physical incapacity resulting from causes beyond your control; or (2) physical disability. Other uses are prohibited and will be subject to disciplinary action.

Exhibit 2.13 *Child-Care Options Recommended by Anderson's Department Stores' Task Force on the Work/Family Interface*

1. *Alternative One: Establish and operate a daycare centre in each department store.*
   Estimated capital investment required for this option will be $58,000 per store or a total corporate investment of $4,872,000. Then the annual operating costs will average $108,000 per store or $9,072,000.

2. *Alternative Two: Contract out daycare services to Child Care Services, a private corporation.*
   Child Care Services rates average about $3.25 an hour per child for an eight-hour day and $3.75 per hour for shorter periods in their own facilities. They also are willing to provide the service in the department stores for $3.50 and $4.00 per hour, respectively.

3. *Alternative Three: Contract out daycare services to public schools in the local communities.*
   The rates average about $3.00 an hour per child, but the service is typically available for limited hours.

4. *Alternative Four: Provide a voucher system whereby parents may choose their own daycare services and use redeemable vouchers to pay for this service.*
   Vouchers would limit reimbursement to $3.50 an hour per child.

Form 3 *Recommendations for the Task Force on Work/Family Interface, Anderson's Department Stores*

Policy or Program	Time Frame for Implementation*
1.	
2.	
3.	
4.	
5.	
6.	
7.	
8.	
9.	
10.	
11.	
12.	

*short-term = within the next year
intermediate-term = one to two years
long-term = more than two years

Authorized Absence with Pay

Employee Benefits

Leave without Pay

Sick Leave

Form 5 *Task Force Recommendations Regarding Daycare Services, Anderson's Department Stores*

Daycare Options	Expected Advantages or Benefits	Expected Disadvantages or Costs
1. Establish and operate daycare centre		
2. Contract with private corporation		
3. Contract with public schools		
4. Establish voucher system		

Human Resource Forecasting Assignment

I. *Objectives:*
  A. To give you practice in forecasting an organization's human resource needs.
  B. To familiarize you with some of the factors that affect an organization's future human resource needs (growth, automation, turnover).
  C. To familiarize you with the complexities involved in making human resource forecasts.
  D. To point out that all human resource forecasting is based on assumptions and that these assumptions are critical to the accuracy of the forecast. Incorrect assumptions lead to erroneous forecasts.
II. *Time Required to Complete Assignment:* 1 to 2 hours
III. *Instructions:* You have been given the assignment of forecasting the human resource needs of the National Credit Union, which currently employs approximately 1,100 people. The credit union currently has 50 branch offices located throughout a major urban area, each of which employs approximately 14 individuals. The credit union expects to add 38 branches during the next three years. Branches within the credit union differ considerably in size, so the figures given represent averages.

During the past month, the credit union has placed an order for 30 automated teller machines to be placed in its old branch offices. These machines are scheduled to be in operation December 31, one year from now. The credit union has found that for each new machine purchased, one less teller is needed, on average.

A breakdown of the credit union's current staffing is shown in Table 1 below.

Table 1 *Present Staffing*

Total Employees	1,100
Number of Branches	50
Supervisors per Branch	4
Number of Supervisors	200
Tellers per Branch	10
Number of Tellers	500
Branch Employees	700
Main Office Employees	400

The credit union has asked you to perform three human resource forecasting tasks. First, based on the assumptions given below, you are required to determine employee turnover for the main office, the old branches, and the new branches. Your boss would like to know this information for each of the next three years and for each of the major employee categories (i.e., supervisors, tellers/clerical, and main office). Your job is to complete Table 2 shown below.

Table 2 *Turnover*

Employee Category	Year 1	Year 2	Year 3
Old Branch Supervisors			
Old Branch Tellers			
Main Office			
New Branch Supervisors			
New Branch Tellers			
Totals			

Second, your boss would like to know the number of new employees the credit union will need to hire for each major employee category for each of the next three years. Your job is to complete Table 3 shown below.

Table 3 *Number of Employees to Be Hired*

Employee Category	Year 1	Year 2	Year 3
Old Branch Supervisors			
Old Branch Tellers			
Main Office			
New Branch Supervisors			
New Branch Tellers			
Totals			

Finally, your boss would like to know the total number of employees who will be working for the credit union at the end of each of the next three years. Your job is to complete Table 4.

Table 4 *Year-End Employment*

Employee Category	Year 1	Year 2	Year 3
Old Branch Supervisors			
Old Branch Tellers			
Main Office			
New Branch Supervisors			
New Branch Tellers			
Totals			

In order to complete your assignment, your boss has told you to make a number of assumptions. These are:

A. You are making all projections in December for subsequent years ending December 31.
B. With regard to old branches, assume
   1. The 50 old branches employ 4 supervisors and 10 clerical employees/tellers each.
   2. Thirty teller machines will be placed in operation on December 31 (one year hence) and will replace 30 tellers.
   3. The credit union does not terminate any employees because of the new teller machines. Rather, as tellers quit throughout the year, they are not replaced.

    4. Annual turnover is 30 percent for tellers/clerical employees, and 20 percent for supervisors.
C. With regard to new branches, assume
    1. New branches are added as follows: 10 in Year 1, 12 in Year 2, and 16 in Year 3.
    2. Each new branch employs 14 individuals (4 supervisors and 10 tellers/clerical).
    3. New branches are added evenly throughout the year. Thus, for the purpose of calculating turnover, on average, there are 5 new branches in Year 1 (50% × 10); 16 in Year 2 [10 in Year 1 plus 6 (50% × 12)]; and 30 in Year 3 [22 plus 8 (50% × 16)].
    4. Turnover is 30 percent for tellers/clerical employees, and 20 percent for supervisors.
D. With regard to the main office, assume that turnover will be 10 percent per year.

37. SKILL BUILDER

Phased Retirement Options

    I. *Objectives:*

        A. To give you practice in using the Internet to generate information relevant to solving human resource problems.

        B. To familiarize you with the various options to traditional employee retirement.

    II. *Time Required to Complete:* 1 to 2 hours

    III. *Instructions:* Read the "Situation" below and then search the Internet for the following: (1) phased retirement options; (2) advantages or benefits of each option for employees and the employer; and (3) disadvantages or costs of options for each.

        Possible websites are as follows:

        http://www.rrq.gouv.qc.ca/an/flashretraiteqc/capsule_retraite_037.htm

        http://www.hrsdc.gc.ca/en/lp/spila/wlb/caowc/11chapter_6.shtml

        http://www.moneysense.ca/planning/retirement_living/article.jsp?content=551021

        Then fill in Form 6 (provide at least one advantage and disadvantage for each of the listed options) and be prepared to present your findings and recommendations to the class.

Situation

The Owens Engineering Company provides a full range of engineering services to a wide variety of governmental and private organizations. Ron Owens, the company president, has become increasingly concerned about his company's demographics. Two-thirds of their 82 engineers are in the age range of 50 to 67. The company's current retirement policy is to offer retirement to all employees who reach age 55 or more, with 25 or more years of service.

Within the next few years, Owens has determined that 42 percent of the engineers will be eligible for retirement, and, based on past company data, 70 percent will retire within two years of their actual eligibility. This means he expects to lose 29 of 82 engineers to retirement over the next four years. In addition, the "normal" annual turnover rate among engineers has been 8 percent per year. This would reduce the company's "pool" of engineers by another 7 per year, or 28 over the next four years.

After discussing the situation with Susan Barber, the Human Resources Manager, Owens concluded most voluntary turnover was "unavoidable." While the company provides competitive salaries and benefits for the region, the local unemployment rate is extremely low (averaging 2.8 percent), and there are virtually no unemployed engineers in the area. Future forecasts are for a continued "tight" labour market for engineers in the region.

Owens and Barber determined that the best way to deal with their potential engineer shortage was to retain older engineers as they become eligible for retirement. This decision was not only based on the numbers but also on the qualities and qualifications they anticipated losing. For example, when four senior civil engineers retired during the past year, the company lost their contacts and influence, their knowledge of their customers, special requirements in the contract-bidding process, and their knowledge about who to see and how to get things done internally.

Barber is a friend of your instructor in "Human Resource Management" this term. Your instructor has assigned your student team the term project of assisting Owens Engineering in assessing its options for retaining its older engineers.

Option 1

Advantages/Benefits to the Company	Advantages/Benefits to the Employee
1.	1.
2.	2.
3.	3.
Disadvantages/Costs to the Company	Disadvantages/Costs to the Employee
1.	1.
2.	2.
3.	3.

Option 2

Advantages/Benefits to the Company	Advantages/Benefits to the Employee
1.	1.
2.	2.
3.	3.
Disadvantages/Costs to the Company	Disadvantages/Costs to the Employee
1.	1.
2.	2.
3.	3.

Option 3

Advantages/Benefits to the Company	Advantages/Benefits to the Employee
1.	1.
2.	2.
3.	3.
Disadvantages/Costs to the Company	Disadvantages/Costs to the Employee
1.	1.
2.	2.
3.	3.

RECRUITING AND SELECTION

38. CASE

Recruiting Recreational Vehicle Surveyors

Liberty Engineering Co. is located in Quebec. The company was founded during the 1940s and does a considerable amount of drafting and design work for the major automotive companies and their suppliers. When sales in the auto industry are high, Liberty Engineering experiences a significant volume of work. However, when recessions hit the automotive marketplace, work at Liberty also sharply decreases.

In an attempt to stabilize revenues, the president of Liberty Engineering decided it would be prudent to diversify the company by bidding on federal government contracts. The company had little experience in this kind of work, but the president felt that this would not preclude it from bidding on contracts and obtaining them.

Within a six-month period, the company had bid on and lost two contracts. However, a third bid pertaining to the safety and use of recreational vehicles proved to be successful. The contract was for several hundred thousand dollars. The government was interested in obtaining information regarding how people actually use recreational vehicles such as pickup truck campers, motor homes, and various kinds of recreational trailers. Ultimately, the purpose of the study was to determine what additional safety rules, if any, should be established relating to the manufacture and use of recreational vehicles. Among the pieces of information desired by the government were how much weight citizens place in their recreational vehicles, what kinds of trailer hitches are in use, whether recreational vehicles have proper suspension systems, and to what extent citizens are aware of the safety features of their recreational vehicles.

In Liberty's proposal to the government, the company stated that it would recruit, select, and train qualified individuals to survey over 1,000 recreational vehicles. The surveying would be done at three different sites: a forest location, a seashore site, and a mountainous locale. At a meeting with government officials, three locations were selected: Prince Edward Island National Park (seashore), Banff National Park in Alberta (mountains), and Prince Albert National Park in Saskatchewan (forest). Two other important decisions were also made at the meeting. First, to ensure consistency of data collection, all surveyors would be trained together at a campground at Prince Albert National Park. Second, the employees would then be divided into survey crews and sent to their respective job sites. It was also decided that each survey crew would consist of one leader and four surveyors, and that two crews would be sent to each data collection site.

All responsibility for recruiting and training the 30 employees (6 leaders and 24 surveyors) fell on the shoulders of Bob Getz, the new Human Resource Director. Bob had worked as a designer for Liberty for 20 years before being transferred to human resources. At the same time that a project Bob had been working on for two years ended, the former director of human resources quit, so Bob was a logical choice. In addition, Bob was well-liked by most of Liberty's older employees and knew a great deal about the company's policies and procedures. Bob's major shortcoming was that he knew little about staffing activities.

Before recruiting potential job applicants, Bob knew that he would first need to develop a set of job descriptions for all 30 employees. Since crews would be doing essentially similar jobs, albeit at different locations, Bob needed only to develop job descriptions for each of four survey positions and that of the leader. Hence, Bob obtained the list of data to be collected for each vehicle, determined the tasks required to collect the data, and divided the task into four job positions. Bob realized that the job duties of each surveyor would ultimately need to be changed based on actual experience. Nonetheless, he roughed out the following job descriptions:

Surveyor I: Take pictures of recreational vehicle with a camera. Interview driver and record information received.

Surveyor II: Read and record scale weights for each recreational vehicle tire. Take tire pressures and measure tread depth. Record make, size, and air capacity of each tire.

Surveyor III: Unhook trailer hitch, if present, and record make of hitch, ball diameter, and whether levellers are present. Determine type of suspension on recreational vehicle and count number of leaf springs, if present.

Surveyor IV: Stop recreational vehicle as it enters campground, explain to driver the purpose of the study, ask the driver to participate in study. When survey of recreational vehicle is complete, discuss the findings with the driver.

The leader's responsibilities would be to plan daily work activities, motivate the employees to do the surveying, complete all forms, and do occasional troubleshooting.

With job descriptions in hand, Bob met with Norm Larson, vice president of Liberty, who was ultimately responsible for conducting the recreational vehicle surveys. During the meeting, Bob learned that all 30 employees were to meet at the campground in Prince Albert National Park on June 10. They were to be trained on the job for four days, and the company would provide them with lodging and food while they were there. All employees were to provide their own transportation to the park, to their subsequent job sites, and then back home. The company would pay them for travel time but would not provide any mileage allowance, lodging, or food. Upon arrival at their assigned job site, employees would need to find accommodations for July and August, and would receive no lodging or food allowance from the company during their stay. Once work commenced at each job site, employees would be responsible for providing their own transportation to and from the campground.

All employees were to be paid $8.45 per hour. The company would provide the minimum level of benefits mandated by law, such as employment insurance and workers' compensation, and would pay a small additional percentage on top of the hourly pay rate in lieu of giving vacation time. No other benefits would be offered. No one under the age of 18 would be hired for safety reasons.

After the meeting with Norm, Bob decided he should check with park supervisors at the different job sites. He learned that most recreational vehicles leave campgrounds early in the morning and enter late in the afternoon. Few arrive or depart between 10 a.m. and 4 p.m. In order to survey a maximum number of vehicles, crews would need to work from 6 a.m. to 11 a.m. and from 3 p.m. to 8 p.m., a total of 10 hours a day. Therefore, each crew could work a four-day-on and a four-day-off schedule. Bob was told the locations where the crews would work at Prince Edward Island National Park and Banff National Park were not shaded; hence, employees at these sites would need to work in the sun and wear uniforms, including hats. The Prince Albert National Park location would be cooler than the others and surveying could be done in shaded areas. When Bob asked the park supervisors whether they knew of any people who would be interested in working on the survey project, their response was, "You've got to be kidding." A supervisor at Prince Edward Island National Park flatly told Bob that he couldn't conceive of any person being willing to drive to Prince Edward Island and back under the conditions Bob outlined. He suggested that Bob put a Help Wanted ad in a Montreal newspaper.

After talking with the park supervisors, Bob was quite depressed. He knew that he had to hire 30 employees within the next few weeks. He knew that six of them had to have sufficient leadership skills to get the job done while not antagonizing the employees so much that they would quit. He further realized that the 24 surveyors would have to enjoy the outdoors and be willing to tolerate uncomfortable weather conditions. He realized, too, that the ideal surveyor would be one who had above-average knowledge of auto mechanics, legible handwriting, reasonable communication skills, and an ability to work well with others under adverse conditions. What Bob didn't know was how he could recruit and hire 30 people who fit these descriptions.

Questions

1. If you were Bob, how would you recruit the needed employees?
2. Evaluate the suggestion that Bob recruit employees by placing a Help Wanted ad in a Montreal newspaper.
3. What should the firm do if they are unable to recruit sufficient employees for the job?

Selecting Patient Escorts

Mason Hospital is located in the heart of a large Canadian city. It is one of five major hospitals in the area. Mason Hospital has about 1,200 hospital beds and employs 4,500 individuals, including approximately 40 patient escorts.

The job of patient escort is a rather simple one, requiring only minimal training and no special physical talents. When patients need to be moved from one location to another, patient escorts are summoned to assist in the move. If the move is only a short distance, however, a nurse or orderly can move the patient. Of particular importance is the fact that patient escorts almost always take patients who are being discharged from their hospital rooms to the front door of the hospital. A wheelchair is always used, even if the patient is able to walk unassisted. Thus, the typical procedure is for the nurse to call for a patient escort; the escort then gets a wheelchair and goes to the patient's room, assists the patient into the wheelchair, picks up the patient's belongings, wheels the patient down to the hospital's front door or to his or her car in the parking lot, and returns to the work station.

The job of patient escort is critical to the hospital since the escort is always the last hospital representative the patient sees, and hence has a considerable influence on the patient's perception of the hospital. Of the approximately 40 escorts, about 30 are men, and 10 are women. Most are high-school graduates in their early twenties. Some, particularly those on the early morning shift, are enrolled in post-secondary education and are working for the hospital to earn money to pay tuition expenses. Four of the escorts are older women who had previously served as hospital volunteers and then decided to become full-time employees instead. Turnover among patient escorts is quite high and has averaged 25 percent in recent years. In addition, the potential for moving to other employment in the hospital is quite good, and as a result, another 25 percent of the escorts typically transfer to other jobs in the hospital each year. Thus, about half of the patient escort positions need to be replaced annually.

The hospital follows a standard procedure when hiring patient escorts. When a vacancy occurs, the Human Resource Department reviews the file of individuals who have applied for the patient escort job. Usually the file contains at least 20 applications, because the pay for the job is good, the work is relatively easy, and few skills are required. The top two or three applicants are asked to come to the hospital for interviews. Typically, the applicants are interviewed first by the Human Resource Department and then by the patient escort supervisor. The majority of those interviewed know some other employees of the hospital, so the only reference check is a call to these employees. Before being hired, applicants are required to take physical exams given by hospital doctors.

Every new escort attends an orientation program the first day on the job. This is conducted by a member of the Human Resource Department. The program consists of a complete tour of the hospital; a review of all the hospital's human resource policies, including a description of its promotion, compensation, and disciplinary policies; and a presentation on the hospital's mission and philosophy. During this orientation session, employees are told that the hospital's image in the community is of major importance and that all employees should strive to maintain and enhance this image by their conduct. After orientation, all patient escorts receive on-the-job training by their immediate supervisor.

During the last two-year period, the hospital has experienced a number of problems with patient escorts that have had an adverse effect on the hospital's image. Several patients have complained to the hospital administration that they have been treated rudely, or in some cases roughly, by one or more patient escorts. Some complained that they had been ordered around or scolded by an escort during the discharge process. Others stated that the escort had been careless when wheeling them out of the hospital to their cars. One person, in fact, reported that an escort had carelessly tipped him over. All escorts are required to wear identification tags, but patients usually can't remember the escort's name when complaining to the hospital. Additionally, the hospital usually has difficulty determining which escort served which patient because escorts often trade patients. Finally, even when the hospital can identify the offending escort, the employee can easily deny any wrongdoing. He or she often counters that patients are generally irritable as a result of their illness and hence are prone to complain at even the slightest provocation.

At the hospital administrator's request, the Human Resource Manager asked the Chief Supervisor of patient escorts, the head of the Staffing Section within the Human Resource Department, and the assistant manager of the Human Resource Department to meet with her to review the entire procedure used to select patient escorts. It was hoped that they could develop a new procedure that would eliminate the hiring of rude, insulting, or careless patient escorts.

During the meeting, a number of suggestions were made as to how the selection procedure might be improved. Criticisms of the present system were also voiced. The Chief Supervisor of patient escorts argued that the problem with the hospital's present system is that the application form does not collect any really useful information. He stated that the questions that really give insight into the employee's personality were no longer on the application form. He suggested that applicants be asked about their hobbies, outside activities, and personal likes and dislikes on the form. He also suggested that each applicant be asked to submit three letters of recommendation from people who know the applicant well. He wanted these letters to focus on the prospective employee's personality, particularly the applicant's ability to remain friendly and polite at all times.

The assistant manager of human resources contended that the hospital's interviewing procedure should be modified. He observed that during the typical interview little attempt is made to determine how the applicant reacts under stress. He suggested that if applicants were asked four or five stress-producing questions, the hospital might be in a better position to judge their ability to work with irritable patients.

The head of the Staffing Section noted that patient escorts require little mental or physical talent and agreed that the crucial attribute escorts need is the ability to always be courteous and polite. He wondered whether an "attitude" test could be developed that would measure the applicant's predisposition toward being friendly or displaying other appropriate attitudes toward patients. He suggested that a job analysis could be done on the patient escort job to determine those attitudes that are critical to being a successful patient escort. When the job analysis was complete, questions could be developed that would measure these critical attributes. The test questions could be given to the hospital's present patient escorts to determine whether the test accurately distinguishes the best from worst escorts. The head of the Staffing Section realized that many of the questions might need to be eliminated or changed, and that if the test appeared to show promise, it would probably need to be revalidated in order to meet government requirements. He felt, however, that a well-designed test might be worth the effort and should at least be considered.

The meeting ended with all four participants agreeing that the suggestion of trying to develop an "attitude test" was probably the most promising. The assistant manager of Human Resources and the Chief Supervisor of patient escorts stated that they would conduct a thorough job analysis covering the patient escort position and develop a list of attitudes that are critical to its success. A second meeting would then be scheduled to prepare the actual test questions.

Questions

1. Critique each of the alternative approaches suggested for solving the problem of selecting patient escorts.
2. Recommend a procedure for recruiting and hiring patient escorts.
3. Besides improving its selection procedures, what other actions could the hospital potentially take to improve the behaviour of the patient escorts?

A Solution for Adverse Impact

A provincial government agency was in need of assistance regarding its staffing practices. Recently, some of the job applicants had complained that the selection procedures for one of the entry-level law enforcement jobs were discriminatory. The staffing specialists, who had previously ignored this possibility, were now alerted to the potential problem of adverse impact against women and minorities.

Bob Santos was a staffing specialist for the agency and had been employed with the staffing division for almost three years. He had kept up with the laws and regulations on discrimination and equal employment opportunity. About two months ago, he had attended a training seminar on identifying indirect discrimination in hiring practices and reducing the "adverse impact" of such practices. Upon returning to the agency, Bob decided that an evaluation of the agency's current staffing practices was necessary because these had been developed more than 10 years ago.

The Selection Process

The selection of entry-level agents for the law enforcement job involved a two-step multiple-hurdle process. Applicants were first required to pass a cognitive ability test, similar to but somewhat easier than the cognitive components in most high-school graduation equivalency exams. The exam was made up of 25 verbal items and 25 quantitative items. A candidate was required to receive a passing score of 70 (35 of the items correct) in order to be eligible for the second step of the selection process: an interview.

In the interview, a three-member panel of supervisors asked each applicant questions on how they would deal with various hypothetical job situations. After an initial period of questions regarding the applicant's education and experience, the applicant was given a situation and then asked to respond to the situation. Typically, after each candidate's initial response, further questioning would ensue from the panel to determine the full response of the candidate. The interview would last about half an hour. At the end of the interview, the three interviewers would rate the candidate on 10 dimensions, such as attitude, motivation, and communication. Candidates receiving high scores on most of the dimensions would pass the interview. After a physical examination and a security check, the candidate was hired and asked to report to training.

The Determination of Adverse Impact

Bob learned at the training seminar that employers should make adverse impact determinations at least once a year. Although records of information about applicants and successful candidates had been kept, the agency had not calculated the selection rates over the past three years. Bob thought that these calculations were long overdue and decided to have them done as soon as possible. A week later, the selection rates were tabulated. The data are presented in Exhibit 2.14.

After calculating the adverse impact for both the test and the interview, Bob decided that a discussion with the personnel psychologist in the agency would be necessary. A meeting was arranged between Bob, his supervisor (the head of the staffing division), and Ron Burden, the personnel psychologist. A discussion ensued regarding the data that had been collected. It was decided that the original job analysis was poorly done and that very little documentation had been retained by the agency. Although there was a task inventory, the major tasks or job duties had not been rated for qualities such as importance, frequency, difficulty, and trainability. Ron pointed out that this documentation would be critical if they ever needed to defend the selection procedures in court. By the end of the meeting, the group decided that it would probably be a good idea to do another job analysis. Ron felt that the selection procedures would have to be modified to fit the results of the job analysis. Ron was asked to determine how the job analysis would be done, while Bob would coordinate the project in the field.

Job Analysis

Human resource professionals recognize that there is no "one best way" of analyzing a job. Ron had to decide on a method or technique that would generate information from the officers and supervisors on the important work responsibilities and the tasks associated with them. After much deliberation, he decided to use the critical-incident technique. Ron knew that if the agency wanted to continue using situational questions in the interview, the critical-incident job analysis technique readily lends itself to the development of this type of question. The method involves collecting reports of behaviours that are "critical," in that they distinguish between successful and unsuccessful work performance. The officers and supervisors were instructed that their descriptions of the critical incidents should include (1) the circumstances that preceded the incident, (2) the setting in which the incident occurred, (3) what the agent did that was effective or ineffective, and (4) the consequences of the incident.

Ron asked a sample of officers to describe three critical incidents and to indicate the task associated with each critical incident. After receiving the data on the critical incidents, Ron and Bob derived an inventory of work behaviours. This list of work behaviours was then sent back to the officers, who were asked to rate the importance of each behaviour, how frequently it was performed, and the amount of training that was required to learn that behaviour.

When this information was collected, Ron and Bob generated a list of major job tasks or job duties. They assigned all the important work behaviours to their associated tasks. This list of tasks and work behaviours was then sent out to a group of supervisors who were asked to review the list. This same group of supervisors were also asked to meet for a two-day conference later in the month to determine the important knowledge, skills, abilities, and other characteristics (KSAOs) required to perform these work behaviours. Ron also planned for these experts to select the critical incidents to be used for the new interview.

Supervisory Conference

At the conference, the supervisors were given the inventory of tasks and their corresponding work behaviours. They were asked to derive the KSAOs and then rate how important the skill or ability was for the performance of the work behaviours. The most important knowledge, skills, abilities, and other characteristics are shown in Exhibit 2.15.

The job experts were asked to evaluate the current staffing practices in light of this list of KSAOs. Ron, Bob, and the supervisors agreed that the content of the exam would have to be changed to reflect the first three KSAOs. Ron proposed a reading comprehension exam in which the content would be a small sample of the procedures, laws, and regulations that are taught at the training academy. Applicants would read a section and then answer questions regarding the laws and regulations taught in that section. This type of test has been called a miniature training and evaluation test. All the parties agreed that this job-related procedure would be a good way of assessing the first three KSAOs.

The job experts wanted to retain the interview. Ron and Bob agreed as long as the following conditions were met:

1. All interview questions would have to be job-related.
2. Critical incidents from the job analysis would be selected to assess the last five KSAOs.
3. Sample answers to each critical incident would be determined in advance. Interviewee responses would be rated on a five-point scale defined explicitly in advance.
4. The same scoring method would be used for each applicant. All procedures would be used consistently for each applicant so that all applicants had the same chance of being selected.
5. All interviewers would be required to attend a training session to learn how to administer and assess the structured interview.

The supervisors agreed to these conditions. However, they did not want the interview to be completely structured. They felt that the interview should begin with a few questions regarding the applicant's past education and experience. Bob and Ron agreed to this with the stipulation that this information should not bias the candidate's assessment and scoring at the end of the interview.

When Bob and Ron returned to the agency, they were happy about what had transpired at the supervisory conference. The question that remained was the type of validation to be used on the newly developed selection procedures. Ron felt that they should validate the selection procedures with a criterion-related validity strategy. They would collect the scores for both the interview and the test and later compare them to the successful candidates' evaluations during training or their performance appraisal ratings at the end of their first year on the job. Since Ron was familiar with these procedures, he felt that this was a preferred strategy over a content validity strategy. On the other hand, Bob felt that a predictive validity study was too costly and unnecessary. Since their newly developed procedures were job-related, a content validity approach was sufficient. Instead of arguing over which type of validation strategy to use, they decided to discuss the matter with Bob's supervisor and meet again later in the week.

Questions

1. Is there any evidence of adverse impact against any groups of applicants to the agency?
2. If the total selection process for a job has no adverse impact, should the individual components of the selection process be evaluated for adverse impact?

3. Which type of validation would you use? Why? What are the differences between content and criterion-related validity studies?
4. Evaluate the job analysis procedures used in this case. Is it necessary to do such a thorough analysis?
5. If you are doing a criterion-related validity study, should your criterion be success in training or on-the-job performance ratings?

Original case prepared by Ronald J. Karren, Isenberg School of Management, University of Massachusetts.

Exhibit 2.14 *Tabulation of Selection Rates*

Pass Rates for the Test

Group	Number Who Took Test	Number Who Passed	Pass Rate %
Whites	282	134	47.5
Blacks	36	10	27.8
Asians	102	44	43.1
Aboriginals	0	0	0
Men	385	170	44.2
Women	35	18	51.4
Total	420	188	44.8

Pass Rates for the Interview

Group	Number Interviewed	Number Who Passed	Pass Rate %
Whites	112	87	77.7
Blacks	8	5	62.5
Asians	40	22	55.0
Men	148	109	73.6
Women	12	5	41.7
Total	160	114	71.2

Note: The number interviewed for each group is less than the number who passed the test. The difference represents individuals who did not wish to continue through the second part of the selection process.

Exhibit 2.15 *KSAOs Derived from the Task/Behaviour Inventory*

1. Knowledge of applicable laws
2. Knowledge of procedures and regulations
3. Reading and verbal comprehension
4. Ability to perform effectively in dangerous situations
5. Ability to communicate effectively
6. Skill in interpersonal relations
7. Judgment ability
8. Ability to solve problems quickly and effectively

Evaluating the Recruiting Function

I. *Objectives:*

A. To make you aware of the necessity of evaluating the efficiency and effectiveness of various recruitment sources.

B. To provide you with practice analyzing data, drawing conclusions, and planning a strategy to remedy identified problems or deficiencies.

C. To make you aware of the linkages among staff turnover, recruitment sources, recruitment methods, and adequate staffing.

II. *Out-of-Class Preparation Time:* 2 hours

III. *In-Class Time Suggested:* 45 minutes

IV. *Procedures:* Read the entire exercise, including the "Background" on St. Vincent's Hospital. Then, using the data provided in Exhibit 2.16, do the calculations on Form 7. A yield ratio is the number of applicants necessary to fill vacancies with qualified people. It is the relationship of applicant inputs to outputs at various decision points. For example, the yield ratio for all recruitment sources in Exhibit 2.16 shows that 273 nurse applicants were generated over the three-year period from 1992 to 1995. Since only 221 were classified as potentially qualified, the yield ratio is 273/221 or 1.24 to 1. The yield ratio for "potentially qualified" among "walk-ins" is 1.26 (53/42). The average cost per nurse hired among "walk-ins" is $119.23 ($1,550/13). Yield ratios at other steps in the process are also shown for all recruitment sources on Form 7. These data show that the hospital needs to start with more than 5 times as many applicants as it needs to fill job openings and more than 13 times as many applicants as it hopes to have as "above average" performers.

Do the calculations on Form 7 on your own prior to class. Think about the implications of these data for future recruitment at the hospital. Then look at Exhibit 2.17 in conjunction with the background description and think about the implications for the recruiting process. During the class period, form groups of three to five, who will act as a consulting team for the hospital. Discuss and answer the "Questions" in your group. At the end of the class period have a spokesperson for each group discuss the group's answers and rationale with the entire class.

Background

St. Vincent's Hospital is a 260-bed hospital in Saskatoon. During the last decade, the hospital operated with a nursing staff of approximately 450 registered nurses and experienced a nursing turnover rate of about 25 percent per year. The turnover rate was comparable to the average rate at Canadian hospitals of similar size during the past 10 years. However, the rate has accelerated to an average of 35 percent over the past three years.

These higher turnover rates have put additional pressure on the recruiting process to provide larger numbers of qualified candidates. However, Sam Barnett, director of human resources, has reported more difficulty locating qualified nurse candidates over the last three years. Barnett's office has prepared the recruitment data shown in Exhibit 2.16. The data show that 273 applicants (from all sources) had to be screened to produce 52 qualified candidates who accepted a job offer. One year later, 19 of these 52 had left the hospital. The last column shows the direct and indirect costs of recruitment by source, including clerical time, supervisor time, and direct costs such as travel and postage. The Human Resource Department has also conducted a telephone survey of all the nurses they could locate who did *not* accept a job offer from the hospital during the most recent three-year period. Reasons for such rejections are shown in Exhibit 2.17.

Mary Larsen, the 62-year-old director of nursing services, has been conducting all the off-site recruitment for many years. This includes both the nursing Job Fair and the provincial Nursing Association meeting. She has begun to feel "burned out" because of all her external recruiting and internal evaluation of candidates over the years.

At a recent meeting, she suggested that an outside group (your group) be brought in to analyze the whole recruiting process, identify problems and opportunities, and suggest improvements. Larsen and Barnett both readily agreed to use an outside consultant because they are aware of current severe nursing shortages due to declining nursing school enrollments. St. Vincent's itself contributed to this enrollment decline by closing its own School of Nursing due to fewer applications and the high cost of operation.

Since recruitment of new nurses has begun to fall behind turnover of nurses employed at St. Vincent's, the vacancy rate has begun to increase. Five years ago, only 11 percent of staff nursing positions were unfilled. This percentage has now increased to 23 percent. One result has been an exhausting workload on the existing nursing staff. In addition to increased turnover, the symptoms of staff burnout (e.g., stress, conflict, absenteeism) are becoming more evident.

Questions

1. How would you evaluate the nurse recruiting strategy currently being used by the hospital? Is the hospital using too few or too many recruiting sources? Why?
2. If you feel the hospital is using too many recruitment sources, which ones would you eliminate and why?
3. What stage or stages in the recruitment process seem to be most amenable to improvement? What specific improvements would you suggest to decrease the yield ratios? Why?

Exhibit 2.16 *Data on Recruitment Sources for Registered Nurses at St. Vincent's Hospital, 1996–1999*

Recruitment Source	Number of Applicants	Potentially Qualified	Invitation for Interview	Qualified and Offered Job	Accepted Job	One-Year Survival	Above Average Rating	Total Recruitment Costs
1. Direct applications								
write-ins	53	42	30	20	13	8	4	$ 1,550
walk-ins	64	47	38	24	11	5	2	1,500
2. Employee referrals	13	12	7	5	4	3	2	400
3. Newspaper ads	24	16	8	4	2	1	0	750
4. Journal ads	19	18	10	8	4	2	2	450
5. Educational institutions:								
community colleges	16	13	11	6	2	2	1	1,200
hospital-based schools	8	8	3	2	1	0	0	800
university programs	24	24	16	14	10	8	7	1,300
6. Private employment agency	9	9	8	5	2	2	1	4,000
7. Public employment agency	8	4	2	1	1	0	0	300
8. Direct mail	15	14	4	3	1	0	0	450
9. Job fair	13	7	5	3	1	1	1	900
10. Provincial Nursing Association meeting	7	7	4	3	0	0	0	1,150
Totals	273	221	146	98	52	33	20	$14,750

Exhibit 2.17 *Reasons for Nurse Rejection of a Job Offer from St. Vincent's Hospital, 1996–1999*

Reason	Number	Percent
Recruitment Processes		
Job attributes not communicated	2	4.3
Negative perception of recruiter	12	26.1
Negative perception of hospital	2	4.3
Lack of timely follow-up	13	28.3
Perceived lack of honesty in recruitment process	1	2.2
Negative information from recruiter	1	2.2
Job Attributes		
Location of hospital	3	6.5
Salary offer	2	4.3
Hours of work	2	4.3
Promotional opportunities	0	0.0
Fringe benefits	0	0.0
Working conditions	3	6.5
Perceived poor job "match"	5	10.9
Totals	46	100.0

Form 7 *Yield Ratios at Each Step in the Recruitment Process and Recruitment Cost per Nurse Hired, St. Vincent's Hospital, 1996–1999*

Recruitment Sources	Yield Rates						Average Cost per Nurse Hired
	Potentially Qualified	Accepted Interview	Offered Job	Accepted Job	One-Year Survival	Above-Average Rating	

1. Direct applications
  write-ins
  walk-ins							

2. Employee referrals							
3. Newspaper ads							
4. Journal ads							

5. Educational institutions:
  community colleges
  hospital-based schools
  university programs							

6. Private employment agency							
7. Public employment agency							
8. Direct mail							
9. Job fair							
10. Provincial Nursing Association meeting							
Averages for all sources	1.24	1.87	2.79	5.25	8.27	13.65	

42. EXERCISE

Selection Decisions

I. *Objectives:*
   A. To make you aware of the complex criteria often used to select candidates for administrative positions.
   B. To help you develop skills in planning and implementing semi-structured interviews.
   C. To give you practice in preparing for, participating in, or evaluating the selection interview.

II. *Out-of-Class Preparation Time:* 2 hours

III. *In-Class Time Suggested:* 45 minutes

IV. *Procedures:*
   A. Read the entire exercise including the "Background," "Questions for the Semi-Structured Interview," and the various forms. During the previous class period, the instructor will have divided students in the class into groups of seven: four executive committee members, two applicants, and one observer.
   B. Prior to class, prepare for your role in the group. Committee members should fill in the first two columns of Form 8 and the interviewer questions on Form 9 in pencil or on a separate sheet of paper. This will facilitate committee discussion, reduce the amount of class time needed for interview preparation, and save the forms themselves for the *final* list of criteria (Form 8) and interview questions (Form 9). Committee members should be prepared to play their roles (Form 9) as they would expect the described individuals to behave in real life. The observer for each group should read Form 10 in advance. Then he or she should fill it out during the interview and be prepared to discuss it at the end of the class period.

   The two applicants in each group should review their résumés in either Exhibit 2.18 or Exhibit 2.19 and be prepared to elaborate on any of the data in the résumé as well as provide supplementary information not on the résumé to the committee. An alternative to using two class members as job applicants is to use two individuals from *outside* the class.
   C. During the class period, each committee should spend 10 to 15 minutes comparing notes and designing a *final* set of criteria and weighting system for Form 8 and interview questions for Form 9. An option is to have the different committees come together and agree to a given set of selection criteria and their weight.

   Neither the applicants nor the observers should be present during these discussions. When the committee is ready, the applicants should be called from outside the room one at a time. In the meantime, the applicants should be doing final preparations for their interviews, including consideration of how they will respond to hypothetical questions that may be asked.

Possible selection criteria the committee may want to consider are: previous experience as a hospital CEO, educational background, ability to "fit" into the organization in terms of personal views and goals, knowledge of Brookdale Hospital and its problems, ideas for solving the hospital's problems, interpersonal skills, communication skills, and administrative skills.

D. Each candidate is then interviewed for 10 to 15 minutes. After each interview, board members fill out the remainder of Form 8 including the rating of each candidate on each criterion, the total score for each, and any additional comments. The observer will take notes and make an evaluation on Form 10 during the interviews. At the conclusion of these interviews, the committee compares notes and makes a decision concerning which candidate should be recommended for the position and why.

E. When all the groups have finished the interview and assessment process, the instructor asks each group to report to the entire class in the following order: the committee decision and rationale, the performance of the two applicants, and the observer's report. Lessons concerning the selection interview process are presented by both interviewers and interviewees. Depending on class size, this "wrap-up" phase should take 10 to 15 minutes.

Background

Brookdale Hospital is a 420-bed hospital located in a large Ontario city. The hospital was originally founded by a group of local physicians in 1948. It is now part of a larger group of hospitals, which includes 10 hospitals with a total of about 5,000 beds. The regional health authority that runs the system follows a policy of decentralization. Consequently, while some centralized support services have been provided, each hospital has continued to operate with a great deal of autonomy.

Recently, the hospital has begun to experience declines in occupancy rates and increased annual deficits. John Rhodes has been the chief executive officer for the past eight years. Two months ago, he suffered a stroke and, on the advice of his physician, has decided to retire at age 55.

The Board of Directors has appointed the associate administrator, Terry Bradford, as the acting administrator and chief executive officer while a search for Rhodes's replacement is made. The Executive Committee of the board has advertised the position widely over the past six weeks in a variety of professional publications.

As a result of the résumés generated through this recruitment process, the board has selected the two top candidates for the position: Chris Smith, an administrator of a small 60-bed hospital, and Terry Bradford. Résumés for each are shown in Exhibits 2.18 and 2.19. The committee has also developed a job description for the position as shown in Exhibit 2.20.

Hiring a new CEO requires a formal vote by the entire board, as well as concurrence by the resident of the corporation. However, the latter two steps have always been formalities. The critical decision is the recommendation of the

Executive Committee. This committee consists of the following four individuals: Sam Gordon, Amanda Simpson, Steve Bailey, and Jane Sears.

Gordon is a physician and the chief of the medical staff and has been with the hospital for 13 years. He is 58 years old and has a specialty in general surgery. He has been concerned about what he views as the eroding power of physicians vis-à-vis administrators and outside regulators over the past few years. Consequently, he would like the committee to recommend someone who can work well with physicians, understand their needs, and generally support their desires to provide high-quality patient care.

Simpson is a city councillor and was selected for both the board and the Executive Committee because of her political contacts. Her goals are to make sure the hospital survives, keeps its costs under control, and continues to provide some care for indigents. Since Brookdale is one of the major hospitals in the city serving her constituents, Simpson naturally is concerned that the hospital may close due to the deficits it has been experiencing. She feels the hospital has to be more innovative in developing and marketing new services to offset the declines in inpatient services.

Bailey is resident and chief executive officer of Applied Electronics, a very successful company that he founded 18 years ago. He admits he still doesn't know much about health care, but has been a member of the board for 12 years due to his entrepreneurial talents and his business contacts. His view is that the hospital needs to become more "businesslike," and focus on services that are not losing money. He also believes that the hospital has not done enough to raise funds through private philanthropy.

Sears is the president of a local bank. She has an M.B.A. and has been in banking for 22 years. Her major concern is the deteriorating financial position of the hospital. In her view, the new CEO should have excellent financial management skills as well as an ability to work well with physicians. She views the previous CEO (Rhodes) as deficient in these areas.

The committee has invited both Bradford and Smith to interview for the position of CEO. The outline for the selection process is shown on Form 8 and the form for questions to be developed by the committee is on Form 9.

Questions for the Semi-Structured Interview

In its purest form, a structured interview occurs when the interviewers bring to the interview a list of predetermined questions to ask the interviewee. The advantage is that the interviewers have previously discussed and agreed upon the relevant criteria. During the interview, all interviewers focus upon these criteria. Weighting of these criteria is often used as well. This systematic process usually results in higher levels of consistency among interviewers than is the case with unstructured interviews.

However, structured interviews do not allow the interviewee to discuss a topic of his or her choice or to provide additional information on areas that require further explanation. An unstructured interview emphasizes creating a supportive climate and helping the interviewees discuss values, goals, objectives, and career plans.

A compromise that retains the benefits of a structured interview while also creating the openness of the unstructured interview is the semi-structured interview. Here, the interviewers not only develop a set of structured questions to evaluate the candidate based on the agreed-upon criteria but also ask open-ended questions, such as "What are your long-term career goals?" and "Why is that important to you?"

Develop a list of up to 10 questions to ask the two applicants and decide which committee members should ask which questions. Be sure to consider the criteria identified on Form 8 as well as some open-ended questions designed to learn more about the applicant. Write these questions on Form 9.

Exhibit 2.18 *Résumé 1*

TERRY A. BRADFORD
119 Brook Hollow Lane
Toronto, Ontario

Job Objective

To secure a position as chief executive officer for a large Canadian hospital.

Education

1972–1976:	University of Western Ontario
	Major: Sociology
	Degree: B.A., June 1966, Cum laude, GPA 3.52
1982–1983:	York University
	Major: Business Administration
	Emphasis: Organizational Behaviour
	Degree: M.B.A., June 1973, GPA 3.86
	Graduated with Honours
Other:	After completing my M.B.A. degree, I have taken two additional graduate courses in accounting and one additional course in finance at the University of Toronto.

Employment History

February 1995–Present:	Associate Administrator; Brookdale Hospital, Toronto, Ontario
	Duties: liaison between the CEO and the medical staff, nursing staff, and other major hospital departments; represents administrator at various functions; strategic planning and marketing; reviews financial and occupancy data.
June 1988–February 1995:	Assistant Administrator; Oakland Hospital, Edmonton, Alberta
	Duties: worked with the administrator and associate administrator on a variety of administrative functions in finance, personnel, marketing, and public relations.
August 1983–June 1988	Personnel Assistant; Bayview Municipal Hospital, Owen Sound, Ontario
	Duties: designed personnel appraisal form, conducted selection interviews, designed and taught courses for supervisors, and designed advertisements for positions.
June 1976–September 1982:	Various sales and administrative positions in a variety of organizations.

Personal

Date of Birth:	September 6, 1954
Height:	173 cm (5 ft. 8 in.)
	Weight: 68 kg (150 lbs.)
Marital Status:	Divorced, no children
Hobbies:	Music, travel, and swimming

Exhibit 2.19 *Résumé 2*

CHRIS A. SMITH

Home Address	**Office Address**
2057 Hickory Street	Administrator
Windsor, Ontario	Morningside Hospital
	204 Jefferson Street
	Windsor, Ontario

Personal: Married, two children

Educational Background

B.S.—University of Guelph (1977)
M.B.A.—Dalhousie University (1982)

Experience:

Morningside Hospital, Windsor, Ontario	November 1991–Present
Acting Administrator	June 1999–Present
Associate Administrator	June 1993–June 1999
Assistant Administrator	November 1991–June 1993
Eastside Hospital, Toronto, Ontario	
Financial Manager	June 1988–November 1991
McLains Department Store, Saint John, New Brunswick	
Financial Manager	January 1986–June 1988
Financial Trainee	June 1982–January 1986
City of Guelph, Ontario	
City Planner	July 1977–August 1981

Member: Rotary Club and First Baptist Church

Interests: Snow skiing and politics

Exhibit 2.20 *Job Description: Chief Executive Officer, Brookdale Hospital*

Description of Work

General Statement of Duties: Supervises and coordinates administrative work of a complex nature involving the entire hospital and all its components; represents the hospital to the external community.

Supervision Required: Implements policies developed by the Board of Directors.

Supervision Exercised: Plans, organizes, motivates, coordinates, and directs a staff of administrative and clerical personnel. Total direct supervision involves over 15 individuals.

Examples of Duties

1. Initiates and coordinates activities related to long-range planning and delivery of the hospital's services.
2. Develops and enforces policies and procedures related to administrative functions.
3. Coordinates major staff services, including budget, personnel, medical services, nursing services, dietetics, and housekeeping.
4. Develops and compiles administrative reports as required by the board or external regulatory agencies.
5. Performs related work as required.

Required Knowledge, Skills, and Abilities

Extensive and broad knowledge of complex management systems (internal and external) in a health care environment. Skill and ability in planning, personnel management, and budgetary control. Ability to relate to external stakeholders, including the Board of Directors.

Qualifications for Appointment

Education: Graduation from a college or university with major coursework in business administration, public administration, or health administration.

Experience: Ten years or more of progressively responsible experience in administration or management.

Form 8 *Criteria for Selecting a Chief Executive Officer and Ratings of Applicants Based on These Criteria*

Criteria: Major dimension of job description and personal characteristics desired	Weight of the Criteria (1–5)	Job Applicant Rating on the Criteria (1–10)		Total Score (Weight X Rating)		Comments about Each
		Bradford	Smith	Bradford	Smith	
1.						
2.						
3.						
4.						
5.						
6.						
7.						
8.						
9.						
10.						
Total Scores						

Form 9   *Questions for Interview**

1.

2.

3.

4.

5.

6.

7.

8.

9.

10.

*Develop interview questions that are not biased or illegal, but which relate to the performance dimensions developed in Form 8.

1. How well did the committee establish rapport with each applicant?

2. How well did each of the candidates respond to the committee's questions? What improvements would you suggest? Why?

3. Approximately what percentage of the 15-minute interview time was spent listening to the applicant and what percentage consisted of committee questions and/or comments? How appropriate was this breakdown?

4. Did the committee overemphasize negative information, ask illegal questions, show bias based on irrelevant factors, or otherwise treat either applicant unfairly?

5. Did the committee probe unclear areas, or did it allow short answers that did not provide necessary information?

6. What is your overall assessment of the success of the committee in eliciting relevant information for making this selection decision? Why?

43. EXERCISE

Selection Interview Role Play

I. *Objectives:*
   A. To help you develop skills in conducting selection interviews.
   B. To provide you with practice in applying the basic principles of effective interviewing.
II. *Out-of-Class Preparation Time:* 30–90 minutes, depending on role played (students who play the applicant will need to prepare a résumé)
III. *In-Class Time:* 45 minutes
IV. *Procedures:* The class should be divided into groups of three: an interviewer, applicant, and observer. Roles should be assigned ahead of time so you will have time to prepare for your role. This is especially important for those of you who will play the role of interviewee since you are to use your own résumé and qualifications during the role play. The interviewer should prepare a set of interview questions. Read the scenario that follows and the role description provided by the instructor. Participants should assume that the interview is taking place in a campus placement office. The role play begins when the applicant arrives for the interview, and ends when both individuals have accomplished their objectives. At the end of the role play, the interviewer completes the interviewer's report (Form 11) and shares it with the applicant. Next, the observer provides feedback on his or her observations to the group (Form 12). The group then identifies and discusses the hardest part of the interview from both the interviewer's point of view and the applicant's perspective. If time permits, the entire class then discusses the reliability and validity of the interview as a method of selecting applicants for jobs.

Scenario

The director of university recruiting for Duro Insurance Company is presently recruiting students for its administrative trainee program. The one-year training program involves a combination of on-the-job training and formal classroom training. Upon successful completion of the training, a candidate is assigned a position as assistant department supervisor.

Duro Insurance Company ranks in the top 15 percent of life insurance companies nationally. Duro markets all forms of insurance, bonds, and pension products on an individual and group basis. More recently, the company added diversified financial services, including discount brokerage services, real estate financing, and mutual funds. The company is divided into six major divisions (Employee Benefits, Commercial Insurance, Individual Life, Automobile, Homeowners, and Diversified Financial Services) and functionally into several major operating departments: Sales, Underwriting, Administrative, Loss Prevention, Actuarial, Claims, Legal, Financial and Investments, Advertising and Public Relations, Personnel, and Research and Policy Development. Duro has over 8,000 employees and more than 100 field offices throughout the country. Management at each field office consists of a manager, several department heads, and their assistants. The company has enjoyed a pattern of steady growth and expansion over the years.

Job Description for Administrative Trainee

1. Handle day-to-day administration of field office, including direct supervision of office clerks.
2. Plan and oversee the use of space, furniture, and equipment on a continual basis and recommend changes as necessary.
3. Supervise computer processing operations for issuing and servicing insurance policies, including claims.
4. Implement and maintain accounting and collection procedures.

The trainee works closely with the department head in learning these duties.

Job Qualifications

1. Bachelor of Science or Bachelor of Arts degree with business management background (knowledge of accounting desired).
2. Ability to communicate effectively.
3. Ability to handle detail.
4. Ability to plan and direct activities of subordinates.
5. Demonstrated leadership potential.
6. Knowledge of computers and software packages including Simply Accounting.

Additional Job Data

1. The trainee position reports directly to a department head.
2. Expected career progression is to assistant department supervisor (1–2 years) and, with continued development, to department head (4–5 years after supervisory assignment).
3. The position requires relocation.
4. The company offers competitive salaries and benefits, including a tuition repayment plan and in-house career planning and development.

Form 11   *Interviewer's Report*

Applicant _____   Position _____

Date _____   Interviewer _____

Rate the applicant's background and behaviour, taking into consideration the factors listed for each area.
Circle a rating for each factor. Give an overall rating also.

1. Presentation (appearance, manner, oral communication skills, interest, motivation):

Poor   1   2   3   4   5   Excellent

2. Education (major, intellectual abilities, academic achievement, knowledge of field):

Poor   1   2   3   4   5   Excellent

3. Work experience (related experience, skill and competence, job performance, interpersonal skills, leadership):

Poor   1   2   3   4   5   Excellent

4. Summarize candidate's strengths:

5. Summarize candidate's weaknesses:

6. Overall evaluation and recommendation:

Poor   1   2   3   4   5   Excellent

Recommendation: ( ) Invite for field visit   ( ) Do not invite

Comments:

1. What was the quality of the interaction between the interviewer and applicant?

2. What type of interview did the interviewer use (structured, semi-structured or non-structured)? How well did it work?

3. Were the questions job-related?

4. What did the interviewer do to put the applicant at ease?

5. Did the interviewer listen? Did the interviewer spend too much time talking?

6. Did the interviewer follow up on questions not completely answered?

7. Did the interviewer gain enough information to make a decision about the applicant?

8. General observations.

Which Selection Procedure Is Most Effective?

I. *Objectives*:
    A. To examine the strengths and weaknesses of four different methods for selecting new employees.
    B. To enhance your oral communication skills.

II. *Out-of-Class Preparation Time:* 30 minutes to prepare for the debate

III. *In-Class Time Suggested*: 50–75 minutes

IV. *Procedures*: Your instructor will divide the class into five groups at the end of class prior to conducting this exercise. There will be four debating groups consisting of three to five members each and one or more groups of "judges" that consist of the remaining class members. Debaters will be assigned one of four positions and told to prepare to argue in favour of that position. Judges will be told to read the textbook chapter pages that cover those positions. The issue to be debated is: Which approach to selecting new employees is most effective? The positions are: (1) the structured interview; (2) the unstructured interview; (3) ability and personality tests; and (4) reviewing applications and résumés, and talking to or getting letters from listed references.

At the start of the next class, your instructor will announce that a four-way debate will be held. The judges' role in the debate is to "search for the truth." They are to listen to the different sides presented and then, after the debate is over, tell the class what they believe is the "correct" answer to the debate question, not who "won" the debate.

The debate consists of two rounds. The purpose of Round One (15–20 minutes) is for each team to learn the position of the other debating teams. Hence, each team has up to 5 minutes to explain their position as comprehensively as possible. At the completion of Round One, the debating teams are given up to 10 minutes to prepare criticisms of each of the other three teams for Round Two. During this intermission, judges are to discuss what they have heard and begin to formulate their own position.

In Round Two (15–20 minutes), each debating team is given up to 5 minutes to criticize the position of each of the other teams. Unlike a traditional debate, teams are not allowed to rebut the criticisms made by others. They must simply listen to them. Round Two ends when Team Four has finished criticizing the position of the other three teams.

After the debate has ended, the judges have 5 minutes to discuss the case among themselves and to arrive at a consensus, if possible. The judging team(s) then explains its decision to the debaters.

45. INCIDENT

The Ethical Selection Dilemma at Integrity Motors

Background

Integrity Motors has been retailing quality used cars and trucks for 10 years. It has become the largest and most successful used car dealership in the region. Integrity Motors employs 11 full-time salespersons. Timmy Blackburn, the owner, wants to maintain a policy of having a lean yet highly productive staff, which means that the employees have to be dependable, highly competent, and willing to work at a high level of productivity for long hours each day.

After 10 years at Integrity Motors, the sales manager was resigning to start his own business. Timmy felt he needed the same type of employee he currently had in the position—someone who had considerable experience as a sales manager, was creative and a good motivator, who had good communication and management skills, and who would be committed to the dealership for a long time. Although Timmy felt it prudent to take the necessary time to carefully select a new sales manager, time was of the essence because the end of the year was approaching and the inventory needed to be drastically reduced.

Applications for the job started pouring in almost immediately. After a week, 45 applicants had expressed interest in the job, and 10 potentially suitable candidates were invited for interviews. A panel consisting of Helen, the office manager, Joe, the service manager, and Timmy interviewed the 10 applicants. Based upon the interviews, it was clear that one candidate, Gladys Morrison, was outstanding compared to all the other applicants. Gladys had recently moved to the area from a city where she had been a sales manager for 15 years. Everyone agreed that she was the perfect candidate. The next morning an offer would be extended to Gladys. Everyone left the meeting feeling satisfied that they had made an excellent choice.

A New Development

The next morning when Timmy arrived at the dealership he was met by Helen and Joe, who seemed troubled. Apparently, after the meeting the prior evening, Helen happened to meet an old friend at a convenience store. The friend told Helen she was four months' pregnant and that, coincidentally, her new neighbour was also four months' pregnant. To Helen's surprise, the pregnant neighbour was Gladys Morrison, the person to whom the dealership intended to extend a job offer the next morning. Helen said absolutely nothing to her friend about Gladys's employment inquiry or pending job offer, yet throughout the night, Helen worried about the potential hire.

The next morning, as Helen shared this development with Timmy and Joe before Gladys was contacted, all three discussed the potential consequences of hiring Gladys. Joe was astounded that Gladys had not informed them of her pregnancy. Timmy quickly told him that legally she did not have to tell them about it, and furthermore, an employment decision could not be based on her pregnancy. Helen observed that, though legally this was true, from a practical standpoint the dealership could not afford to be without a sales manager for an extended period of time. Timmy agreed. He too was concerned about her potential absence as well as her potential inability to work for long periods under intense pressure, especially when they needed to reduce inventory. Helen also reminded them that, although Gladys was clearly the best applicant, there were at least nine other applicants who would be suitable sales managers.

Questions

1. What are the legal and ethical issues involved in this case? Was it ethical for Gladys to have applied for the position in the first place?
2. Should the owner hire Gladys or some other applicant? Should the information about the pregnancy be considered?
3. If Gladys is hired, how could Integrity Motors accommodate her pregnancy?

Original case contributed by James C. Wimbush, Indiana University.

The Exit Interviews

Mr. William James has recently been hired as the director of human resources for a call centre in New Brunswick. While he was interviewing for the position, several administrators and managers told him there was a severe employee morale problem, particularly among customer service representatives. James later learned that the annual turnover rate of customer service representatives has averaged 18.4 percent, compared to 11.6 percent at other Canadian call centres over the past three years.

James was aware that all exiting employees are required to complete an exit interview questionnaire and interview prior to receiving their final paycheque. He asked his assistant to pull the files for all exit interviews of departing customer service representatives and to prepare a summary of the major reasons for leaving and specific suggestions on how the facility could increase its retention of customer service representatives.

When the results were compiled, James was disappointed. The utility of these data was very low. Most of the respondents indicated they were leaving for "personal reasons," "family responsibilities," or "job offer." Very few volunteered recommendations for how the call centre could improve employee retention, even when asked directly on both the questionnaire and during the interview. The recommendation mentioned most frequently was "better parking."

The prevailing opinion of the individuals with whom James spoke was that departing employees are reluctant to discuss any "sensitive" issues or concerns for fear of alienating the interviewer or supervisor. He was told no one wanted to possibly jeopardize their recommendation to other employers due to anything they might say during the exit interview. Through his informal conversations with customer service representatives and supervisors, he knew there were many problems and concerns shared by many employees, including inadequate staffing, lack of respect and support from supervisors and top management, favouritism in salary increases and promotions, and high stress levels due to all of the above. Yet he was unable to document these problems and others with the current exit interview data.

James is now attempting to determine the best methods of identifying employee problems and assessing employee reaction to the organization, its various components, and various human resource policies and programs. He is also interested in determining the factors which cause many of the long-tenured employees to stay.

Questions

1. Discuss the nature and causes of the problem.
2. Should James attempt to improve the exit interview process? If so, how should this be done?
3. What other assessment alternatives should he consider in addition to, or rather than, exit interviews?
4. How can James use the information generated about why employees stay or leave to improve employee retention?

Nepotism

Jim was the office manager whose branch of a large architectural firm had 25 architects and eight personal assistants. While Jim was in charge of the entire office, Doris was in charge of the assistants who were not assigned to work for particular architects. These assistants were assigned to tasks by Doris on an as-needed basis. The newest assistant was Ellen, and although she had been with the firm for less than six weeks, she had already caused considerable problems for Jim, Doris, and the architects.

One day, Ellen had been brought to the office by her father, one of the firm's founders who worked at a different office. The father announced that he had hired his daughter to work for Doris during this and future summer vacations from college. Unfortunately, Ellen had no skills whatsoever that related to the duties required. In addition, the office was fully staffed and did not need any additional help.

Doris was irate when she learned that she was supposed to find work for Ellen and supervise her. She was particularly upset that Ellen had been hired without the firm following the standard selection process, and that Ellen had just been dumped on her doorstep. She told Don, "Ellen has no knowledge of architecture whatsoever. I have no work for her. I don't want to have anything to do with her!"

On her first day of work, Ellen was shown to her desk but was assigned no specific tasks. Within a few days, she had introduced herself to all of the architects and started spending more and more time in their offices. Wanting to make a favourable impression on Ellen's father, the architects willingly talked with her at length. One of the young architects was particularly taken by her, and vice versa. She spent more time in his office than in any other. Meanwhile, the other personal assistants were starting to complain about all of the attention that Ellen was receiving and the fact that she wasn't doing "her share" of the tasks. In addition, the architects were falling behind in their work. A vicious rumour was circulating that Ellen had a brother that also might be thrust upon the office. During all of this, Doris refused to have anything to do with Ellen and reminded Jim that she was *his* problem.

Questions

1. What are the major problems in this case?
2. If you were Jim, what steps would you take to solve the problems depicted in this case?
3. What are the advantages and disadvantages of having a "no nepotism" policy?

48. SKILL BUILDER

Evaluating Job Application Forms

I. *Objectives:*
A. To familiarize you with the criteria for selecting questions to put on an application form.
B. To give you practice in evaluating the questions on an application form.

II. *Time Required to Complete:* 1 hour

III. *Instructions:* Review the application form that appears in Exhibit 2.21. This form is used by Holy Radio Network for their administrative and clerical employees. You should thoroughly review the legal requirements for pre-employment inquiries and other relevant information on application forms found in your text. Use the guide below to evaluate the questions that appear on the application. Prepare a short write-up summarizing your findings and make specific recommendations for improving the questions.

Questions to Be Asked in Evaluating Appropriateness of Application Form Items

1. Is this question job-related?
2. Will answers to this question have an adverse impact (i.e., disqualify a significantly larger percentage of members of one particular group than of others)?
3. Is this question really needed to judge an applicant's qualifications and suitability for the job?
4. Does the question constitute an invasion of privacy?
5. Can the applicant's response to this question be verified?

Exhibit 2.21 *Job Application Form*

HOLY RADIO NETWORK APPLICATION FOR EMPLOYMENT

Name: _____

    (Last)   (Middle initial)   (First)

Street Address: _____

PHOTO

_____

    (City)   (Province)

Sex: Male   Female   Age: _____

Own home: Yes No   How long? _____ Rent: Yes No   How long? _____

Phone No. (_____)_____

Marital Status: Married   Divorced   Never Married   Widowed   (circle one)

If married, indicate name of spouse: _____

Exhibit 2.21 *continued*

Of what country are you a citizen? _____

Indicate languages spoken fluently: _____

List all physical disabilities: _____

Religion: _____

Church membership: _____

Name of minister: _____

How often do you attend church? _____

List church activities: _____

Do you smoke?   Yes   No   Do you consume alcoholic beverages?   Yes   No

Have you ever been arrested?   Yes   No   Indicate offences: _____

Military experience: _____   Type of discharge: _____

Education

High school name: _____   Date of graduation: _____

Business or technical school name: _____   Degree: _____

Attended: _____   Date of graduation: _____

Junior/community college name: _____   Degree: _____

Attended: _____   Date of graduation: _____

University name. _____   Degree: _____

Attended: _____   Date of graduation: _____

Work Experience

Name of employer: _____   Job title: _____   No. of years: _____

Reason for leaving: _____

Name of employer: _____   Job title: _____   No. of years: _____

Reason for leaving: _____

Name of employer: _____   Job title: _____   No. of years: _____

Reason for leaving: _____

_____

I certify that all the information that I have given in this application is true, accurate, and complete. I understand that any misstatement or omission of a material fact may be a cause for dismissal.

Date _____   Signature _____

Source: Adapted from Robert D. Gatewood and Hubert S. Feild, Human Resource Selection (New York: Dryden Press, 1987), 279.

Staffing for a Telecommuting Job

I. *Objectives:*
    A. To give you practice in revising a job description for a telecommuting job.
    B. To enhance your understanding of how to prepare a staffing plan for a telecommuting job.
    C. To familiarize you with some of the differences between staffing for telecommuting job environments versus staffing for traditional job (office) environments.

II. *Time Required to Complete:* 1 to 2 hours

III. *Instructions:* A large pharmaceutical company located in the Prairies is one of the leading pharmaceutical manufacturers in Canada. Because of the intense competition in the industry and the heightened competition for highly skilled personnel, the company believes that quality-of-work-life (QWL) is a key factor for achieving competitive advantage. In support of this belief, the company is considering the adoption of a telecommuting work arrangement for selected jobs.

The job of public relations (PR) specialist has been identified as an appropriate job for telecommuting, due to the fact that the job responsibilities are mostly information-related activities that require independent mental effort with no supervisory responsibilities. Exhibit 2.22 contains the current job description for the PR specialist, which reflects the primary job activities and qualifications for a full-time, in-office PR specialist. There is currently only one job incumbent, and that person has resigned.

You have been asked to develop a plan for recruiting and hiring a replacement who will telecommute from home.

    A. What method of job analysis do you recommend to determine the job requirements and job specifications for a telecommuting job? Is the method you recommend different than the method you would use if the job were performed in a traditional office environment?
    B. What procedures do you recommend for recruiting and hiring a telecommuter? Are the procedures you recommend different than the procedures you would use if the job were performed in a traditional office environment?
    C. What changes would you make to the job description in Exhibit 2.22 to reflect the telecommuting nature of the job?
    D. What other recommendations would you make to ensure the successful implementation of a telecommuting work arrangement?

Original case contributed by Diana Deadrick, Old Dominion University.

Exhibit 2.22 *Job Description*

Job Title: Public Relations Specialist

Department: Public Relations

Reports To: Director of Public Relations

General Summary: Serves as a writer on numerous firm publications; coordinates materials; writes, edits, and proofs articles, public relations publications, and advertising copy using Microsoft Word software and Macintosh graphic and layout programs.

Essential Job Functions:
1. Writes, edits, and proofs public relations articles, newspaper copy, and human interest stories.
2. Writes advertising copy in conjunction with the marketing department.
3. Writes, edits, and coordinates printing and layout of company newsletter.
4. Meets with executives to determine public relations needs.
5. Meets with media officials and the public to publicize firm's accomplishments.
6. Attends information meetings at the main office on an as-needed basis.
7. Gives presentations at meetings and other public events.
8. Performs other related duties as assigned by management.

Education and Experience Required: Degree in Art/Graphic Design; demonstrated ability to use Macintosh and PC computer hardware/software; some experience in television presentation or public speaking; considerable knowledge of journalism principles, English grammar and usage; demonstrated ability to write newspaper, news, and human interest articles, reports, brochures, and advertising copy; demonstrated ability to work and communicate effectively with others.

Developing Effectiveness in Human Resources: Training, Career Development, and Performance Appraisal

Part 3

50. CASE

Career Development at Electronic Applications

Electronic Applications Corporation is a major producer of silicon chips for the computer industry. It is located near Ottawa in an area that is home to many high-technology firms. Since its founding in 1972, the company has grown rapidly in terms of sales and profits, thus enhancing its stock price many times over.

However, human resource policies have tended to lag behind company growth. The policy emphasis has been on developing reactive policies to meet the requirements of external organizations such as the federal government. Proactive human resource policies have not been a high priority.

Recently, Harold Sweeney has been hired as director of human resources for the company. Sweeney had previously served as an assistant personnel director for a large "blue-chip" corporation based in British Columbia. He took his current position not only because of an increase in pay and responsibility, but also because of what he termed "the challenge of bringing this company from a 1950s human resources mentality to one more compatible with the realities of the 21st century."

Sweeney has been on the job for four months and has been assessing the situation to determine the more significant human resource problems. One significant problem seems to be high turnover among the electrical engineers who work in Research and Development. This department is the core of the research function, and turnover rates have averaged about 30 percent per year over the past three years.

In assessing the cause of the problem, Sweeney checked area wage surveys and found Electronic Applications paid 5 to 8 percent above the market for various categories of electrical engineers. Through informal conversations with a large number of individuals, including the engineers themselves, he learned that many of the engineers felt "dead-ended" in the technical aspects of engineering. Since the company did not have a formal exit interview system, he could not check out other possible explanations through that mechanism.

In particular, the Research and Development Department had lost some of the younger engineers who had been considered to be on the "fast track." Most had gone to work for competitors in the local area.

One particular Research and Development employee who impressed Sweeney was Helen Morgan. Helen was 29 years old, had a Bachelor of Science degree from the University of Waterloo, and was studying at night for her M.B.A. at Carleton University. Helen had been employed at Electronic

Applications for seven years: three in an entry-level engineering position and four as a section chief. The latter promotion was to the highest position in Research and Development other than the position of director of research and development.

Helen claimed that "the company doesn't really care about its good people." In her view, the present director, Harry James, doesn't want to allow his better people to move up in the organization. He is more interested in keeping them in his own department so he can meet his own goals without having to orient and train new people. Helen also claimed she was told she "has a bright future with the company" by both James and the former director of human resources. Her performance appraisals have been uniformly excellent.

She went on to criticize the company for using an appraisal form with no section dealing with future potential or future goals, and for having no rewards for supervisors who develop their subordinates; no human resource planning to identify future job openings; no centralized job information or job positioning system; no career paths and/or career ladders; and attitudinal barriers against women in management positions. She recommended that steps be taken to remedy each of the problems she identified.

Sweeney checked out the information Morgan had provided and found it to be accurate. Moreover, he heard through the "grapevine" that she is being considered for an excellent position with a nearby competitor. Clearly, he has an even greater challenge than he had anticipated. He realizes he has an immediate problem concerning high turnover of certain key employees. In addition, he also has a series of interconnected problems associated with career development. However, he is not quite sure what to do or in what order.

Questions

1. Describe the nature and causes of the problem faced by Sweeney.
2. What additional questions should Sweeney ask or what additional information is needed before proceeding toward a solution to this problem? Why?
3. What are the individual and organizational benefits of a formalized career development system?
4. If Sweeney decides to develop a formalized career development system at Electronic Applications, what components or types of services should be offered? Why?
5. Should the career development activities be integrated with other human resource management activities? If yes, which ones? Why?
6. What criteria should Sweeney consider to evaluate good candidates for promotion? What criteria could be used to evaluate the performance of supervisors in development of their subordinates?

The Safety Training Program

Houghton Refrigeration Company builds refrigerators for large appliance companies. It employs about 300 people, mostly assembly-line workers, and is located in a small rural town in New Brunswick. The company typically builds chest-type freezers and small bar-type refrigerators on a contract basis. On occasion, however, it also builds standard-size refrigerators. The president of the company is a former engineer, as are most of the other executives. These individuals are very knowledgeable about engineering, but have received little training in the basic principles of management.

During the summer months, volume at the factory increases significantly, and the company needs to hire about 40 new employees to handle the heavy workload. Most of these new employees are students who attend the university in the nearby city. Some high school students are hired as well.

When a new employee is hired, the company asks him or her to complete an application form and then to show up at the plant gate ready for work. Employees receive no orientation. The worker is shown to a work station and, after a minimum amount of on-the-job training, is expected to start performing a job. Most of the jobs are quite simple; hence, the training is typically completed within 10 minutes. The first-line supervisor usually shows the employee how to do a job once, then watches while the employee does the job once, leaves, and comes back about 20 minutes later to see how the employee is progressing. Typical jobs at the plant include screwing 14 screws into the sides of a freezer, placing a piece of insulation into the freezer lid, and handing out supplies from the tool room.

The company has had excellent experiences with employing university students over the years. Much of the success can be attributed to the older workers coming to the aid of the new employees when difficulties arise. Most new employees are able to perform their jobs reasonably well after their on-the-job training is completed. However, when unexpected difficulties arise, they are usually not prepared for them and therefore need assistance from others.

The older workers have been especially helpful to students working in the "press room." However, Joe Gleason, the first-line supervisor there, finds it amusing to belittle the university students whenever they make any mistakes. He relishes showing a student once how to use a press to bend a small piece of metal, then exclaims, "You're a hot-shot university student; now let's see you do it." He then watches impatiently while the student invariably makes a mistake, and jokingly announces for all to hear, "That's wrong! How did you ever get into university anyway? Try it again, dummy."

One summer, the company experienced a rash of injuries to its employees. Although most of the injuries were minor, the company felt it imperative to conduct a series of short training programs on safe material-handling techniques. The company president was at a loss as to who should conduct the training. The director of human resources was a 64-year-old former engineer who was about to retire and was a poor speaker. The only other employee in the Human Resource Department was a new 19-year-old secretary who knew nothing about proper handling techniques. Out of desperation, the president finally decided to ask Bill Young, the first-line supervisor of the "lid-line," to conduct the training. Bill had recently attended a training program himself on safety and was active in the Red Cross. Bill reluctantly agreed to conduct the training. It was to be done on a departmental basis with small groups of 10 to 15 employees attending each session.

At the first of these training sessions, Bill Young nervously stood up in front of 14 employees, many of whom were university students, and read his presentation in a monotone voice. His entire speech lasted about one minute and consisted of the following text:

> Statistics show that an average of 30 persons injure their backs on the job each day in this province. None of us wants to become a "statistic."
>
> The first thing that should be done before lifting an object is to look it over and decide whether you can handle it alone or if help is needed. Get help if there's any doubt as to whether the load is safely within your capacity.
>
> Next, look over the area where you're going to be carrying the object. Make sure it's clear of obstacles. You may have to do a little housekeeping before moving your load. After you have checked out the load and route you're going to travel, the following steps should be taken for your safety in lifting:
>
> 1. Get a good footing close to the load.
> 2. Place your feet about 25 cm (or 8 to 12 in.) apart.
> 3. Bend your knees to grasp the load.
> 4. Bend your knees outward, straddling the load.
> 5. Get a firm grip.
> 6. Keep the load close to your body.
> 7. Lift gradually.
>
> Once you've lifted the load, you'll eventually have to set it down—so bend your legs again—and follow the lifting procedures in reverse. Make sure that your fingers clear the pinch points. And, finally, it's a good idea to set one corner down first.

After Bill's speech ended, the employees immediately returned to work. By the end of the day, however, everyone in the plant had heard about the training fiasco, and all, except the president, were laughing about it.

Questions

1. Evaluate the company's on-the-job training program. Should it be changed?
2. Should the company install an employee orientation program for new factory workers, or is one unnecessary?
3. What changes should be made in the company's safety training program?
4. What other ways might a firm emphasize safety and curtail accidents, other than training?

The Mentoring Problem at Walnut Insurance

Tom Morrison, president of Walnut Insurance, was sitting at his desk reading a letter he had just received and thinking about a recent meeting with his vice presidents. He knew he had to make a decision regarding whether to implement a new mentoring program, but he did not know what that decision should be.

Walnut Insurance has been selling liability insurance to firms in one particular industry for over 50 years. Its specialized niche in the insurance industry has made it highly successful. It employs about 2,400 individuals who work in 12 regional offices throughout Canada and in its Manitoba headquarters.

Walnut Insurance has six senior male vice presidents (VPs) who report directly to Tom Morrison. Over the years, these individuals have travelled between the various regional offices, working primarily with the insurance sales representatives. The VPs perform numerous functions when visiting the regional offices. They go out on overnight sales trips with the representatives to learn about customer problems; they assist agents with policy questions and provide training; they evaluate agents to determine who has the potential to be promoted; they pass on the firm's values and culture, which places heavy emphasis on honesty and satisfying customer needs; they assist agents in interpreting company policies; and they determine what new policies need to be developed.

Over the years, these VPs have performed one other valuable service to new employees—they have informally mentored some of them. Typically, each VP would pick out five or six promising agents and take them under his wing. He would get to know the agents well, point out strengths and weaknesses, and help them develop plans for achieving management positions. Over the years, this approach has worked quite well.

However, in the last two years the firm has hired over 50 new agents, almost two-thirds of whom are women. These individuals are university graduates who majored in a variety of disciplines. They were hired based on their sales skills, initiative, self-confidence, assertiveness, and physical appearance. Previously, almost all of the new hires were men. Tom Morrison believed that the present informal mentoring system might result in women being excluded from opportunities within the company, so he thought that a formal system should be considered.

At one of the firm's regular retreats, Tom broached the subject with his VPs. He commended them for their willingness to mentor agents voluntarily in the past, noted that many of the regional managers were a product of this mentoring, explained his concerns regarding the need for female agents to receive equal mentoring treatment, and asked them if they thought the process should be formalized by assigning specific agents to specific VPs.

Tom's suggestion went over like a lead balloon—not a single person liked the idea in the least. In fact, they strongly opposed it and told Tom this as tactfully as they could. One VP explained that he was an elder in the church and had strong religious convictions. He did not want to travel with female employees on overnight sales calls because it might tarnish his image among his evangelical friends. He had no problem working with females in regional offices and had done so for many years. But he did not want to travel with them.

Three other VPs were opposed to the idea because they were fearful of harassment complaints being filed against them. They noted that a recent insurance trade publication article described numerous cases in which managers in several other insurance firms had been charged with harassment. The article explained how, even if one is innocent of a charge, one's career can be ruined. The VPs demanded to know how and whether the firm would stand behind them if they were charged with harassment.

One other VP objected to the idea because he wanted free choice in selecting employees to mentor. He argued that only the best agents are deserving of mentoring and that it would be a waste of time to mentor everyone. He asked, "Why should we mentor someone who does not have the potential to become a manager?"

The last VP objected because he knew that his wife would not approve of any plan that would require that he work closely with young female agents, particularly at night in faraway locations.

After hearing all of these objections, Tom asked the VPs to give further thought to the issue. He restated that mentoring was critical to the firm's success and that it was important for women not to be left out of the process.

In the week that followed, Tom did not hear anything more regarding the issue from any VP. However, he did receive a letter from one wife (see Exhibit 3.1) and it was clear what she thought of the idea. Nonetheless, the final decision was his to make.

Questions

1. If you were Tom, would you implement a formal mentoring program? If so, how would you address the VPs' concerns?
2. What alternatives to a formal mentoring program are available to Tom?

Exhibit 3.1 *Letter from a VP's Wife*

January 23, 2003
1105 Edgewater Dr.
Winnipeg, Manitoba

Mr. Tom Morrison
President
Walnut Insurance Company

Dear Tom,

I am writing to you regarding the new mentoring proposal that is being considered. My husband told me about it at dinner last week and I have been worried about it ever since.

As you may know, my husband and I have been married for 28 years and have raised three lovely children. We are dedicated to each other and have strong family values. We try to act as good role models to our children and to others.

To be honest, I am very concerned about what effects the new mentoring program might have on our marriage. My husband is faithful to me and I trust him with other women under typical circumstances. However, the new program involves special circumstances and I do not trust the women he might need to mentor. Some of these women may be so ambitious that they will stop at nothing to get promoted. They would not hesitate to destroy a marriage or my husband's career if they thought it would help them get ahead.

I would appreciate it if you would find a different alternative. Surely, some other approach would accomplish your goals.

Sincerely yours,

Joyce Butler

Joyce Butler

53. EXERCISE

Conducting a Training Needs Assessment

I. *Objectives*:
   A. To illustrate the importance of needs assessment for organization change efforts.
   B. To show you the linkages between organization-wide, job-wide, and individual training needs.
   C. To help you learn how to identify training needs and collect supporting data.
II. *Out-of-Class Preparation Time*: 60–90 minutes
III. *In-Class Time*: 45 minutes
IV. *Procedures*: Read Case 29, "Strategic Human Resource Management," and the following "Update" on the School of Business Administration at Riverside University. Then use Form 1 to conduct a needs assessment. In general, a needs assessment is used to identify any discrepancies between desired and current performance behaviours. Although the outcome of the assessment might be the identification of training needs, it could identify other organization development needs that are not necessarily met through training programs.

Part I of Form 1 is to be used for the Organization Analysis phase of the needs assessment, which identifies "where" there is a need for improvement within the school and whether there are "system-wide" problems that exist. Factors to be analyzed include any recent or anticipated organization-wide changes and how that will affect the organization's goals, structure, culture, and/or climate. The result of this analysis is a determination of whether the "problem" (discrepancy) is an organization-wide problem as opposed to an individual training problem. Part II of Form 1 is to be used for the Job/Task Analysis, which identifies "what" tasks are in need of improvement and whether there are job-wide problems that exist. Factors to consider here include any recent or anticipated changes in the job demands and how that might affect the nature of the job requirements (tasks, skills), goals, resources, and/or performance opportunities. The result is a determination of whether the "problem" is a job-wide problem as opposed to an individual training problem. Part III of Form 1 is used for the Person/Performance Analysis and identifies "who" is in need of training and what type of training is needed. The result is a determination of whether the problem is a motivation-related training problem or an ability-related training problem.

Complete Form 1 on your own before class. Think about the implications of your analysis for organization development programs in addition to training programs. During class, form groups of three to five, who will act as the consulting team for the school. Share your individual analyses and come to a consensus about what should be done. At the end of class, have a spokesperson from each team discuss the team's recommendations and the rationale to support them.

Since your last visit to the college, the Dean has implemented those changes pertaining to the strategy of focusing on adult learners. Specifically, the school now offers (1) more evening courses for both undergraduate and graduate students, (2) a teaching schedule that accommodates students that want to earn their degree in the evening, (3) credit courses in suburban locations, and (4) M.B.A. concentrations in a variety of areas. In addition, the Dean has implemented a "TQM" philosophy for the school whereby students are treated like customers and "customer service" is the new goal for faculty to pursue. These changes had been in place for a year when the Dean decided to evaluate their effectiveness. A "customer satisfaction" questionnaire was sent out to recent graduates; the results were disappointing. Of particular concern were the findings that the graduates were dissatisfied with the quality of their education and that they would not recommend that their friends, family, or colleagues attend Riverside's School of Business Administration.

The Dean has hired a consulting team (your group) to develop a training program for faculty in order to improve the quality of teaching in the school. However, your team has decided to first conduct a needs assessment to determine whether there really is a need for faculty training.

Original case contributed by Diana Deadrick, Old Dominion University.

Form 1 *Training Needs Assessment*

Part I: Organization Analysis

"Where" is there a need for improvement within the school?

1. What school-wide changes have occurred or are anticipated to occur? How have these changes affected faculty performance? What evidence is there to suggest that a "problem" exists?

2. In what way are the changes described above conflicting with the school's original organizational structure, culture, and/or climate? What type of data should be collected and analyzed in order to identify these conflicts?

3. What recommendations would you make to alleviate these conflicts?

Part II: Job/Task Analysis

"What" tasks are in need of improvement?

4. What job-wide changes have occurred or are anticipated to occur with respect to faculty members? How have these changes affected faculty performance?

5. In what way are the changes described above conflicting with the faculty members' previous job expectations and responsibilities? What type of data should be collected and analyzed in order to identify these constraints?

6. What recommendations would you make to alleviate these conflicts?

Part III: Person/Performance Analysis

"Who" needs to improve?

7. Do faculty members need any training? If so, what type of training is needed, and how would you conduct it?

Design and Evaluation of Training Programs

I. *Objectives:*
  A. To help you determine which training methods are most appropriate for achieving particular objectives.
  B. To show you the linkages between training objectives, training methods, and training evaluation.
  C. To help you learn how to identify and write training objectives.
  D. To build skill in the evaluation of training programs.

II. *Out-of-Class Preparation Time:* 1 hour

III. *In-Class Time Suggested:* 45 minutes

IV. *Procedures*: Prior to the class meeting in which this exercise will be discussed, read the entire exercise and use a pencil to complete Forms 2 and 3. You may also use a separate sheet of paper. At the beginning of the class period, the instructor should divide the class into discussion groups of three to five students.

Each group should begin by completing Form 2. If you are unfamiliar with any of the training methods listed, consult your text or ask your instructor.

Look at each training objective/outcome and then determine which training methods would be most appropriate for achieving each of the six training objectives. Since each group member comes into the class period with his or her own ideas on which training method is most appropriate, there may be a need for some discussion and negotiation before a group consensus can emerge.

Put an "X" beside the method that seems most appropriate for achieving each objective or outcome. For example, if you believe that a lecture with questions would be a good method of facilitating knowledge acquisition on the part of a training program participant, put an "X" in that space. Then put an "X" wherever the particular training method seems appropriate for achieving particular training objectives or outcomes. For each of the six objectives or outcomes, you should have at least three, but no more than eight, training methods that are identified as most appropriate.

Now look at the data in Exhibit 3.2. These data are taken from a training needs analysis of Corporation X. The number opposite each occupation group indicates the percentage of members in that group citing any training need at all. The numbers under that, opposite each of the two training needs identified for each group, indicate the percentage of that group requesting training in those subject areas.

This company has had no previous formal training programs for its employees and the newly hired director of training has asked your group to answer the following questions:
  1. Which two occupational groups should I provide training programs for during my first year? Why?

2. What training objectives should I set for each occupational group and training need?
3. What training methods should I use to meet these objectives?
4. What training evaluation method should I use to evaluate each training method or program?

Before completing Form 3, review the information in Form 2 and Exhibit 3.2. Select the two occupational groups that you feel should be the new director of training's top training priority for the coming year. Then select only one training need for each occupational group. For example, if you feel training programs for executives are a priority, choose either strategic planning or marketing. Write down the two occupational groups you choose and one training need for each on Form 3.

Now develop specific objectives for each of the two training programs you are recommending. If your group selected strategic planning for executives as one of the two programs, then possible objectives might be increased knowledge about the process of strategic planning or successful development of a strategic plan for the corporation or the executive's department. Likewise, an objective for a performance appraisal program for middle managers might be the design of an appropriate performance appraisal form and process for the individual middle manager's particular situation.

Once the objectives are determined, they usually fit under one of the six major objectives or outcomes listed on Form 2. Based upon your previous analysis in Form 2, select up to three training methods for achieving these objectives with the particular occupational group. For example, achieving the objective of helping executives improve their strategic planning skills might involve on-the-job coaching by consultants or other executives skilled in this process, as well as business games, lectures, or cases.

The final step is to determine the most appropriate method of evaluating the particular training program or programs. The four major methods of evaluation, in order of their degree of complexity and difficulty, are as follows:

1. Participant reaction—usually determined by a questionnaire immediately at the conclusion of the training program.
2. Learning—assessment of knowledge about or attitudes toward a particular subject, both before and after a training experience.
3. Behavioural change—changes in on-the-job behaviour or performance as measured by performance appraisals, subordinates' perceptions, supervisor's perceptions, and/or individual productivity data.
4. Organizational effectiveness—decreases in departmental or organizational costs, turnover, absenteeism, and grievances; and increases in departmental or organizational sales, income, or productivity as compared to a control group of those not attending training.

Now look at the questions on Form 4 and answer them in your group. Once all the questions are answered, raise your hands and let the instructor know your group has finished the exercise. Appoint a spokesperson to discuss your group's recommendations. When all groups have finished, compare results in each of the groups and discuss possible reasons for differences between the groups.

Exhibit 3.2   *Results of a Training Needs Assessment Survey*
by Occupational Group

Top Two Areas of Training Needed by Occupational Group	Percentage Citing Need
1. Executive	67
Strategic planning	38
Marketing	27
2. Middle managers	84
Performance appraisal techniques	44
Employee motivation	32
3. Professionals	27
Effective communication skills	16
Principles of supervision	14
4. Salespeople	28
How to close a sale	22
Effective communication skills	12
5. First-line supervisors	47
Employee motivation	31
Principles of supervision	21
6. Production workers	22
Discipline	16
Production scheduling	10
7. Office/clerical staff	38
Time management	25
Assertiveness training	20

Form 2 *The Effectiveness of Alternative Training Methods for Achieving Various Training Objectives/Outcomes*

Training Method	Training Objectives					
	Knowledge Acquisition	*Attitude Change*	*Problem-Solving Skills*	*Interpersonal Skills*	*Participant Acceptance*	*Knowledge Retention*
Information Processing:						
Lecture (with questions)						
Conference (discussion)						
Sensitivity training						
Laboratory training						
Observation						
Closed-circuit TV						
Programmed instruction						
Correspondence courses						
Videos						
Reading lists						
Simulation:						
Cases						
Incidents						
Role playing						
Business games						
In-basket exercises						
On-the-Job:						
Job rotation						
Committee assignments						
On-the-job coaching						
Feedback from performance appraisal						
Apprenticeships						

Occupational Group:

Training Need:

Training Objectives	*Training Methods*
1.	1.
2.	2.
3.	3.

Occupational Group:

Training Need:

Training Objectives	*Training Methods*
1.	1.
2.	2.
3.	3.

1. Why did you select the particular two occupations for the highest priority in training?

2. Once you had determined the occupational group, training need, and training objectives, how did you determine which training method would be most appropriate?

3. Select one occupational group from Form 2. Identify one or two training evaluation methods for one training method you recommended. Why did you choose this evaluation method?

4. What problems might you encounter if you attempted to implement evaluation processes based on improvements in individual participant behaviour or organizational effectiveness? Why?

5. What are the most effective training or educational methods to facilitate your own learning? Why?

6. Consider the most complex job you have ever had. What would have been the most effective method of training for that job? Why? What method (if any) was actually used?

55. EXERCISE

On-the-Job Training

I. *Objectives*:
  A. To make you aware of the problems a supervisor may encounter when training employees.
  B. To provide you with practice in conducting on-the-job training.
  C. To teach you how to prepare training aids.
  D. To teach you how to evaluate on-the-job training.
  E. To familiarize you with the major on-the-job training steps.

II. *Out-of-Class Preparation Time*: 1 to 2 hours

III. *In-Class Time Suggested*: 45 minutes

IV. *Procedures*: An important task for most supervisors is to instruct new employees on the methods and procedures necessary to perform various operations involved in a job. Initially, the employee may be totally unfamiliar with a particular task. This places an additional burden on the manager to make his or her instructions as clear and precise as possible. In this exercise, you will be asked to train one or more members of the class on how to perform a task. After the training is complete, it will be critiqued.

Preparation for the training can be done individually or in groups of three to five members, at the instructor's option. If groups are used, the instructor will divide up the class during the class period prior to the one in which this exercise will be conducted. Each group will then meet outside of class to prepare for the training. Each individual or group should begin by selecting a task to teach one or more class members. For example, one of the following could be picked:

  1. How to lift heavy objects safely.
  2. How to fold a napkin as is done in fancy restaurants.
  3. How to tie a special knot used by tree surgeons, marine personnel, or those in the Armed Forces.
  4. How to fix a dripping faucet.
  5. How to use a volt-ohm meter such as an electrician might use.

In selecting a task, pick one that is performed in the industry, one that most class members don't already know how to perform, and one sufficiently complicated that trainees can't perform it instantly. Remember, you will have to provide all of the materials necessary to perform the task.

Once a task has been selected, your group should develop a training aid and make copies for each class member. It might include:

  A. Training objectives.
  B. Benefits of performing the task for the employee, the company, and the customers.
  C. A list of tools, materials, and equipment necessary to perform the task correctly.

D. A list showing each step in sequence necessary to perform the task, including the necessary illustrations.

E. A form to evaluate the trainee.

Finally, you must choose the best approach for conducting the training (e.g., lecture, demonstrations, simulations) and the steps that will be followed when conducting the training. If you are working in groups, a spokesperson (the one who will actually conduct the training for the group) should also be selected.

At the start of class, the instructor will select four or more groups/individuals to actually conduct on-the-job training. Depending upon the task, the instructor will also select one or more students to serve as trainees. At this point, the trainer will hand out a copy of the training aid to each class member and, one at a time, conduct training. This will be followed by a critique of each training session and training aid by all class members. Toward the end of class, those groups/individuals that did not actually conduct training during class will be asked to distribute a copy of their training aid to all class members.

The Orientation Problem

Carol Burgess is a letter carrier and a part-time trainer of letter carriers for Canada Post in a major western Canadian city. She trains all new letter carriers in her service area, which encompasses the northern half of the province. Over the past five years, she has trained 318 new letter carriers. Typically, the training is offered prior to the new letter carrier's entry to the job, although sometimes it occurs shortly thereafter.

The training program typically encompasses both the orientation of new employees to Canada Post and the development of specific skills needed by the new letter carrier. The latter involves practice in casing mail (i.e., sorting) to appropriate locations in preparation for delivery, reading maps, determining appropriate sequencing of deliveries, and customer relations. The total training program takes three full days: one day of orientation and two days of skills training.

The orientation part of the training program encompasses both an orientation packet and a discussion of various Canada Post policies and procedures. The orientation packet typically includes information about employee benefits, holidays, copies of certain standard forms (e.g., income tax withholding forms), outline of emergency and accident procedures, key terms used in Canada Post operations, copies of the health and life insurance options, and telephone numbers and locations of the human resource department and other important offices. In addition, an explanation is provided that covers Canada Post's mail delivery operations and purpose, the training to be received, the letter carrier's duties and responsibilities, job standards and production levels, rules and regulations, and the chain of command for reporting. Burgess concludes her orientation with an offer of help and encouragement for the future.

The assumption built into the orientation is that the information given in the orientation will be supplemented at the job site by the direct supervisor, who will provide all the necessary information about the particular facility, the personnel at the facility, and the area covered by the route or routes to which the new employee will be assigned. It is assumed that the direct supervisor will also provide additional printed information such as the employee handbook and the collective agreement. According to policy, each new letter carrier should get three days of on-the-job training, one of which is paid for by the training division and two that are charged to the supervisor's production budget.

Burgess learned from subsequent conversations with her former trainees over the past five years that the orientation provided by the direct supervisor varied from practically nothing to fairly extensive. In some stations, the supervisor greeted the new employee, introduced the person to one other employee, and explained their own expectations regarding attendance, personal conduct, and productivity. Then the employee was given an assignment and allowed to "sink or swim." Several supervisors were known to be "S.O.B.s." While 83 percent of new hires have survived their probationary 90-day period over the past three years, less than 20 percent survived in certain stations.

Last night, Burgess received a telephone call from Edith Jones, one of her former trainees who finished training 10 weeks ago. Jones is a single parent with two school-age children who had left her job as a secretary and taken the letter carrier job in order to make more money. She was in tears as she described her experience at her station.

Her supervisor gave her no printed materials, introduced her to only one other employee, and has shifted her from route to route over the 10 weeks she has worked at the facility. No help or support of any kind has been offered, but the supervisor has continually berated her for the number of hours she has taken to case and deliver routes. She had tried to study maps during her days off in order to learn the areas covered by various routes, but this only helped a little. Each route had to be delivered in a particular order and it took time to learn the sequence. The other letter carriers were all stressed out and working overtime themselves. Consequently, they ignored her and offered no assistance. Jones told Burgess that she was on the verge of quitting. Burgess told her to "hang in there because it does get easier with time."

As a result of all the complaints she had received from former trainees (some of whom survived the 90-day probationary period), Burgess decided to recommend that the area Postmasters implement a program to train supervisors in how to orient new letter carriers. However, she wasn't sure what specific items the supervisors should include in their new employee orientation and how to train them to do it.

Questions

1. Describe the nature and causes of the orientation problem.
2. What types of orientation for new employees should direct supervisors provide at the work site?
3. What training methods should be used to train the supervisors, assuming approval of the proposal?
4. What printed materials should the supervisor provide for new letter carriers in light of what Burgess already provides?
5. In addition to the printed materials discussed in the previous question, what else should the supervisor do to orient new letter carriers?

57. SKILL BUILDER

Identifying Training Needs through Task Analysis

I. *Objectives*:
   A. To introduce you to the process and purpose of assessing training needs.
   B. To give you practice in determining training needs for a job.
II. *Time Required to Complete*: 2 to 3 hours
III. *Instructions:* There are generally three analyses used to determine an organization's training needs: organization analysis, task or operations analysis, and person analysis. This assignment allows you to perform a task analysis for a particular job by interviewing and observing a job holder. A task analysis involves systematic collection of data about a specific job. Its purpose is to determine what an employee should be taught to perform the job at the desired level. It generally includes a description of the major tasks of the job, standards of performance, how the tasks are to be performed to meet the standards, and the skills, knowledge, and abilities necessary. You will conduct the task analysis by following the steps described below.

Step 1: Select a job to analyze. You may choose a job currently held by a relative, friend, or fellow student. (If you completed Exercise 34, Writing Job Descriptions, in Part 2, you may use the job you described to complete that exercise.) Ask the job holder if you may interview him or her about the position and/or also observe him or her performing the job.

Step 2: Obtain a job description for the job you selected or prepare one by interviewing the job holder. The job description should describe in general terms the worker's major duties and responsibilities. For example, a job description for an accounts receivable clerk might include the following duties and responsibilities:
   1. Invoice shipments to customers on a monthly basis.
   2. Prepare journal vouchers at the end of the month to record cash receipts and sales by product lines.

When preparing the job description, be sure to include those things that are critical to performing the job satisfactorily, no matter how infrequently or briefly they occur, and the knowledge, skills, and abilities needed.

Step 3: This step involves identifying the tasks associated with performing each of the major duties of the job. You are to identify the overt, observable behaviours that are involved in performing the job. Arrange (if possible) to observe the worker performing his or her job and develop a list of the tasks involved. A task listing includes behavioural statements of how the job is to be performed. Using the example of the accounts receivable clerk, the tasks associated with invoicing customers might include:
   1. Pull and review invoice master.
   2. Extend and update invoice master.

3. Add correct discount and freight charges.
4. Make necessary amount of copies on copy machine.

When you complete this step, you should have a report that includes the title of the job, the major duties (responsibilities) of the job, the tasks associated with each duty/responsibility, and the knowledge and skills required of job incumbents.

Step 4: Once you have completed Steps 1–3, answer the following questions and include them in your report:

1. What training would benefit a person performing the job? If you had to design a training program for the job, what content areas would be needed, based on your analysis?
2. What training method would be best (e.g., on-the-job training, seminars, apprenticeships, vestibule)? Why?

PERFORMANCE APPRAISAL

58. EXERCISE

EvalSim—A Performance Evaluation Exercise

I. *Objectives:*
   A. To familiarize you with some of the problems related to the use of performance appraisals and to provide alternative approaches for solving these problems.
   B. To give you practice in making decisions and writing memos to employees regarding performance appraisal issues.
   C. To familiarize you with the major duties or tasks that staffing specialists must perform with regard to a firm's performance evaluation system.

II. *Out-of-Class Preparation Time:* 20 minutes to read exercise, plus 1 hour to determine responses to e-mail items, either individually or with group members, and write memos

III. *In-Class Time Suggested:* 45 minutes to discuss all e-mail items

IV. *Procedures:* This exercise can be done individually or in groups of three to five members, at the instructor's option. First, you are to begin by reading all of the material presented in this exercise. Assume that you are responsible for developing and maintaining the O'Leary Organization's performance appraisal system. You are to assume further that the items that follow were waiting in your e-mail account when you returned to work after a three-week vacation. You (or your team) is to respond in writing to each employee who sent you an e-mail. Second, explain on a separate sheet of paper what additional actions you would take with reference to each item. For example, if you believe that you should gather additional information before making a final decision on an item, explain what information you would want. Or, if you believe that additional memos or discussions with someone in the company are needed, explain this. You (or your team) should bring both the memos and the "Additional Action" sheets to class. Be prepared to present and defend these materials during the class discussion.

Situation

The O'Leary Organization is a medium-sized organization with headquarters located in central Canada. You may assume that the organization is a manufacturing company, a hospital, an insurance company, a university, or virtually any other medium-sized organization with which you are familiar.

The O'Leary Organization's Human Resource Department is organized in the manner shown below:

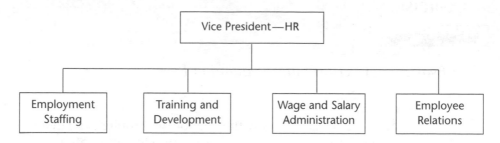

The Training and Development section consists of you or your team. In addition to conducting training, you have full responsibility for the organization's performance evaluation system. Included among your duties are:

1. Determining which employees will be evaluated.
2. Determining how frequently employees will be evaluated.
3. Determining which appraisal format should be used.
4. Determining which job categories will be used to evaluate the employee's job performance.
5. Determining who should evaluate each employee.
6. Ensuring that all evaluators know how to complete the organization's performance appraisal form and how to conduct evaluation interviews.
7. Establishing the performance appraisal system and ensuring that all employees adhere to it.
8. Maintaining all performance appraisal records.

The O'Leary Organization's present performance appraisal system, which you are to assume you or your team designed, requires that all employees be evaluated by their supervisor on a periodic basis. All employees are evaluated at the end of a 90-day period (the probationary period) and on a yearly basis thereafter. The performance appraisal form used by the organization is shown in Exhibit 3.3. Supervisors are required to complete this form for each of their employees at the appropriate time, discuss the evaluation with him or her, ask the employee to sign the form at the end of the evaluation interview, and return the completed form to the Human Resource Department.

Exhibit 3.3   *The O'Leary Organization Performance Appraisal Form*

NAME	SOCIAL INSURANCE NO.
TITLE	DEPARTMENT
TODAY'S DATE	APPRAISAL PERIOD FROM_____ TO_____ Annual 90-day

PART I Performance Rating

(All Employees)

	1	2	3	4	5
Ability					
Attendance					
Attitude					
Appearance					
Conduct					
Initiative					
Work with Group					
Promotability					
Quantity of Work					
Quality of Work					
Overall Level of Performance					

REMARKS

Prepared by_____   Title_____

COMMENTS BY REVIEWED EMPLOYEE:

Employee's Signature_____   Date_____
(Employee signature does not indicate agreement, merely acknowledgment of having seen this report.)

1—Unsatisfactory   2—Below Average   3—Satisfactory   4—Good   5—Excellent

E-Mail Items

Item 1

Memorandum

To: HR Department
From: Tom Morrison, Accounting Department
Subject: 90-Day Employee Evaluation

I just received my 90-day employee evaluation and received mostly "3's" on it. My boss explained his evaluation to me by saying that I was making good progress on the job. He added that if I continue to show improvement I will receive "4's" and "5's" like the more experienced employees do. Why am I being evaluated against older, more experienced workers? That doesn't seem right. I believe that, considering my limited experience, I deserve "excellent" evaluations.

Item 2

Memorandum

To: HR Department
From: Paul Lands, Computer Centre
Subject: Performance Evaluation

Joe Meena and I started together at the O'Leary Organization two years ago. We are both in the Computer Centre doing the same job, only he works one shift, and I work another. Two weeks ago, when we compared our performance evaluations, I discovered that he received all "5's" whereas I received mostly "4's." The thing that irks me is that he and I both know we are doing an equally good job. His boss is just more lenient in his evaluation than is my boss. I don't think this whole system is fair, particularly since he may get promoted (based on his performance evaluation) before I do. Can't something be done about this?

Item 3

Memorandum

To: HR Department
From: Jill Best, Manager
Subject: Lost Performance Appraisal Form

Six weeks ago when our offices were being remodelled, one of the janitors accidentally threw away a small stack of papers. Included in the stack was a performance appraisal form that I had just completed on one of my subordinates, Karen Whitmore. I know you need this form, but it is gone. What should I do?

Item 4

Memorandum

To: HR Department
From: Sue Peters, Supervisor
Subject: Administering Employee Evaluations

I have recently received from your office a request to conduct evaluations this month on three of my employees. As you probably know, I was promoted to this supervisory position just one week ago as a result of the former supervisor's termination. I don't feel that I can presently conduct a fair evaluation of these employees. Do you want me to do them anyway?

Item 5

Memorandum

To: HR Department
From: Sandra Kelly, Supervisor
Subject: Evaluation of Karen Bicknell

Yesterday afternoon, I conducted an evaluation interview with Karen Bicknell. When I told her I gave her a "3" on "Work with Group" she got quite upset and defensive. She said the evaluation should have been at least a "4" and probably a "5." I attempted to explain my evaluation to her, but she wouldn't listen. Instead, she continued to argue with me. Karen received a "4" evaluation last year on "Work with Group" and a "3.5" overall evaluation this year. What should I do if this happens again?

Item 6

Memorandum

To: HR Department
From: Howard Adams, Supervisor
Subject: Necessity of Signing Evaluation Forms

Recently, I conducted a performance evaluation interview with Harold Wallace. At the end of the interview, when I asked him to sign the appraisal form at the bottom, he refused. I asked him if the evaluation was accurate, and he said yes. I also explained to him that signing the form only represented an acknowledgment that he had been evaluated and had seen the completed evaluation. He replied that he had nothing to gain from signing the form, and, therefore, why should he sign it? I don't know what I should do. Harold is somewhat of a problem and is often quite stubborn.

Item 7

Memorandum

To: HR Department
From: Margaret Windell, Purchasing
Subject: Annual Performance Review

I have a rather troublesome question to ask you. I would ask it of my boss but she is currently in the hospital. For the last 23 years, I have received an overall performance review, and my evaluations have all shown that I am an excellent employee. I am six years from retirement and, frankly, I have reached the point where performance evaluations aren't of any consequence to me. I know I am doing a good job. I know I won't get promoted or transferred, and I am at the top of my pay grade. So why should I continue to be evaluated formally?

Item 8

Memorandum

To: HR Department
From: Sarah Wade, Maintenance Engineer
Subject: Employee Appraisal Form

When I was over in the HR Department yesterday, looking at my personnel file, I saw the appraisal form that was completed on me one month ago. I was shocked to see the following statement written on it under "Remarks": "Sarah has a very poor work attitude and doesn't appear willing to change it." My boss, Marilyn Turner, had also changed my evaluation on "Attitude" from "4" to a "2." I am positive the negative statement was not on the evaluation form when I signed it. Needless to say, I want you to do something about this!

Item 9

Memorandum

To: HR Department
From: Chris Green, Supervisor
Subject: Performance Evaluation of Bill Young

Next week, I must conduct a performance evaluation interview with Bill Young, who works by himself in the evenings. While I was completing the evaluation form on him, I realized that it was impossible for me to evaluate him on one of the evaluation categories, "Work with Group." What should I do? I am afraid if I leave it blank it will affect his "Overall Level of Performance" score and, hence, his chances for a promotion.

Item 10

Memorandum

To: HR Department
From: Jeff Skala, Finance Department
Subject: Confidentiality of Performance Evaluation

As you know, I have been experiencing a series of personal problems during the past year, all of which have adversely affected my job performance. These problems reflected themselves on my recent performance evaluation as my "marks" slipped from mostly "4's" to mostly "2's." I can't disagree with my evaluation, but I don't think it was right for my boss, Helen Jackson, to tell two of my coworkers that she had given me a "1" on "Quality of Work." It seems to me that this type of information should be none of their business.

Performance Appraisal Interview Role Play

I. *Objectives*:
  A. To allow you practice in conducting a performance appraisal interview.
  B. To compare and contrast different approaches to the performance appraisal interview.
  C. To help you develop sensitivity toward communication problems in performance appraisal interviews.
II. *Out-of-Class Preparation Time:* 20–30 minutes
III. *In-Class Time Suggested:* 45 minutes
IV. *Procedures*:
  A. Read the exercise before coming to class.
  B. Four students should be selected to participate in two different performance appraisal interviews (A and B). Two will play the role of the employee and two will play the role of the supervisor. Role assignments should be made in the prior class period or before class begins. The instructor will provide role sheets.
  C. The persons playing the role of the employee should read "Employee's Role."
  D. The person playing the role of supervisor A should read "Supervisor Role A," and the person playing the role of supervisor B should read "Supervisor Role B."
  E. During the class period in which the role plays will occur, all role play participants should be taken outside of the classroom and given time to prepare their respective roles. All other members of the class are to observe the two different sets of interviews and record their observations on separate sheets of paper.
  F. Supervisor A conducts a 10–15 minute appraisal interview with one of the employees in front of the class. The other role play pair remains in the hall outside the classroom until their turn.
  G. After the first role play is completed, the second role play pair enters the classroom and conducts its appraisal interview. The first role play team joins the rest of the class to observe the interview.
  H. The entire class discusses both interviews.

Situation

Tri-City Health Services is a large non-profit organization providing basic outpatient health services and health education programs to low-income families. It employs over 40 physicians and nurses and more than 200 other workers in various staff positions. Pat Smith, who previously worked in the children's health care program, has been working as a junior assistant in the Fundraising and Grants Department for the past two years. Pat has done well in performing the job—all performance objectives have been met or surpassed for the year. However, this year Pat has been consistently late for work on many occasions. Each year, on the anniversary date of the employee's hire, his or her supervisor must conduct a performance appraisal interview. Chris Jackson, the supervisor, has completed the performance evaluation form shown in Exhibit 3.4 and is ready to discuss the evaluation with Pat.

Instructions for Observers

Your task is to evaluate two different sets of performance interviews. As you observe the interviews, consider the following:

1. How did the supervisor begin the interview? Was the purpose of the interview clearly stated?
2. What type of interview approach did the supervisor use? Who did most of the talking?
3. Did the supervisor learn how the employee feels about the job? About his or her performance?
4. Did both parties gain a clear understanding of the problem and its solution?
5. Were any specific action plans made to resolve the problem(s)?
6. Are there any ways in which the supervisor could improve the interview? How?
7. Which interview was most effective? Why?

Exhibit 3.4 *Performance Evaluation Form*

I. Rating Categories

Performance Dimensions	Performance Level	Points (Maximum = 5)
Quality of Work (The degree to which the employee's work is free of flaws)	Excellent	5
Quantity of Work (The total amount of acceptable work completed within time and resources available)	Excellent	5
Attendance (Includes absences and tardiness)	Poor	1
Cooperation (The degree to which the employee cooperates with and is respected by coworkers)	Average	3
Initiative and Self-Reliance (The degree to which the employee is independent and self-directed)	Excellent	5
Work Timeliness (The degree to which the employee exhibits skill in planning and scheduling activities)	Average	3
Responsibility (The degree to which the employee is willing to accept responsibility for details in work)	Above Average	4
Total Points		26

II. Objectives and Goals

A. Did the employee set any specific work-related goals this performance period?
   Yes (X)   No ( )
B. If yes, what were they?
   To complete and implement a fundraising program by April 1.
   To obtain a 15 percent increase in federal grants by April 1.
C. To what extent were they met?
   Employee met or exceeded both objectives. The fundraising effort was very successful (over $125,000 was raised) and federal grants have increased by 18 percent this year.

Overall evaluation of goal achievement?   Excellent

III. Overall Evaluation of Employee Performance
   ## (Support evaluation with comments)

The employee has done a fine job on performance objectives but continues to have a problem with tardiness. Based on this, the overall rating for the year is average (26 out of 35 points). I do not recommend the employee for a promotion at this time.

Supervisor Signature	Date	Employee Signature		Date

Performance Appraisal Interview Role Play **Exercise 59**

60. EXERCISE

Which Performance Appraisal Format Is Most Effective?

I. *Objectives*:
  A. To examine the strengths and weaknesses of four different methods for appraising employees.
  B. To enhance your oral communication skills.
II. *Out-of-Class Preparation Time:* 30 minutes to prepare for the debate
III. *In-Class Time Suggested:* 50–75 minutes
IV. *Procedures:* Your instructor will divide the class into five groups prior to conducting this exercise. There will be four debating groups consisting of three to five members each, and one or more groups of "judges" that consist of the remaining class members. Debaters will be assigned one of four positions and told to prepare to argue in favour of that position. Judges will be told to read the textbook chapter pages that cover those positions. The issue to be debated is: Which approach to appraising employees is the most effective? The positions are: (1) trait appraisal instruments such as the graphic rating scale; (2) behavioural appraisal instruments such as the behaviourally anchored rating scale; (3) a ranking or forced distribution system; and (4) outcome appraisal instruments such as management by objectives.

At the start of the next class, your instructor will announce that a four-way debate will be held. The judges' role in the debate is to "search for the truth." They are to listen to all four different sides presented and then, after the debate is over, tell the class what they believe is the "correct" answer to the debate question, not who "won" the debate.

The debate consists of two rounds. The purpose of Round One (15–20 minutes) is for each team to learn the position of the other debating teams. Hence, each team has up to 5 minutes to explain their position as comprehensively as possible. At the completion of Round One, the debating teams are given up to 10 minutes to prepare criticisms of each of the other three teams for Round Two. During this intermission, judges are to discuss what they have heard and begin to formulate their own position.

In Round Two (15–20 minutes), each debating team is given up to 5 minutes to criticize the position of each of the other teams. Unlike a traditional debate, teams are not allowed to rebut the criticisms made by others. They must simply listen to them. Round Two ends when Team Four has finished criticizing the position of the other three teams.

After the debate has ended, the judges have 5 minutes to discuss the case among themselves and arrive at a consensus, if possible. The judging team(s) then explains its decision to the debaters.

Ethical Performance Appraisal Issues

I. *Objectives:*
   A. To make you aware that many performance appraisal decisions involve ethical issues.
   B. To familiarize you with some of the many ethical performance appraisal issues.
   C. To familiarize you with various criteria that can be used to determine if an action is ethical.
   D. To make you aware of some of the reasons why a manager may be tempted to act unethically when evaluating subordinates.

II. *Out-of-Class Preparation Time:* 15 minutes to read each of the situations presented and answer the questions

III. *In-Class Time Suggested:* 20–40 minutes

IV. *Procedures:* At the start of class, the instructor will divide the class into teams of three to five students. Your group should discuss each of the situations below and answer the following questions in the space provided:
   1. Is the manager in the case acting in an Ethical manner? Yes or No? (Answer Y or N under the letter "E" below.)
   2. Would your Group act in the same manner as the manager? Yes or No? (Answer Y or N under the letter "G" below.)
   3. Does your group believe that Most managers would act in the same manner as the manager did? Yes or No? (Answer Y or N under the letter "M" below.)

   In trying to answer the first question, your group may want to consider some or all of the following ethical questions:
   A. Does the action involve intentional deception?
   B. Does the action purposely benefit one party at the expense of another?
   C. Is the action fair and just to all concerned?
   D. Would you or the manager feel comfortable if the action were made public, or must it remain a secret?
   E. Would you need to justify the action by telling yourself that you can get away with it or that you won't need to live with the consequences of the decision?
   F. Would you recommend the action to others?
   G. Will the action build goodwill and better relationships?

Instructions: Read each of the following scenarios and answer questions 1–3 in the space provided below with either a "Y" for Yes or an "N" for No.

Scenario

E	G	M	
___	___	___	1. A supervisor has only two subordinates, one a poor performer and the other a truly outstanding worker. There is a job available in another department that the truly outstanding employee wants. In order to reduce the chances of losing a great employee, the supervisor purposefully rates him lower than deserved on his performance appraisal form.
___	___	___	2. A firm has recently been the subject of a complaint of discrimination against minorities. The firm denies the allegations but asks all supervisors to make sure they do not discriminate. In order to avoid any possible discrimination charges, a manager rates one minority employee with poor performance higher than deserved on her performance appraisal form.
___	___	___	3. A manager has a male subordinate who is married with three children. This employee is a known womanizer and has been spotted by several employees hanging out with women other than his wife, including prostitutes. The supervisor does not believe this is appropriate and rates the employee lower than deserved on the performance appraisal form.
___	___	___	4. A manager has one subordinate who is very argumentative and aggressive. In order to avoid a confrontation during the performance appraisal interview, the manager rates the subordinate higher than is deserved.
___	___	___	5. A firm has a 360-degree performance appraisal system that includes asking all subordinates to rate and evaluate their boss. A manager wants to be promoted so he gives all employees higher performance evaluations than they deserve, in hopes that they, in turn, will rate him higher.
___	___	___	6. A manager realizes that an employee's attendance is so poor that she is likely to get terminated within the next few months. So, in order to build a more solid case against the employee and further justify the inevitable termination, the manager rates the subordinate lower than deserved on the performance appraisal form.

E	G	M
____	____	____

7. A manager wants to get promoted in order to get a substantial raise. He believes that he will be judged, in part, in terms of how effective he has been at developing high-performing subordinates as evidenced by his subordinates' performance appraisal scores. In order to enhance his promotion chances, he rates his employees higher than deserved.

E	G	M
____	____	____

8. A manager wants to give one particular subordinate a big raise in order to keep her from accepting a job elsewhere. However, there is limited raise money available, and it is based on merit. So, he rates another employee lower than deserved, thereby reducing this person's raise, in order to be able to give the other subordinate a larger raise.

E	G	M
____	____	____

9. A manager wants to get rid of a disliked subordinate, so she rates the employee lower than deserved in hopes that the employee will quit.

E	G	M
____	____	____

10. A manager wants to help a subordinate get promoted, so she gives her a higher evaluation than deserved.

Implementing Compensation and Security: Compensation, Incentives, Benefits, and Safety and Health

Part 4

The Overpaid Bank Tellers

The Cooper Bank is located in a semi-rural region with a population of about 50,000. It is one of four bank branches in the region and has the reputation of being the most progressive of the four. Russell Duncan has been the manager of the branch for 15 years. Before coming to this branch of the Cooper Bank, Duncan worked at a large urban bank branch for 10 years. Duncan has implemented a number of changes that have earned him a great deal of respect and admiration from both bank employees and the townspeople. For example, in response to a growing number of people in the area who speak Asian languages, he hired bilingual Asian employees and placed them in critical bank positions. He organized and staffed the city's only agricultural loan centre to meet the needs of the region's farmers. In addition, he established the region's first "uniline" system for handling customers waiting in line for a teller. Perhaps more than anything else, Duncan is known for establishing progressive personnel practices. He strongly believes that the bank's employees are its most important asset and continually searches for ways to increase both employee satisfaction and productivity. He feels that all employees should strive to continually improve their skills and abilities and, hence, he cross-trains employees and sends many of them to courses and conferences sponsored by banking groups such as the Institute of Canadian Bankers.

With regard to employee compensation, Duncan firmly believes that employees should be paid according to their contribution to organizational success. Hence, 10 years ago, he implemented a results-based pay system under which employees could earn raises from 0 to 12 percent each year, depending on their job performance. The amount of the raises is typically determined by the bank branch's Human Resources Committee during February, and the raises are granted to employees on March 1 of each year. In addition to granting employees merit raises, six years ago the bank branch also began giving cost-of-living raises. Duncan had been opposed to this idea originally but saw no alternative to it.

One February, another financial institution in the region conducted a wage survey to determine the average compensation of financial institution employees in the region. The management of the Cooper Bank branch received a copy of the wage survey and was surprised to learn that its 23 tellers, as a group, were being paid an average of $22 per week more than were tellers at other financial institutions. The survey also showed that employees holding other positions in the bank (e.g., branch managers, loan officers, and file clerks) were being paid wages similar to those paid by other financial institutions. (See Exhibit 4.1.)

After receiving the report, the Human Resources Committee of the branch met to determine what should be done regarding the tellers' raises. They knew that none of the tellers had been told how much their raises would be, but that the tellers were all expecting both merit and cost-of-living raises. They also realized that if other employees learned that the tellers were being overpaid, friction could develop and morale might suffer. They knew that it was costing the branch over $26,000 extra per year to pay the tellers. Finally, they knew that as a group the branch's tellers were highly competent, and they did not want to lose any of them.

Questions

1. If you were on the branch's Human Resources Committee, what would you do regarding raises for the tellers?
2. How much faith should the Human Resources Committee place in the accuracy of the wage survey?
3. Critique the branch's policy of giving merit raises that range from 0 to 12 percent, depending on job performance.
4. Critique the branch's policy of giving cost-of-living raises. Should they be eliminated?

Exhibit 4.1 *Wage Survey Results: Comparative Salaries of Local Bank Officers*

Position	Financial Institution 1	Financial Institution 2	Financial Institution 3	Cooper Bank
Commercial Loan Officer	$48,600	$49,500	$47,900	$48,400
Consumer Loan Officer	39,200	34,700	35,760	39,000
Mortgage Loan Officer	47,100	45,900	49,500	47,200
Branch Manager	57,700	59,400	58,800	58,400
Assistant Branch Manager	37,800	37,400	39,600	36,300
New Accounts Officer	33,900	33,800	33,700	33,800
Officer Trainee	33,200	33,000	33,400	33,300
Average Weekly Earnings of Local Financial Institution Employees				
Accounting Clerks	$ 83	$576	$568	$588
File Clerks	546	552	530	543
Tellers	572	569	575	594

Rewarding Volunteers

Background

Eastern University is located in a small town in Atlantic Canada. After several years of political pressure, internal conflicts, and negotiations, the university applied for, and was granted, a Canadian Radio-Television and Telecommunications Commission licence for a new FM radio station. The general goals of the station were to provide quality non-commercial alternative broadcasting with an emphasis on local and national news, jazz, and classical music. The station would have no paid commercials, but would broadcast public service announcements and cultural events.

A short-term objective was to assemble and train a volunteer staff (mostly students and faculty) until funds could be provided for an all-professional administrative staff. A longer-term objective was to develop all-professional announcers.

Exhibit 4.2 shows the organizational structure of the radio station. The general manager, chief engineer, news director, administrative assistant, and program director were all full-time paid positions. These positions were funded through an annual allocation from the budget of the university's student association. All of the other positions were either part-time employees, part-time work study students, or unpaid part-time volunteers.

The largest segment of the staff was the volunteers, made up of college students, faculty, and faculty spouses. The students volunteered to obtain training and experience that they hoped would propel them into careers in the media. Faculty and faculty spouses volunteered either for the new experience or because they liked playing particular types of music. Others volunteered to help the station and to meet new people. Volunteers were trained and used as both announcers and in "behind the scenes" positions, such as board operators. Many of the board operators were told they could become announcers in the future.

The program director's responsibilities included developing the on-air program schedule, developing a volunteer training program (including both equipment operation and on-air announcing), and scheduling/supervising the volunteers and work study students. The program director also did some on-air announcing and worked as the internal liaison, coordinating the various departments. He reported directly to the station general manager, who was responsible for all aspects of internal station management as well as developing and sustaining relationships with external constituencies.

Problems

The person hired initially as program director had a leadership style that did not fit well in a volunteer-oriented organization. Specifically, he was task-oriented and had few skills in managing others. This leadership style contributed to conflicts within the organization, and the program director left the organization by mutual consent after nine months on the job. The position of program director remained unfilled for nine months.

During that time, the general manager and the administrative assistant split the work ordinarily done by the program director, including recruitment, selection, training, and scheduling of the volunteers. However, none of these activities were ever institutionalized in terms of written policies and procedures. For example, there were no written job descriptions for volunteers outlining duties and responsibilities for particular positions. Nor was there any formal feedback system for evaluating volunteer performance and receiving volunteer input. Opportunities for volunteer training were also reduced during this period.

After nine months, a new program director was hired. He had previous experience as a program director at another campus radio station and came highly recommended. His initial statement was one of amazement at the high quality of announcing among the volunteers. In fact, he sent out a memorandum to that effect during his second week on the job. However, as time passed, more and more of the volunteer announcers were told by the program director that their services were no longer required as announcers. They were offered the opportunity to work behind the scenes as board operators with no on-air announcing. Most chose simply to quit.

When challenged by the volunteers, the program director stated that there was too much voice variation among the volunteers and that a professional-sounding station needed more uniformity. Since there was no money to hire full-time professional announcers, the program director (as well as several other paid staff) began to do more of the on-air announcing. The program director himself was working more than 60 hours per week. No new volunteers were being trained. Most of the old volunteers had either quit or been demoted. The five still doing on-air announcing requested a meeting with the general manager.

At the meeting, these volunteer announcers indicated their displeasure concerning the decisions of the program director. They pointed out that they had contributed not only their time but also had made monetary contributions to the station and had encouraged others to do so. The general manager thanked the announcers for their contributions of time and money, but indicated he had given the program director control of the programming, including personnel matters. They were still welcome to do volunteer work at the station and could continue announcing "for the time being." The volunteers were not happy with this response and promptly submitted their resignations.

The general manager now had an even more severe problem. The paid staff were already spread too thin and stretched to the limit even before the latest volunteer resignations. The station was committed to 20 hours of programming each day, and prerecorded tapes could not fill the entire programming gap since they also required staff time to produce. The station was clearly in a crisis situation.

Questions

1. Describe the fundamental problem in this case together with its causes.
2. What specific mistakes were made by (a) the general manager and (b) the program director?
3. What types of rewards are most appropriate for volunteers? To what degree were these provided to volunteers at the radio station?

Exhibit 4.2 *Organizational Structure of the Station*

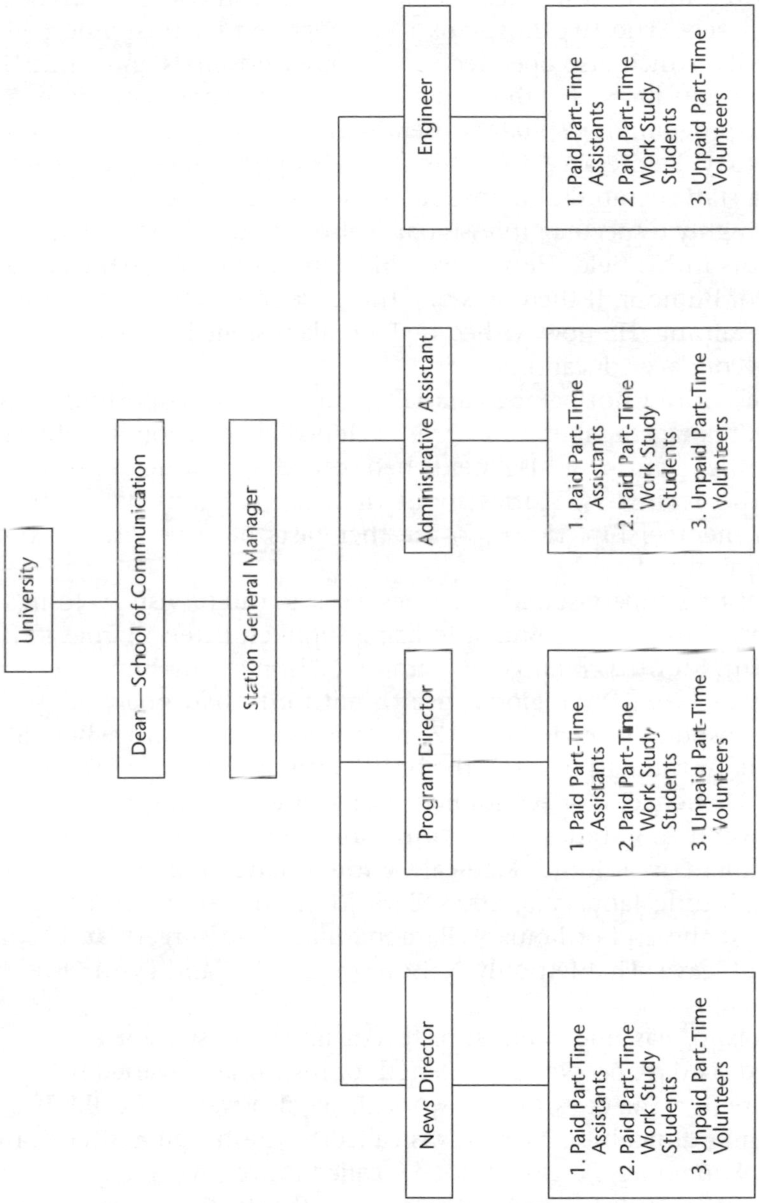

Managing Non-Monetary Compensation

Andrew J. (Drew) Nelson supervised the respiratory therapy department at St. John's and St. Michael's hospitals, located in towns of 16,000 and 2,000, respectively. The two hospitals were operated by the same regional health authority, which also operated several other hospitals and clinics in small and medium-sized towns in the province. Nelson had graduated from a community college program in respiratory therapy and had then earned a bachelor's degree in biology. Before accepting this supervisory position three years ago, he had been a staff therapist at a hospital in another province.

A highly respected professional, Nelson tried to keep up with current developments in his field. He was well liked by staff and patients, and had a good sense of humour. If there was one thing Nelson lacked, it was formal management training. He now wished he had taken some business courses during his post-secondary education.

Nelson did not belong to a labour union, as his position was considered part of management and thus was excluded from union membership. This did not bother Nelson, as his parents had owned a trucking business and had dealt with the Teamsters. Stories about their shenanigans had soured Nelson on union membership. However, the therapists he supervised at both hospitals were unionized.

Nelson's supervisor, Matt Barnes, used to call or visit St. John's regularly to see how things were going or to bring supplies. Lately, Barnes's visits were less frequent. Months could go by without Nelson seeing him.

Since 1963, the regional health authority had operated St. Michael's, a small hospital located about 12 miles west of the town where St. John's was located. At the start of 2004, the health authority Board of Directors decided to close St. Michael's for economic reasons, effective June 30.

Exhibit 4.3 shows an organizational chart for the respiratory therapy department at St. John's Medical Centre in January 2004.

Beginning January 3, 2004, Barb Johnson started a year's paid maternity leave. At the end of January, Ramona Black had surgery and took a six-week medical leave. That left only Nelson, Pam Picha, and Lynn Owens to staff the two facilities.

Nelson was under pressure to cut labour costs. For about a month, he worked six days per week. The length of his workday varied from 8 to 12 hours or more. On the days Nelson worked, he also was "on call." If a patient had breathing difficulties, Nelson was called to the hospital after normal working hours. Sometimes he would not get called in for several days. On other nights, he might get called in two or three times. If a doctor wanted a patient to be on an artificial breathing machine, called a respirator, Nelson had to provide staff at the hospital 24 hours a day.

Since he was an "exempt" (non-unionized management) staff member, Nelson received no overtime pay. Originally he was not paid for on-call hours either. Then he successfully negotiated with the regional health authority to get $1.00 per hour on-call pay. In January and February 2004 combined, Nelson worked more than 140 hours beyond his normal scheduled workweek. His salary was about $44,000.

In March, Pam Picha resigned to move to the United States. Lynn Owens gave two weeks' notice on April 2. She had accepted a position in another hospital. While Nelson attended a respiratory therapists' convention in mid-April, Ramona Black quit without giving notice. Nelson left the conference early to fill in at St. Michael's.

Nelson began to feel he needed some time off work. He was getting burned out. His "earned time" account, which could be used for sick leave, vacation, holidays, and so forth, had almost reached the 400-hour maximum.

On April 21, Nelson asked Barnes if he could take a vacation from May 20 to 26. His wife had to attend a business meeting in New Orleans, and this would be a good chance for the family to spend a few extra days sightseeing.

Receiving no immediate reply from Barnes, Nelson sent him a note with the weekly payroll report of May 5 asking what decision had been made on his vacation request. In the meantime, Barb Johnson found out that Nelson was planning to take time off. She refused to work seven days in a row, which would have been necessary to provide adequate staffing in Nelson's absence. The previous summer, Nelson had worked seven days in a row so that she could take a vacation.

Finally, on May 12, Barnes called Nelson. "Good morning, Drew. Say, about this vacation request.... I really can't let you take off right now. I can't force Barb to work seven days in a row. Besides, if she did, I'd have to pay her overtime." Nelson swallowed hard. Before he could reply, Matt ended the conversation.

The regional health authority's policy on earned time accrual and use is presented in Exhibit 4.1.

Questions

1. What are Nelson's alternatives?
2. What do you think Nelson should do? Justify your answer.
3. Does the hospital administration have any obligation to help alleviate Nelson's situation?

Original case contributed by Margaret Foegen Karsten, the University of Wisconsin, Platteville.

Exhibit 4.3 *St. John's Medical Centre Organizational Chart*

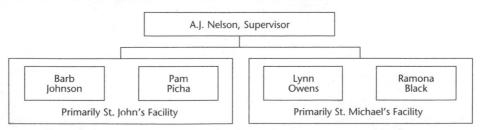

Exhibit 4.4 *Regional Health Authority's Policy on Earned Time Accrual and Use*

Earned Time

Personal time off from the workplace is important in maintaining good health. We are pleased to introduce an innovative program for earned paid time off. The program is called Earned Time, and has been nicknamed "ET."

Earned Time combines traditional programs of paid vacation time, paid legal and personal holiday time, and paid sick time into one "bank" of paid benefit time off. For each hour you work—up to 80 per pay period—an amount of Earned Time is deposited into your personal "Earned Time Account." Then, as you decide you want to schedule time off, the hours accumulated in your personal ET Account are yours to use.

You begin to earn time with your first hour of work. And for each hour you work—up to 80 per pay period—Earned Time continues to accrue. The amount of Earned Time you accrue depends on your length of continuous service with the regional health authority, your exemption status (non-exempt or exempt), and the number of hours you work.

These are also the usual components for determining accrual rates for paid holiday, sick, and vacation time. With this new program, however, you have the flexibility to schedule time off for whatever purpose you choose.

Maximum Accumulation Amounts

The emphasis of Earned Time is to offer you scheduled time away from work for whatever purpose you choose. Full-time employees are strongly encouraged to take 15 days off each year. Because unused Earned Time can be forwarded from year to year, it is possible to reach your Account Maximum if you do not use enough Earned Time each year.

Your personal ET Account has a *maximum accumulation amount of two times your annual accrual rate*. When you near your Account Maximum, it is your responsibility to schedule Earned Time off. If the Account Maximum is reached, no ET will accrue beyond it.

Example of Maximum Accumulation Amounts

Years of Service	Annual Accrual	Maximum ET Accumulation
2–4	200 hours (25 days)	400 hours (50 days)
10	248 hours (31 days)	496 hours (62 days)

Scheduling ET

ET is available as you accrue it. However, requests for paid time off must be approved by your supervisor, who will consider staffing arrangements and departmental operations before granting your request. Schedule ET with your supervisor as far in advance as possible. Often, at least a two-week notice is required for a scheduled absence.

Controlling Employee Benefit Costs

John DeCarlo is president and CEO of Quality Auto Parts, an automotive parts equipment manufacturer and supplier. The company was started by DeCarlo and his father in 1968 and now employs 812 people at four different sites. Revenues and profits increased steadily from 1968 until 1992. Both were down in 1992 and 1993. During the remainder of the 1990s, both were erratic as a result of increased foreign competition in both the auto parts industry and the auto industry itself. From 2000 to 2005, revenues have been increasing, but profitability is decreasing for a number of reasons.

The Problem

DeCarlo recently met with his vice president of finance (David Schramm) and his vice president of human resources (Harriet Foster) to determine how costs could be cut so the company could price its products more competitively, relative to foreign competitors. At this meeting, he learned that employee benefit costs had increased at approximately twice the rate for wages alone (12 percent versus 6 percent yearly) from 1988 to 1998. In particular, the employee health insurance costs increased from $2,184 per employee per year in 1988 to $8,316 in 2005. DeCarlo expressed frustration at these increases and asked what could be done.

Foster and Schramm invited DeCarlo to a meeting of health care providers, insurers, and employers scheduled for the following week. At this meeting, they learned that their problem was quite common and was being experienced by most other corporations in the area. One consultant surveyed a group of chief human resources executives at large companies and found "controlling employee benefit program costs" to be the most critical issue facing these executives. Moreover, health care costs have grown constantly since 1990.

They also learned more about the nature and causes of this problem. Many of the speakers at the conference cited more catastrophic-illness claims, increased use of mental health and substance abuse services, increased use of medical services, the increased costs related to high-technology medicine, the AIDS crisis, and the demographics of employees in the auto industry (i.e., a higher percentage of older employees). One speaker noted: "If businesses in the private sector don't make a profit, they are not going to exist. The continuing escalation of benefit costs is threatening the very survival of some companies, particularly small companies."

Several possible solutions were discussed, although there was no consensus regarding their effectiveness or applicability to particular situations. Among the cost-containment suggestions were more employee-financed benefits, utilization reviews, wellness programs, flexible benefits, and more cost-sharing between employers and employees. Many speakers emphasized that employers should not wait passively for the government to solve the problem because that was unlikely to happen any time soon.

The Challenge

DeCarlo came away from the conference with a greater appreciation of the complexity of the problem and a greater determination to do something about it. However, he wasn't sure what to do. He viewed his company as a "preferred employer" because it had always paid above-average wage rates, and its benefits were always more generous than those of comparable Canadian companies and particularly those of foreign competitors. DeCarlo did not want to do anything to jeopardize his company's advantage in attracting and retaining high-quality personnel. At the same time, he realized that if no changes were made, his benefit costs would be greater than his total projected earnings within the next 10 years.

Quality Auto Parts' current extended health insurance plan is a traditional indemnity insurance plan. All employees have one plan that makes no effort to control the health care services provided. The plan also does not contain any support for preventative practices (e.g., massage therapy, physiotherapy, fitness programs) that might avoid more costly problems for injured or ill employees in the future.

DeCarlo decided to establish an Employee Health Benefits Committee that would report to him in one month with recommendations for containing health benefit costs while minimizing adverse employee reaction. The committee's membership consists of Foster, Schramm, and two employees. You have been asked to serve as an employee member of this committee.

The committee has recommended that DeCarlo consider three general options for the future: (1) stay with the current traditional indemnity policy with an average cost of $5,316 per year, (2) offer a wellness option in addition to the current plan, and (3) establish a special self-insurance fund for employees who want extended coverage and negotiate preferred provider arrangements with local providers.

The committee members are split on the three options. The other employee wishes to continue with the current plan. Schramm wants to adopt the self-insurance option, and Foster wants to offer the wellness option. All three are looking to you to make a recommendation and help them reach a consensus.

Questions

1. Describe the nature and causes of the cost problem in this case.
2. What information should the committee gather before making any recommendations? Why?
3. Given the desire of most employees to pay as little as possible for benefits (i.e., expecting the employer to cover most or all benefit costs), is there any way for the company to continue to attract the best employees while containing benefit costs? Why or why not?
4. On the basis of what you know about this company, which of the three specific proposals would you be likely to recommend? Can the company adopt some combination of the three options? What do you recommend and why?

Evaluating Non-Traditional Incentive Systems: Howe 2 Ski Stores

The Howe 2 Ski Stores are a chain of three ski and windsurfing shops located in the suburbs of a large western coastal city. Maria Howe, a ski enthusiast and business major, opened the first store 10 years ago after her university graduation with financial backing from her family and several friends. From its inception, the Howe 2 store was intended to provide state-of-the-art equipment and clothing for skiers at all skill levels, from beginner to champion. It was to be staffed by employees who were themselves advanced skiers and could provide expert advice on the choice of clothing and equipment, and it was intended to have a quick response time that would permit the last-minute purchase of equipment and clothing prior to a ski trip.

Howe originally drew from a pool of skiing friends and fellow students to staff the stores, and still prefers to hire part-time employees with skiing expertise who might leave in a year over more stable, full-time employees with less expertise and interest in the sport. Whether administrative staff, cashiers, clerks, or moulders (employees who fit bindings to skis), employees were encouraged to keep up to date on the latest skiing equipment and trends, attend ski vendor shows, try out demo equipment, and give feedback on the store's inventory in order to help provide the highest quality equipment and advice for the customer. Suggestion boxes were placed in the store, and Howe herself regularly collected, read, and acted upon the suggestions made by the clerks and customers. She developed special advertising campaigns to build an image for the nearby slopes in order to increase the market. As the business grew, Howe even added a line of rental equipment in order to lower the costs and encourage people to try the sport.

Although profits grew irregularly due to weather effects and the faddish nature of the sport, Howe's efforts paid off in the long term, and within four years business had grown sufficiently to permit the opening of a second Howe 2 Ski Store in another suburb about 16 kilometres from the location of the first store. In order to even out sales across the year, about six years ago Howe took a chance on the growing windsurfing market and the coastal location and added a line of equipment for this sport. The move turned out to be a very good one. The windsurfing market increased by more than 300 percent in four years and continues to experience a slower but stable pattern of growth as families and older adults attempt the sport. This expanded market has enabled her to smooth out the number of sales occurring throughout the year.

Three years ago, Howe was able to open a third store, located within a 25-km radius of the other two locations. Although managers have been hired to run each of the stores and the total number of employees has grown to 65, Howe's basic strategy has remained the same—high-quality, state-of-the-art products, a knowledgeable staff, and quick response time. Profits from the stores have continued to grow, although at a slower rate. Competition from other ski stores has also increased noticeably within the last two years.

The threat of increased competition has been exacerbated by signs that employee productivity has begun to slide. Last year, there were eight occasions where expensive ski orders were not delivered in time for the customer's ski vacation. Although Howe used a variety of maneuvers to retain the customers' patronage (e.g., paying for the customer to rent equipment of equivalent quality, arranging express delivery of the equipment to the customer as soon as it was received at the store, and lowering the price of the equipment), the costs of these late orders were high. She realized that word of mouth about these kinds of incidents could significantly damage the store's reputation. Furthermore, at least 15 percent of all ski orders were delivered more than two days late, even though customers did not miss a trip or vacation as a result.

In an attempt to respond to these difficulties, Howe instituted a merit performance system for the moulders (employees who fit the binding to skis). Although productivity seemed to increase for a while, waves of discontent popped out all over the stores. The moulders felt that their merit ratings were inaccurate because the store managers could not observe them working much of the time. Further, they argued that their performance levels would have been much higher had not other employees interrupted them with questions about appropriate bindings or failed to clearly identify the appropriate equipment on the sales orders. Other employees also complained because they were not given the opportunity for merit pay. The buyers, who visit ski shows, examine catalogues, and talk with sales representatives in order to decide on the inventory, argued that their work was essential for high sales figures and quality equipment. Sales clerks claimed that their in-depth familiarity with an extensive inventory and their sales skills were essential to increasing sales. They also noted their important role in negotiating a delivery date that the moulders could meet. Similar arguments were made by the people in the credit office who arranged for short-term financing if necessary, and the cashiers who verified costs and checked credit card approvals. Even the stockers noted that the store would be in a bad way if they did not locate the correct equipment in a warehouse full of inventory and deliver it in a timely manner to the moulders.

Howe had to concede that the employees were correct on many of these points, so she suspended the merit plan at the end of the ski season and promised to re-evaluate its fairness. Even more convincing were several indications that productivity problems were not limited to moulder employees. Complaints about customer service increased 20 percent during the year. Several customers noted that they were allowed to stand, merchandise in hand, waiting for a clerk to help them, while clerks engaged in deep conversations among themselves. Although Howe mentioned this to employees in the stores when she visited and asked the store managers to discuss it in staff meetings, the complaints continued. A record number of "as is" skis were sold at the end of the season sale because they were damaged in the warehouse or the store, or by the moulders. The closing inventory revealed that 20 percent of the rental equipment had been lost or seriously damaged without resulting charges to the renters because records were poorly maintained. Regular checks of the suggestion boxes in the store revealed fewer and fewer comments. Although less extreme, similar problems occurred in windsurfing season. Employees just didn't seem to notice these problems, or worse, didn't seem to care.

Howe was very bothered by all these factors and felt they could not be attributed to the growth of the business alone. She knew it would be impossible to maintain her competitive position with these events occurring. At a recent Small Business Forum meeting, Howe heard the guest speaker, a university professor, suggest that employers consider a group of non-traditional incentive plans in order to increase employee motivation and involvement and reduce the costs of operating. She decided to investigate the topic further to see whether these plans might be appropriate for her stores.

Questions

1. Given the background information about Howe 2 Ski Stores, discuss the feasibility of implementing lump-sum bonuses, pay for knowledge, profit-sharing, or gain-sharing plans in this situation. What plan or plans would you recommend that Howe look at most closely and why?
2. Assuming that she decides that a gain-sharing plan is feasible, what could be done to increase the likelihood of success?
3. What negative effects are likely to result from even the successful implementation of a gain-sharing plan?

Original case contributed by M. Susan Taylor, University of Maryland, and J. Kline Harrison, Wake Forest University.

Allocating Merit Raises

I. *Objectives:*
   A. To make you aware of the difficulties involved in making merit raise decisions.
   B. To familiarize you with possible criteria a manager can use in making merit raise decisions.
   C. To give you practice in explaining the procedure you used in determining merit raises.
II. *Out-of-Class Preparation Time:* 10–20 minutes to read the exercise and decide each professor's merit raise
III. *In-Class Time Suggested:* 30–40 minutes
IV. *Procedures:* At the beginning of class or before coming to class, you should read the exercise and determine merit raises for each professor.

To start the exercise, the instructor will divide the class into groups of three to five students. Each group should develop a fair procedure that will be used to determine merit raises and then decide the dollar raise to be given to each professor. After each group finishes, one member will write the raise amounts on the board or overhead for all class members to see. Then, once all groups have disclosed their raises, a spokesperson for each group will explain the procedure used to determine their raises.

Situation

Lighthouse University is located in western Canada and has an enrollment of about 8,000 students. The School of Business has 40 full-time and more than 30 part-time faculty members. The school is divided into five departments: Management, Marketing, Finance and Accounting, Decision Sciences, and Information Technology. Faculty members in the Management Department are evaluated each year based on three primary criteria: teaching, research, and service. The evaluation of teaching performance is based on data from student course evaluations over a two-year period. Service to the university, school, profession, and community are also evaluated based on accomplishments in these areas over a two-year period. Research is evaluated based on the number of academic journal articles published over a three-year period. Teaching and research are considered more important than service. In judging faculty performance, the department chair evaluates each professor in the department using one of four possible ratings: Far Exceeds Standards, Exceeds Standards, Meets Standards, and Fails to Meet Standards. The results of this year's evaluations are shown in the next page.

This year the university has agreed to give raises to its employees totalling 3 percent, which means there is $17,400 in raises available to the Management Department. Your task as department chair is to divide the $17,400 among the faculty members. Keep in mind that these raises will likely set a precedent for future years and that the professors will view the raises as a signal of what behaviour is valued and what is not.

Department Chairs' Rating of Job Performance

Professor	Current Salary	Teaching	Research	Service
Houseman	$82,000	Exceeds	Exceeds	Meets
Jones	$106,000	Exceeds	Far Exceeds	Exceeds
Ricks	$135,000	Meets	Meets	Far Exceeds
Matthews	$87,000	New Hire	New Hire	New Hire
Karas	$90,000	Far Exceeds	Exceeds	Meets
Franks	$80,000	Meets	Fails to Meet	Exceeds

A profile of each of the professors is provided below.

Prof. Houseman: 55 years old; 25 years with the university; teaches large sections of Principles of Management; teaches over 400 students per year; has written over 40 articles and given over 30 presentations since joining the School of Business; wants a good raise to catch up with others.

Prof. Jones: 49 years old; 10 years with the university; teaches Human Resource Management and Organizational Behaviour; stepped down as department chair three years ago; teaches about 200 students a year; has written over 30 articles and two books since joining the School of Business; recently received an $80,000 research grant from a local foundation. Wants a good raise as a reward for obtaining the grant.

Prof. Ricks: 61 years old; six years with the university; teaches Labour Relations and Organizational Development; stepped down as Dean of the School of Business two years ago and took a $20,000 pay cut; teaches about 180 students per year; has written only two articles in the last six years due to administrative duties; very active in the community and serves on several charity boards. Wants a good raise to make up for loss of $20,000 annual stipend for service as Dean.

Prof. Matthews: 28 years old; new hire—only four months with university; teaches Employee Relations and Compensation Management; just completed a Ph.D.; will teach about 110 students this year. To be competitive in the job market, the School of Business needed to pay Professor Matthews $87,000 plus provide a reduced teaching load for two years and a $6,000 per year summer stipend; none of the other faculty were given these conditions when they were first hired; had two minor publications while a doctoral student but none since joining the School of Business. Wants a good raise to pay off student loans and buy a house.

Prof. Karas: 32 years old; four years with the university; teaches International Business and Honours sections of Management Principles; teaches about 150 students per year; won Teacher of the Year Award this year; published 12 articles in the last four years; has been interviewing for a new job at other universities and may leave if a good raise is not forthcoming.

Prof. Franks: 64 years old; 18 years with the university; teaches Principles of Management and Human Resource Management; teaches about 150 students per year; principal advisor for Management major students; has not written any articles during the last four years; plans on retiring within two or three years. Wants a good raise to enhance pension plan.

Flexible Benefit Plan Choices

I. *Objectives:*
   A. To familiarize you with how flexible benefit plans work.
   B. To give you an understanding of some of the benefits offered in a flexible benefit plan.
   C. To give you experience in selecting benefits.
   D. To give you an understanding of the criteria individuals use in selecting benefits.
II. *Out-of-Class Preparation Time:* 10 minutes to read the exercise and select benefits
III. *In-Class Time Suggested:* 30–40 minutes
IV. *Procedures:* Assume that you have recently graduated from university and are just starting a new job at a large firm. Your starting rate of pay (net of all taxes and mandatory deductions) is $40,000. Your task is to read the Benefit Policy described below and determine which benefits you would select. Keep in mind that any money you spend on additional benefits will reduce the $40,000 per year you can spend on other things such as housing, entertainment, and travel. After each person in the class has selected the benefits he or she would choose, the instructor will divide the class into groups of three to five. Then, each person explains his or her selections to the rest of the group, along with the rationale behind the decisions. After each person is finished, your group needs to prepare a list of criteria that were used in making the benefit selections. These criteria will then be written on an overhead or blackboard for a class discussion.

Benefits Policy

Your company offers full-time employees the opportunity to participate in a broad range of programs to meet specific needs. Employees are responsible for selecting the benefits that best meet their needs.

Extended Health Care Premium Payments

The extended health care program allows employees to purchase coverage for such services as dental care (including basic services as well as services such as orthodontics and dentures) and vision care. New employees must opt into this program within 31 days of employment to receive this benefit. The firm pays a portion of fees for this coverage. The portion of the fees paid by the employee is as follows:

Monthly Fees

| Employee Only | | Employee Plus One | | Family Coverage | |
Non-Smoker	Smoker	Non-Smoker	Smoker	Non-Smoker	Smoker
$80	$100	$150	$170	$191	$211

Registered Retirement Savings Plan Account

This account allows an employee to set aside pre-tax dollars as a contribution to an RRSP fund administered by the employer.

$5,000 per plan is the maximum annual contribution.

$480 is the minimum annual contribution.

You must make any contributions to this plan by the last day of February in each calendar year to receive the tax benefits of such contributions.

Retirement

Payments into the Canada Pension Plan will be deducted from your paycheque in each pay period effective the first day of employment. You will be automatically enrolled in the firm's pension plan after 1,000 hours of service. Upon retirement or termination of service, you will receive 2 percent of your annual compensation for each year of service. Your pension is vested if you have three years of service with the firm. See your Benefits Office for more details.

Employee Stock Purchase Plan

You are allowed to purchase common stock in the firm at a 15 percent discount off the fair market value through payroll deduction. Contributions are deducted on an after-tax basis. See the Benefits Office for details.

Life Insurance

Full-time employees of our firm have life insurance provided effective the first day of employment as a condition of employment. It provides two kinds of insurance—life, and accidental death and dismemberment. The amount of insurance coverage is equal to the employee's annual salary rounded to the next highest thousand, and then doubled. An amount equal to four times the employee's salary is payable in the event of accidental death. Coverage is also provided for accidental blinding or dismemberment. Premiums are paid by the firm.

Optional Life Insurance

Additional optional life insurance is available and is administered by a large life insurance firm. It is available for employees and their spouses and dependants. Premiums are paid by the employee through payroll deduction. To receive up to $200,000 coverage without providing a certificate of good health, you must request this benefit within 60 days of employment. Your cost will depend upon your age:

Monthly Rate per $10,000 Coverage

Under 25	25–29	30–34	35–39	40–44	45–49
$0.40	$0.50	$0.70	$0.80	$1.30	$2.20

Price quotes are available for those over 50. Check with the Benefits Office.

Long-Term Disability Insurance

Long-term disability insurance is offered to full-time employees, their spouses, parents, and parents-in-law. Employees enrolling within 31 days of hire do not have to complete a health care questionnaire. Long-term disability insurance payments are available to employees enrolled in this insurance program who are absent from work for more than six weeks due to medical problems caused by illness or accident. The payments begin after six weeks of absence have been recorded (it is expected that regular medical coverage will cover any costs incurred during those six weeks). The payments can be used for services providing assistance with day-to-day functions such as dressing, eating, and getting into and out of bed, or for any other expenses associated with treatment of the medical problems. The cost of this insurance is dependent upon one's age and level of coverage. Check with the Benefits Office for specific costs.

Optional Long-Term Disability Income Insurance

Long-term disability income insurance helps to protect your income when, due to a covered illness or injury, you are disabled. It has been designed to cover a disability sustained on or off the job. The plan provides up to 60 percent of your basic monthly earnings after 180 days of disability. The cost varies depending upon age and level of coverage.

Personal Accident Insurance

Personal accident insurance is available for the employee, spouse, and dependent children and helps protect against losses due to accidents. A full benefit is paid for accidental loss of life; loss of use of both upper and lower limbs; loss of both hands, feet, or eyes; loss of speech; or loss of hearing in both ears. Partial benefits are paid in the event of loss of any one hand, foot, eye, both legs or both arms. The firm pays all costs.

Transportation Reimbursement Account

You may contribute to a parking reimbursement account and/or a transportation account that covers mass transit or van pooling. These are two separate accounts. Contributions are deducted from your paycheque. You can contribute up to $185 per month for the Parking Account and $100 per month for the Transportation Account.

Optional Prepaid Legal Plan

The prepaid legal plan, for a monthly payroll deduction of $19.20, provides for legal services such as traffic court representation, court representation for a first offence of impaired driving, will preparation, credit/warranty disputes, financial contract or lease review, uncontested divorce, uncontested adoption, and purchase or sale of a primary residence.

Tuition Assistance

Educational assistance is available for full-time employees with at least one year of service. Our firm will pay for a maximum of 15 credit hours of study per year—6 credit hours in the fall, 6 credit hours in the spring, and 3 credit hours in the summer. Courses must be work- or degree-related and taken at an accredited post-secondary institution.

Executive Perks

I. *Objectives:*
   A. To familiarize you with the wide variety of perks often given to top executives.
   B. To familiarize you with the arguments for and against various executive perks.

II. *Out-of-Class Preparation Time:* none

III. *In-Class Time Suggested:* 30–40 minutes

IV. *Procedures:* At the start of class, your instructor will divide the class into groups of three to five. Your group is to assume that you are all members of the Compensation Committee for a large firm. Your committee is composed of independent members of the firm's Board of Directors. The committee is responsible for establishing annual and long-term performance goals for the firm's executives, for evaluating the performance of these officers, for setting the compensation of these officers, and for making recommendations to the board with respect to new compensation plans. The firm's current chief executive officer (CEO) has announced her retirement, so a new CEO will be chosen soon. Given the controversy regarding executive perks, your committee has been asked by the Board of Directors to review the current CEO's perks to determine if they should also be offered to the new CEO. You are to assume that the current CEO has a base salary of $1 million and earned an additional $2 million from bonuses and stock options. Below is a list of the CEO's current perks. Your task is to evaluate each of the above in terms of whether it should be provided and, if yes, based on which criteria. So, for each item, circle "Y" or "N." Then write below each item, the criteria, if any, that the executive must meet in order to receive that item.

   A. Physical Exams   Y or N
      Criteria: _____

   B. Financial Counselling   Y or N
      Criteria: _____

   C. Company Car   Y or N
      Criteria: _____

   D. Memberships in a Golf Club   Y or N
      Criteria: _____

   E. First-Class Air Travel for Overseas Travel   Y or N
      Criteria: _____

   F. Company Plane for Travel within North America   Y or N
      Criteria: _____

   G. Personal Liability Insurance   Y or N
      Criteria: _____

H. Chauffeur Service   Y or N
    Criteria: _____

I. Reserved Parking   Y or N
    Criteria: _____

J. Clothing Allowance   Y or N
    Criteria: _____

K. Stock Options (allows executive to buy   Y or N
company stock in future years at favourable prices)
    Criteria: _____

L. Golden Parachute/Severance Pay (given if the   Y or N
executive's employment is terminated early)
    Criteria: _____

M. Guaranteed Pension   Y or N
    Criteria: _____

N. Bonuses   Y or N
    Criteria: _____

WageSim—A Compensation Administration Exercise

I. *Objectives:*
   A. To familiarize you with some of the problems involved in building and maintaining a compensation system.
   B. To provide you with alternative approaches for solving some typical compensation-related problems.
   C. To give you practice in writing memos to employees regarding compensation issues.
   D. To familiarize you with job evaluation procedures.

II. *Out-of-Class Preparation Time:* 20 minutes to read exercise, plus 1 hour to determine responses to the e-mail items (either individually or in a group) and write memos

III. *In-Class Time Suggested:* 45 minutes to discuss all e-mail items

IV. *Procedures:* This exercise can be done individually or in groups of three to five members, at the instructor's option. First, begin by reading all of the material presented in this exercise. Assume that you are responsible for developing and maintaining the Mack Organization's wage and salary system. Assume further that the person who previously had these responsibilities has just quit and left you all of the e-mail items that follow. You (or your team) is to respond in writing to each employee who sent an e-mail. Second, explain on a separate sheet of paper what additional actions you would take with reference to each item. For example, if you believe that you should gather additional information before making a final decision on an item, explain what information you would want. Or, if you believe that additional memos or discussions with someone in the company are needed, explain this. You (or your team) should bring both the memos and the "Additional Action" sheets to class. Be prepared to present and defend these materials during the class discussion.

Situation

The Mack Organization is a large organization whose headquarters is in Ontario. It has offices located throughout the country and employs over 700 individuals. You may assume the organization is a chemical company, a manufacturing company, a hospital, a university, or virtually any large organization with which you are familiar.

The Mack Organization's Human Resource Department includes a Compensation Administration section that consists of two individuals, one of whom is you (or your team). The company has several different wage structures, including one for executives and one for clerical personnel. For compensation purposes, all clerical employees are divided into five job classifications. The organization's current wage structure for clerical personnel is shown in Exhibit 4.5.

MACK ORGANIZATION
Compensation Policies
(Excerpts from policy manual)

How Salaries Are Determined

Employee salaries directly relate to the work they do and how well they do it. Two major factors work together to establish the salaries payable for various jobs—position evaluation and salary ranges.

Job Evaluation

Job evaluation is a method of measuring the relative worth of each job in the organization compared to all the other jobs, based on an objective analysis of the duties and responsibilities of the position. The concept is not unique to us; determining the relative value of jobs within an organization is an integral part of any salary administration program, regardless of the company.

At the Mack Organization, job evaluation works like this. First, a description is written for each job. The information used to develop the description comes from a questionnaire completed by the person performing the job. The description defines the function of the job and lists the major duties performed. Each description is then evaluated by a standing committee of people from various areas of the organization who have a broad knowledge of the jobs that exist throughout the organization. Their evaluation is based on "yardsticks," including knowledge required, freedom of action, accountability, contacts with employees and customers, physical effort required, unusual working conditions, research responsibilities, and supervision or management responsibilities. Based on these yardsticks, the job is assigned a point value. By listing all positions according to their point value, the relative worth of each position is established.

When a new job is developed, or duties change on an existing one, the job description is submitted to the position evaluation committee. The committee analyzes it, determines the overall point value, and assigns it to its proper place within the ranking structure. The result is an up-to-date listing of all the jobs in the organization, from entry level to management. This is the first phase in determining salaries. The second phase is the assignment of jobs to grades and the establishment of salary ranges.

Grade Levels and Salary Ranges

Based on the total points received in job evaluation, jobs are assigned to a grade level. Each grade has an entry or minimum rate and a maximum salary payable for the jobs in that grade: the amounts between the entry rate and maximum comprise the salary range for the grade.

To ensure that the organization's salaries remain at a fair, competitive level, ranges and rates are checked continuously against those paid for similar positions in other organizations. Adjustments to the ranges are made periodically as area market rates change.

Usually employees begin at the bottom of each salary grade. Employees are considered for a merit increase after six months of satisfactory service. After this, they may receive an annual merit increase upon completion of satisfactory service. There are a total of six possible merit increases. Cost-of-living increases are granted periodically by the organization to all employees.

Payday

The Mack Organization's staff is paid on a biweekly basis, every other Friday. There are 26 pay periods each year. For pay purposes, a normal week is Friday through Thursday.

Normally a full-time employee is quoted a weekly salary when hired. To compute the annual salary, multiply the weekly salary by 52, or the biweekly salary by 26. The monthly salary equals the annual salary divided by 12.

All employees are paid by electronic direct deposit, and receive a pay statement indicating gross pay, pay to date, deductions required by law, any voluntary deductions, and net pay.

Full-time employees are paid to date on payday—the amount they receive includes what they have earned through that payday. Any overtime or premium earnings are paid in the following pay period. Part-time employees are paid through the previous Thursday so that their hours may be properly credited.

Employees who do not see an indication in the designated financial institution's records that a pay deposit has been made are requested to contact the Human Resource Department, who will investigate the situation and, if necessary, issue a corrected deposit.

Pay Advances

In extreme emergencies, it is possible for employees to be paid for those hours already worked during the current pay period. It is also possible for employees to receive a vacation advance before they go on vacation. All advances need the approval of an employee's supervisor. Six hours are needed to prepare cheques.

Exhibit 4.5 *Mack Organization's Wage Structure for Clerical Personnel*

Job Title	Salary	Number of Employees
Office Services Aide	$26,259 min $34,262 max	40
Office Services Assistant	$27,588 min $36,337 max	30
Secretary	$29,041 min $38,604 max	20
Senior Secretary	$30,628 min $41,083 max	40
Executive Secretary	$32,364 min $43,794 max	20

E-mail Items

Item 1

Memorandum

To: Wage & Salary Division
From: Mary Wallace—Vice President
Subject: Request for promotion

This is to formally request your endorsement of my intent to promote Susan Anthony, an Office Services Aide in my office, to the position of Office Services Assistant. Ms. Anthony has taken the clerk-typist test administered by your office and scored 55 wpm on the typing speed portion of the test. Though I realize the typing speed required for Office Services Assistants is 70 wpm, Ms. Anthony possesses all the other necessary skills to perform all tasks in this office. Ms. Anthony has been with this office for five years and is a loyal and dedicated employee. I wholeheartedly encourage your endorsement of this recommendation. A vacant Office Services Assistant position is available in this office. Please advise as soon as possible.

Item 2

Memorandum

To: Wage and Salary Section
From: Kelly Actor
Subject: Request for pay increase

I have been with this company for 10 years. My present position with this company is Senior Secretary, at the maximum pay level.

The Wispette Company has offered me a position that would give me a 9 percent increase in salary for similar duties.

Since I do enjoy my work, I hate to leave. However, my financial obligations to my family leave me no choice. My husband recently has been disabled, with no hope of employment for three years. As I mentioned, I have enjoyed my 10 years with this company. My supervisor and I get along well. I have not missed any work during the 10 years except for the two-week vacation during the summer.

If you will match the Wispette Company's offer, I would prefer to stay with your company. I understand there is no opening for an Executive Secretary, which would be a comparable position. I need an answer soon.

Item 3

Memorandum

To: Wage and Salary Section
From: Jane Swenk, Supervisor
Subject: Long-term employee wage dispute

Mamie Scott, a secretary, expressed concern that her daughter, also a secretary, was making the same amount of money as her. Mamie has been employed for 28 years, her daughter for five. Merit raises are given yearly only for the first five years, and Mamie has not received one in 23 years. I don't think this policy is fair. Mamie should get something for her longer service. Please respond so I can explain the situation to Mamie.

Item 4

Memorandum

To: Compensation Administration
From: Personnel Director
Subject: Payroll budget for next month

Please prepare a payroll budget for next month for clerical employees. Make whatever assumptions you feel are necessary in doing your calculation. Just let me know what the assumptions are. Many thanks.

Item 5

Memorandum

To: Wage and Salary Section
From: Bob Franklin, Office Services Assistant
Subject: Lost payment

Please issue me a new direct deposit payment for the last pay period. I have no record of it being received. I asked my wife if she had taken the money from the payment out of the bank, and she doesn't remember. I don't think she did because I think she would have remembered if she did make this withdrawal. My pay is $27,588 per year. Please do it as soon as possible.

Item 6

Memorandum

To: Compensation Section
From: Betty Dyer, Supervisor
Subject: Promotion for Tammy Tuff

Tammy Tuff is an excellent secretary in my office. She does an outstanding job with all assignments and performs beyond standards for a secretary in everything she does. She completes her assignments in half the time of other secretaries and voluntarily assumes extra duties after finishing her assignments.

In addition to her outstanding performance, Ms. Tuff has improved morale in the office since she entered on duty nine months ago. She always has a smile on her face and brightens the day for coworkers with her pleasant disposition. Best of all, she makes others feel important, and this has carried over to their work. Everyone seems to take pride in their work; consequently, performance and productivity are up.

Due to Tammy's influence, the turnover rate is zero, leaving her with no promotion potential in this office. Based on Tammy's excellent performance, skills that exceed the requirements of the job, and attitude that has improved morale, I feel that Tammy deserves a promotion within the office even though there is no Senior Secretary vacancy.

Item 7

Memorandum

To: Wage and Salary Section
From: Hal Markley, Supervisor
Subject: Early issuance of pay

I am leaving town in two hours and will be gone for four days on emergency business. I will not have access to an ATM and will not be able to contact my bank during this time. Since I will be away on payday three days hence, it is essential that I receive my payment before I leave.

Item 8

Memorandum

To: Wage and Salary Section
From: McNamara, Department Manager
Subject: Early absence

Mary White, an Office Services Aide, left two hours early yesterday, without permission, to attend a political rally. Should she be paid for this time or not?

Item 9

Memorandum

To: Wage and Salary Section
From: Sue L. Ross, Supervisor
Subject: Promotion for Julie Tate

Julie Tate, Senior Secretary, has been temporarily assigned some of the duties of an Executive Secretary position. The position is temporarily vacant due to the Executive Secretary being on vacation.

Julie has been told by me that she may be assigned higher-level duties on occasion, but she is not satisfied. She has threatened to take her complaint to the Human Resources Office, insisting that she deserves financial compensation for absorbing some duties of an Executive Secretary. None of the additional duties is too difficult for Julie to handle, and she actually does an excellent job on all assignments once she stops complaining about her unfair treatment.

I am recommending that Julie be promoted to an Executive Secretary position so that I can assign her higher-level duties whenever my Executive Secretary is on vacation or sick leave. This way Julie would not complain about the grade level of her work, and the flow of work in the office would proceed smoothly without disruption.

Please respond to this recommendation.

Item 10

Memorandum

To: Wage and Salary Section
From: Doris Pope
Subject: Merit pay increase for Frances Brown, Secretary

I would like you to approve an extra 8 percent pay increase for my personal secretary, Ms. Frances Brown, to be effective immediately. Ms. Brown has served in this position, throughout my eight-year tenure and that of my predecessor, for a total of 25 years. Ms. Brown will be presented with a letter of commendation at a departmental meeting this afternoon. It would be helpful if you could complete the paperwork for this salary adjustment by 5:00 p.m. so that I can present it with the commendation.
Thanks,

Doris Pope

Doris Pope
Department Head

Ethical Compensation Dilemmas

I. *Objectives:*
  A. To make you aware that many compensation decisions involve ethical issues.
  B. To familiarize you with a variety of different ethical compensation dilemmas and issues.
  C. To enhance your ability to identify ethical issues in case situations.
  D. To familiarize you with various criteria that can be used to distinguish between ethical and unethical behaviour.
  E. To examine the interrelatedness between ethical choices, individual values, and ethical organizational climates.
  F. To examine the causes of ethical dilemmas.
II. *Out-of-Class Preparation Time:* 5 minutes to read all or some of the Ethical Compensation Dilemmas below, as assigned by your instructor
III. *In-Class Time Suggested:* 20–75 minutes, depending on how many of the dilemmas below are assigned by your instructor
IV. *Procedures:* At the start of class, you will be divided into groups of three to five and assigned one or more of the following 10 dilemmas to analyze. Your group should answer the following three questions and be prepared to present your decisions:
  A. Are there any ethical issues presented in the dilemma? If so, what are they?
  B. How can the dilemma be resolved most effectively and ethically?
  C. How important are the issues presented in the dilemma?

For the purpose of this exercise, use the following definition of compensation ethics:

Compensation ethics are the rules, standards, or principles that provide guidelines for morally correct behaviour, and for truthfulness in the remuneration and reward of employees.

In answering the three questions, your group may want to address the questions below. They are designed to help you determine if an issue involves ethical considerations.
  1. Does the action involve intentional deception?
  2. Does the action purposely benefit one party at the expense of another?
  3. Is the action fair and just to all concerned? The Golden Rule not only dictates that we "do unto others as we would have them do unto us" but also commands that we treat others as we might wish to be treated.
  4. Would the manager feel comfortable if the action were made public, or must it remain a secret?
  5. Are managers justifying the action by telling themselves that they can get away with it or that they won't need to live with the decision's consequences?

6. Would the decision-maker recommend the action to other managers or firms?

7. Will the action build goodwill and better relationships?

In answering the questions, you also may want to consider three different schools of thought regarding ethical decision-making. The Utilitarian Approach argues that decision outcomes should result in the greatest good for the greatest number of people. The Moral Rights Approach holds that decisions should be consistent with fundamental rights and privileges as set forth in legislation such as the *Canadian Charter of Rights and Freedoms* or other documents such as the United Nations Declaration of Human Rights. The Justice Approach stresses that decisions should be equitable and follow the distributive justice and fairness principle. Some argue that the ideal decision occurs when it is supported by the ethical standards of all three ethical approaches.

After your group has finished its analysis (10 minutes or less), each group will make a short, 2- to 3-minute, presentation to the class. This will be followed by a discussion (6 to 10 minutes long) that focuses on each group's answers.

Ethical Compensation Dilemmas

1. Based on an evaluation of the knowledge, skills, and abilities needed to do each job, a company has determined that two jobs (Job A and Job B) are equal in content and in their value to the organization. However, when the firm studies the labour market, it finds that applicants for Job A are plentiful whereas those for Job B are very scarce. Should the firm offer less to those who apply for Job A, or should the pay offers be equal for both jobs?

2. Assume that the supply of electrical technicians is low, so a firm hires a group of them at $18 per hour. Two years later, due to a recession, the supply of technicians is high, so the market rate for them is now $15 per hour. Should the firm pay new hires $18 or $15? Since the firm bases pay rates on supply and demand, should it lower the pay of existing technicians to $15?

3. Jim is given an extremely large raise because of his superb work record one year. As a result, he is currently earning $55,000 while others at the firm holding the same job are earning $45,000. Everyone expects Jim's performance to continue to be excellent and to enhance the entire unit's productivity. Unfortunately, Jim's performance drops off after the first year and is now just average. What should be done about his pay? Should it be reduced to reflect his current performance, or should he continue to earn more than all of the others?

4. One year, Ethan's performance is truly spectacular (just as good as Jim's had been in the previous case). However, the company has no raise money available that year, so no one, including Ethan, receives a merit raise. Given that Jim received a large raise for past performance, is this fair to Ethan?

5. Mary and Sue both work in the same department. Mary believes that Sue is being paid considerably more than she is. In fact, both employees are being paid about the same amount. Mary wants a pay raise and complains to her

boss and the compensation manager. What should the compensation manager say, assuming the firm follows the policy of not revealing the pay of individual employees? Should Mary be told the amount of Sue's pay? Or should Mary only be told that there is a "misunderstanding" and that her belief is incorrect? Or should some other approach be taken?

6. When Lily was hired as an office employee in a manufacturing facility, she was told verbally that she would receive a raise when she finished her university degree and another raise when she was given additional responsibility. She accepted the job offer based on this understanding. However, during the next two years, the firm experienced slow sales and had to ask all factory employees to accept a 12 percent pay decrease. But Lily, who does not work in the factory, has graduated from university, and has accepted more responsibility. Should she receive a raise?

7. Two firms in the chemical solvent industry decide to merge. Employees in the testing department of Firm A have enjoyed high pay for many years. However, Firm B has a history of paying low wages. As a result, employees in Firm A's testing department earn on average a dollar more per hour than those at Firm B. Upon completion of the merger, what wage levels should prevail? Should wages be cut for those who worked for Firm A? Or should wages be increased for those in Firm B?

8. Sue is a 55-year-old employee of Company A. Her children are out of college and her parents have both died. Company A offers a child care program to all employees, along with an elder care program. However, Sue, like many other employees, has no need for these services, neither now or in the future. Should the firm retain these programs? Should alternative benefits be offered for employees who have no use for such services?

9. Helen works as an accountant for a firm in the textile industry. During non-working hours, she does extensive volunteer work for the Red Cross, Meals on Wheels, and the Heart and Stroke Foundation. Helen's employer wants to maintain a favourable image in the community so it wants every employee to donate money to the United Way. Should the firm pressure Helen to donate money? Keep in mind that if Helen doesn't donate money, other employees may not either, which could result in the firm having an unfavourable image in the community. On the other hand, Helen already donates her labour, which has a monetary value to the organizations she volunteers for, and she may feel that it is unfair to be asked to donate even more.

10. Frank works 25 hours per week for a mail order firm in the packaging department. He receives no benefits beyond those required by law. Frank does the same work as three other employees, all of whom work full-time. These employees qualify for benefits such as additional pension contributions, extended medical care, long-term disability, and employer-financed child care. Is this ethical? Assume that Frank would like to work full-time, really wants to receive benefits, and feels harmed because of this shortfall. On the other hand, the firm is not legally required to pay Frank these benefits. Frank only works part-time, and it would be expensive to pay benefits to all part-time employees, including Frank.

Developing Bioterrorism Policies and Procedures

I. *Objectives:*
   A. To sensitize you to the potential human resource challenges of bioterrorism resulting from the anthrax attacks that occurred in the United States in late 2001.
   B. To familiarize you with various bioterrorism websites that might prove useful in developing policies and procedures for handling potential bioterrorism events.

II. *Out-of-Class Preparation Time:* 30 minutes

III. *In-Class Time Suggested:* 20 minutes

IV. *Instructions:*
   A. Students will break up into groups of three to five students. All students will read the "Situation" and then search the websites listed to become familiar with the general societal issue of bioterrorism. In the "Situation" described below, the employer is a municipal government that incorporates one "first responder" (i.e., the municipal health authority) and numerous other government entities.
   B. Based on your website research, each group will be responsible for identifying appropriate policies and procedures for addressing one of the four bioterrorism challenges listed on Form 1.
   C. On Form 1, each group will write a policy addressing their assigned challenge to be added to the municipal Policies and Procedures Manual given to all municipal employees. Be sure to differentiate those policies and procedures that apply only to the municipal health department (if any) as well as those that apply to all entities of the municipal government.

   Some useful websites for the search might be:

   http://www.phac-aspc.gc.ca/publicat/ccdr-rmtc/01vol27/dr2704ea.html

   http://www.bccdc.org/category.php?item=7

   http://www.science.bio.org/bwc.news.html

Situation

Joel Walsh is the director of human resources for a municipal government. The municipality encompasses suburbs of a large city and rural areas, with a total population of about 250,000 people. After 9/11 and the subsequent anthrax scares, the municipal clerk, Mr. Kevin Reinhart, called Joel into his office to tell him that "we need to get ready for possible future attacks and not assume it couldn't happen here." More specifically, he asked Joel to update the current municipal Policies and Procedures Manual to incorporate policies and procedures addressing preparedness, detection, diagnosis, and response to bioterrorism events, including the role of the regional health authority.

Joel immediately recognized he did not have the background or information base to prepare such policies and procedures. He asked Professor Bruce Arden if one of his classes could help him develop those policies and procedures. Your group in his class has been given this assignment. Prepare Form 1, turn it in to your professor, and be prepared to report to the class if so requested.

Category	Appropriate Policies and Procedures
1. Preparedness and prevention	
2. Detection and surveillance	
3. Diagnosis of biological agents	
4. Response to bioterrorism/ communication	

Safety and Health Programs

I. *Objectives:*
   A. To familiarize you with contemporary health and safety policies and procedures.
   B. To give you an understanding of the possible gaps that may develop between health and safety policies and procedures and actual practices on the job.

II. *Out-of-Class Preparation Time:* 3 hours

III. *In-Class Time Suggested:* 45 minutes

IV. *Procedures:*
   A. You or your group of two or three students (at the option of your instructor) select one organization and obtain its policies concerning health and safety. Examples of issues covered by health and safety policies might include workplace injuries, AIDS, employee assistance programs, and smoking. The information is often contained in the employee handbook or policy manual.
   B. You or your group then interviews one person in the organization who is knowledgeable about these policies.
   C. You or your group then writes up a short report which answers the following questions:
      1. What safety and health policies/procedures currently exist? Are any changes in these policies contemplated for the near future? If so, why?
      2. What safety and health problems were the policies above designed to eliminate or minimize?
      3. To what extent do employees abide by these policies? How do employees feel about these policies? Why?
      4. Are these policies enforced and who is responsible for enforcement? If the policies are not enforced, why not?
      5. What impact does occupational health and safety legislation have on the organization?
      6. What future changes does the organization anticipate in the areas of health and safety?
   D. At the option of the instructor, you or your group reports the results of your study either (1) to the class as a whole or (2) to a small group.
   E. The reports are then turned in to the instructor.

74. INCIDENT

The Safety Problem

Belcher Manufacturing Company employs 300 workers in its main plant. One of its major product lines is compressors for air conditioners. All compressors are tested when they come off the assembly line. William Carlson was one of the employees assigned to inspect the completed compressors, using a standard testing procedure. He was 28 years old, a high-school graduate who had been employed in the compressor division for five years when he was promoted to the job of inspector.

Each inspector goes through an extensive training program where proper procedures for testing compressors are explained and demonstrated. In addition, inspectors are required to follow the detailed procedures for testing each unit specified in the company manual. The company's policies do not permit any deviations from those procedures.

Two years ago, Carlson was testing a compressor when it exploded. He was killed on the spot. The company expressed sympathy to the family but also indicated that the company had provided proper training, proper clothing, proper warnings, and proper procedures. It reiterated its commitment to employee safety and implied that the cause of the explosion was probably due to improper employee testing procedures that were neither known nor approved by the company.

The family hired an attorney to pursue a lawsuit against the company. Recently, the case was heard in court. Testimony during the trial revealed that most of the inspectors, including Carlson, had developed various "shortcuts" to reduce the time required to test each compressor. Some inspectors continued to use the shortcuts even after the fatal accident occurred. The family's lawyer argued that it was not clear that Carlson had violated procedures, but even if he had, the company had an obligation to know about the deviations and to take steps to bring inspectors back to the proper testing procedures. In addition, the lawyer argued, the company was responsible for providing training, periodically reinforcing proper procedures, and monitoring practices to assure conformity to procedures. After hearing the evidence, the jury then retired to consider a verdict and, if the company is found guilty of safety violations, to assess appropriate penalties.

Questions

1. In this particular case, was the company guilty or innocent of safety violations that resulted in the death of Carlson?
2. Irrespective of the jury's decision in this case, what should the company do now to avoid a similar incident in the future?

Retiree Health and Pension Benefits

Frank Sears was a blue-collar worker for a large Ontario-based chemical company for his entire career, and retired in 1993 at age 60. Sears felt quite secure about his situation at the time of retirement. The union had negotiated very generous extended health insurance and pension benefits for the company's retirees. His home mortgage had been paid off in 1992, so his only household expenses were property taxes, repairs, and routine maintenance.

The health and pension benefits that Sears and his wife receive have failed to keep up with inflation since 1993. They have adapted by eating out less often and postponing some needed home repairs. Since their pension benefits were not indexed to inflation, they had reconciled themselves to learning to live on less.

However, their retiree extended health insurance premiums, purchased through Sears's former employer, were a particular concern. The premiums had increased 21 percent and 26 percent, respectively, for each of the past two years. Mrs. Sears called a number of other insurance companies to determine how much it would cost to purchase this insurance on their own directly from another insurer. To her amazement, she learned that direct purchase would cost them less.

After checking with two other retired couples who were insured with the original company, she learned that both couples had switched their coverage a year ago when they found out that the original company had viewed retiree health insurance as a source of profit and had charged accordingly. Mrs. Sears promptly switched to a new insurer and felt the problem had been solved.

Yesterday, she received a letter from an executive of a company she had never heard of, indicating that his company had purchased the original company who had sold Mrs. Sears the insurance. The letter went on to say that, effective immediately, no more health or pension benefits would be paid by this company or any other firm. Mrs. Sears was no longer concerned about the health insurance benefits, since these were paid directly out-of-pocket anyway. However, their ability to pay for the health insurance was dependent upon continued lifetime pension benefits, as the collective agreement stipulated at the time of Sears's retirement.

Questions

1. Do companies have either a moral or legal obligation to honour all terms and conditions associated with an employee's retirement that were in effect at the time of that retirement? Why or why not?
2. Does the purchase of the original company by another company, or changing economic circumstances, eliminate the employer's obligation concerning retiree benefits? Why or why not?

Merit Increases

Dr. Carl Jones is chairperson of the Department of Management in the School of Business Administration at a large university in Eastern Canada. He has been a member of the department for 14 years and a full professor for 5 years. Last summer, he was asked to assume the position of chairperson after a screening committee reviewed résumés and conducted interviews with him and three other candidates.

Carl is very excited about the new challenges and has begun several innovative projects to enhance faculty research and consulting. The teaching function in the department has always been considered first-rate, while research productivity has been somewhat weaker. Carl has continued to be very productive as a scholar, publishing three articles and two book chapters and making one conference presentation over the past year. He also made considerable progress on a management text he was co-authoring. Finally, he remained active in his professional association, the Academy of Management, where he served as chair of one of the professional divisions.

The university's policy is that all salary increases are based only on merit. Carl had developed a very sophisticated performance appraisal system for his faculty members to help him quantify salary recommendations. His point system considers and weighs different items in the areas of teaching, research, and service. Teaching and research are given weights of 40 percent each and service is weighted at 20 percent. For the coming academic year, his recommended salary increases averaged 7 percent and ranged from 3 to 14 percent. Carl felt he had good documentation for all his recommendations.

Carl submitted his recommendations to Dean Edmund Smith and was pleased when all the recommendations were accepted. He then proceeded to schedule appointments to meet with each faculty member to discuss his recommendation for each individual and the reasons for the recommendation, and to develop goals for the coming year. While a few of the faculty members receiving lower increases indicated dissatisfaction with his weighting system, particularly with the emphasis on research, these meetings generally went well.

Carl then submitted his own annual report detailing his accomplishments as chair as well as his personal accomplishments. From his perspective, he felt he deserved at least a 10 percent increase, since his department had made major strides in a number of areas while the other departments had been standing still. Moreover, none of the other department chairs were professionally active on the national level, and none had published articles or textbooks in the past year. His teaching evaluations were also in the top 15 percent of faculty in the college.

Dean Smith sent letters to all the department chairs in August. Carl was shocked to learn that his salary increase was just 7 percent. Information he received through the "grapevine" indicated that all the chairs had received a

7 percent increase. He also learned from one of the other chairs that the Dean always gave the chairs equal percentage increases each year. Contrary to the official university policy, there were no distinctions based on merit.

Carl was visibly upset about what he considered to be a major inequity. He then called the Dean's secretary to schedule an appointment to discuss the situation with Dean Smith.

Questions

1. Describe the nature and causes of the compensation problem described in this incident.
2. Are "merit" salary increases always based on "merit"? Why or why not?
3. Why did Dean Smith have a policy of equal percentage salary increases for all department chairs despite the stated university policy? Are all the chairs equally meritorious?
4. How do you think Dean Smith's "merit" increases will affect Carl and his performance as department chair and faculty member? Why? What can Dean Smith do to motivate Carl if a large differential pay increase based on performance is out of the question?
5. What are the long-range benefits of a true "merit" program? What are the problems associated with the lack of such a "merit" system for department chairs?

77. INCIDENT

The Medical Leave Problem

Maura Currier has been working for ComputerTech for four years as a lead supervisor. During the past two years, Maura's mother has needed frequent medical attention for her diabetes. As an only child, Maura has helped her mother, Jane, as often as her work schedule would allow. Unfortunately, during the past two years, Jane's condition has worsened.

Maura asked the firm for, and was granted, an unpaid leave to care for her mother, in accordance with company policy (see policy in Exhibit 4.6). The agreement stated that Maura could miss work every Friday for 60 weeks, rather than take off 12 straight weeks. At the end of 60 weeks, Maura returned to work full-time, but immediately began missing work to care for her mother until all of her allotted vacation and sick leave days were exhausted. She then asked that her Friday leave be extended indefinitely, because her mother's condition remained serious and required her ongoing assistance.

The firm's Human Resource Director was uncertain what the appropriate response should be. The firm needed Maura to be at work regularly because of the increasingly heavy workload and because her job duties were critical. Also, other supervisors and employees preferred not to have to cover for her. On the other hand, Maura was an excellent supervisor and had worked four years for ComputerTech. In addition, everyone was concerned about Maura's, and her mother's, welfare and wanted to be supportive of them.

Questions

1. What are the advantages and disadvantages of extending Maura's leave?
2. If you were the Human Resource Director, would you grant Maura's request? Explain your answer.

Exhibit 4.6 *Family Medical Leave Policy*

Employees who have worked for at least one year and worked 1,250 hours during the 12-month period preceding the commencement of the leave are eligible to take up to 12 weeks of unpaid job-protected leave for one or more of the following reasons:

1. Because of the birth of a son or daughter of the employee and the need to care for such son or daughter;
2. Because of the placement of a son or daughter with the employee for adoption or foster care;
3. To care for the spouse, son, daughter, or parent of the employee, if such spouse, son, daughter, or parent has a serious health condition; or
4. Because of a serious health condition that makes the employee unable to perform the functions of the position of such employee.

Employees who wish to take advantage of this policy must fill out a Leave Request Form at least 30 days prior to the date they wish the leave to commence or as soon as possible in cases where the reason for the leave (such as sudden illness) was unforeseeable. They will be entitled to return to the same job or an equivalent position as the one they held before, and all normal benefits will be restored. Eligible employees will also be entitled to maintain benefit coverage during the period of leave to the same extent as if they had continued to work during the leave period.

The Educational Leave Problem

Rollermakers Corporation is a manufacturer of rollers used by most industrial firms to move products and packages from one location to another. For example, many delivery companies use rollers to slide packages from one area of the warehouse to another, thereby minimizing the lifting of heavy items. Coal companies use rollers underneath conveyor belts to move coal from the mine into empty coal train cars. Rollers are usually made to customer specifications rather than mass produced. Typically, customers determine the type of rollers needed with the help of design engineers or Rollermakers's sales staff.

Rollermakers's staff consists of a production crew, an inside sales force, an outside sales force, and administrative offices. The administrative offices and the inside sales force work together to process quotes, orders, and invoices in the most efficient manner possible. The inside sales force is hired using a placement firm and employees are trained internally. Administrative staff are usually hired from the same recruiting agency, with some exceptions. Purchasing managers and accounting positions are salaried and are filled through advertising and recruiters. In the recent past, the company has faced threats of racial discrimination complaints from former inside sales employees. No complaints have been filed but management has become more careful in all human resource matters.

The present purchasing manager was hired from his position at a competing company a little over a year ago. At that time, the manager was also attending an evening M.B.A. program at a local university and, as part of his compensation package, was given tuition reimbursement and time off to attend classes, with the understanding that the classes would not cause a major disruption to the daily work schedule. For the past year, this has worked well because classes do not start until 5:45 p.m.

With the new fall semester starting, two inside sales employees informed the inside sales manager of their intentions to return to college on a part-time basis. Jan, a black female, wants to continue attending university to finish a degree in accounting. She is in her third year of studies and hopes to finish within the next two years. She is scheduled to take two accounting courses in the fall semester: one with classes scheduled on Tuesday and Thursday from 11:00 a.m. until 12:20 p.m., and the other with classes scheduled on Monday, Wednesday, and Friday from 2:00 p.m. until 2:50 p.m. These are the only times the courses are offered, and the courses are required for completion of the degree. The university campus is located about five minutes from work. Jan has made it known that she will be leaving the company upon graduation. She has been with the company for 18 months and is well liked and competent. She is one of the more efficient and accurate members of the inside sales staff.

The second employee, Josephine, is a white female starting community college after achieving her high-school equivalency diploma. She would like to take classes that meet from 2:00 p.m. until 2:50 p.m. and from 3:00 p.m. until 3:50 p.m. on Monday, Wednesday, and Friday. The community college campus is located within 20 minutes of work. She plans to earn a degree or certificate in accounting and has stated that she wishes to stay with the company "for as long as they will have me." She wants to earn more money, and was told that if she obtained her degree she would be eligible to be promoted to an appropriate position. The current bookkeeper is planning on retiring in three years and Josephine has her eye on this job. Josephine is likewise well-liked by most, but not all, of the inside sales force. Her error rate on specifications and pricing of specialty work is higher than most others.

Josephine submitted her request to take the classes to the inside sales manager; she has not registered or paid for the classes. Jan had registered and paid for her classes. The schedules chosen by the employees drastically conflicted with the regular business day. Nonetheless, both employees demanded that their schedules be worked around and accommodated. They contended that the precedent set by accommodating the schedule of the purchasing manager should apply to them. Rollermakers does not currently have any formal policy regarding educational leaves. However, both employees were told when they were first hired that they were expected to be at work during business hours.

Questions

1. Should the firm allow the two inside sales people to miss work in order to attend classes? Should it pay for the tuition? Why?
2. Should the firm continue to allow the purchasing manager to attend the evening M.B.A. program and to pay his tuition?
3. Should there be a formal policy regarding educational leave or should it remain informal? If the firm decides to formalize its policy, what provisions should it contain?

The Lost Vacation Days

Ships, Inc. is a yacht-building company located on the west coast of Canada. One September afternoon, the firm made the decision to shut down operations due to an approaching storm. This was based on the forecasted arrival of storm-force winds to the area as early as noon on Wednesday. The firm's owners made the decision to close at approximately 2:00 p.m. on Tuesday afternoon, and some employees were told Tuesday by supervisors that the shutdown would occur beginning with the next morning's shift and that they were not to report to work. They were also told that the time they lost would be excused with pay.

By Tuesday evening, it was very clear that the storm would not hit the area until Thursday at the earliest. Nonetheless, the firm decided to maintain the decision to shut down on Wednesday. The emergency hotline message confirmed this information, but also said that missed time for salaried employees would be charged against each employee's vacation allocation.

By Wednesday evening, the emergency hotline message was updated to state that the shutdown would be continued through the first shift on Thursday with normal operations commencing on the second shift. The storm subsequently hit the area Thursday night (during the second shift), leaving many roads littered with branches and debris.

On Friday morning, when the employees reported for work again (many of them without electricity at their homes), they were hit with the fact that they had just lost two days of vacation—two days gone with the wind. Part-time employees had the option of using two days of their vacation allocation or taking time off without pay, but full-time employees did not have a choice—they were required to take the two days from their allocated vacation time. This action was in line with the company's policy for complete shutdowns despite what some employees had been told prior to the shutdown.

Within a few days, many people became very upset with the way the company had handled the situation and with the fact that they had just lost two vacation days for no good reason. Why did the firm close down operations so soon instead of waiting for the storm to hit? Why didn't it close down operations on Thursday, the day the storm actually did arrive? Some had already scheduled vacation time for over Thanksgiving and the Christmas holidays and now realized that they had insufficient vacation days left. Those who had already paid for their airline and cruise tickets were particularly upset. Others were offended by the fact that the firm now expected them to work uncompensated overtime to make up for the work missed.

The company's vacation policy states that full-time employees accrue vacation time based on length of service. Employees with less than five years' seniority receive one day per month, those with five to ten years' experience earn one and one-half days per month, and those with more than ten years earn two days per month. Employees have the right to carry over unused vacation time to the next year. The policy also states that, if the shipyard is shut down for any reason, the time lost by full-time employees will be taken from each person's allocated vacation time. Furthermore, the policy states that, in the event of a partial shutdown, full-time employees who report to work and are then sent home will be paid for any time missed and will not be required to take lost time from their allocated vacation time.

Questions

1. What, if anything, should the company do with regard to employees who have vacations planned later this year and now don't have enough vacation time?
2. What, if anything, should the firm do regarding the lost vacation time for all of the other employees?
3. Should the firm change its current policy that requires full-time employees to take time from their allocated vacation time whenever a shutdown occurs?

Developing a Wage Structure

I. *Objectives:*
    A. To familiarize you with how data obtained when using the point-system approach to job evaluation can be used to develop a wage structure.
    B. To give you practice in developing a wage structure.
II. *Time Required to Complete:* 1 hour or less
III. *Instructions:* Examine all of the pay data below.

Pay Grade	Job Evaluation Points	Top of Grade	Position
1	100–200	$28,000	Office Services Aide
2	201–300	$29,500	Personal Assistant
3	301–400	$33,750	Secretary
4	401–500	$36,900	Admin. Secretary

Exhibit 4.7 shows a partially completed pay structure for office staff positions. Your task is to complete the chart for pay grades 2, 3, and 4. Construct pay steps for each of the remaining pay grades based on the following guidelines for "time in service" in each pay grade (round total to nearest $10).

Pay Step Data

Entry wage = 65.5 percent of top for each pay grade

Step 1: After 1 year within the pay grade = 70 percent of top

Step 2: After 3 years within the pay grade = 75 percent of top

Step 3: After 5 years within the pay grade = 82 percent of top

Step 4: After 8 years within the pay grade = 90 percent of top

Top of grade: After 10 years within the pay grade

In addition, listed below are the names of employees in each pay grade and their current salaries. Plot each one on Exhibit 4.7. Which of the current salaries fall outside the appropriate pay grade? What action should the firm take with regard to the pay of these individuals?

Office Services Aides:

Charles Hamilton—6 years' service—paid $25,109

Mary Richardson—10 years' service—paid $26,125

Personal Assistants:

Jerry Smith—2 years' service—paid $24,625

Theresa Jones—5 years' service—paid $25,800

Secretaries:

Alicia Wadsworth—5 years' service—paid $29,475

Connie Johnston—7 years' service—paid $30,190

Velda Prescott—1 year's service—paid $26,625

Administrative Secretaries:

Gloria Lopez—3 years' service—paid $30,175

Rosemary Jensen—5 years' service—paid $32,060

Original case contributed by Steve Maurer, Old Dominion University.

Exhibit 4.7 *Pay Structure for Office Staff Positions*

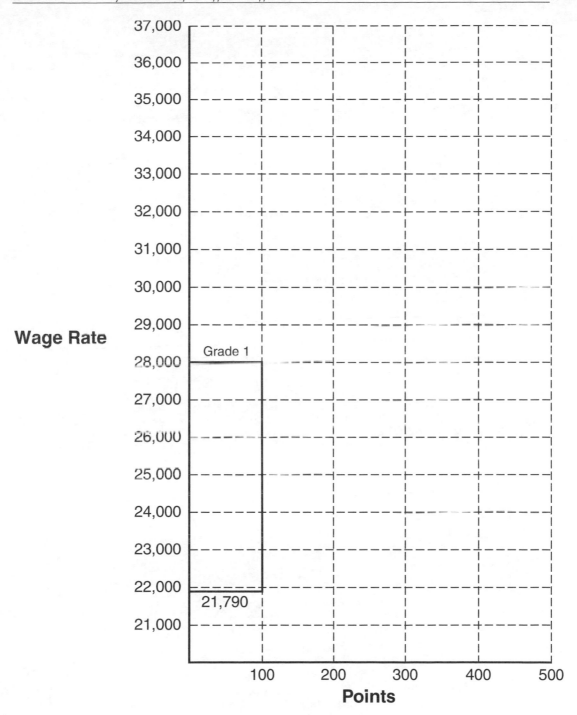

Wage Rate

Grade 1

21,790

Points

Enhancing Employee Relations: Employee Rights and Discipline, Labour Relations, and Collective Bargaining

Part 5

MOTIVATION AND DISCIPLINE

81. CASE

The Broken Employment Contract?

Arthur Wayne walked out of Sara Bell's office in shock. It was hard for him to understand what had just transpired. Bell, treasurer of EcoCare, a large insurance company, had just told Wayne of the decision to terminate his employment, and had requested his immediate resignation in return for a severance pay arrangement whereby he would continue to receive his salary for six months or until he found other employment. As he looked at the date on his watch calendar, May 7, Wayne realized that he had been hired exactly five years ago by Bell.

Bell had told Wayne that EcoCare was not satisfied with his administration of the company's employee car program and that, due to the number of complaints about the program from other employees, it was in the best interest of the company to ask for his immediate resignation. Wayne, assistant to the treasurer, had been in charge of the program for the past year. During a meeting the day before with both Bell and the vice president of operations, George Findlay, Wayne had been unable to explain why there were so many complaints about the program. One such complaint had involved a claim that someone had "set back" the odometers on several company-owned cars while the vehicles were under Wayne's control.

After his termination, Wayne requested that the decision to ask for his resignation be reviewed by the company president and by the chairperson of the EcoCare Board of Directors. Wayne felt that he had been wrongfully discharged, as he was under the impression that he had a contract for continued employment as long as his performance was satisfactory. He further maintained that his supervisor had not properly followed EcoCare's termination policies and procedures.

In preparation for the review, the president asked the director of Human Resources, Chris Miller, to investigate the facts of the situation and the events leading up to Wayne's termination.

The Human Resource Department's Investigation

In order to prepare his report for the president, Miller decided not only to review Wayne's personnel file but also to interview Wayne, Bell, and others involved in the case. Two weeks later, Miller prepared the following summary of what had been learned.

"After seven years with a local bank in Michigan, Arthur Wayne sought the assistance of an employment agency to obtain a job that would give him more opportunities for advancement. Wayne was a university graduate with a bachelor's degree in Business Administration; he also had completed 15 credit hours toward an M.B.A. degree in Finance. The employment agency referred him to our company. After several pre-employment interviews and a psychological test, Wayne was hired as an assistant to the company treasurer, Sara Bell. His duties primarily consisted of analyzing and preparing certain financial reports under the direction of Bell. Wayne came to us with excellent work experience and admirable references from his previous employers.

"According to Wayne, he felt that at the time his employment began he had a 'contract' with EcoCare that was partly oral [based on Bell's statements during the job interview] and partly written. Wayne told us that during his pre-employment interview with Bell, he had specifically asked about job security, and was told that 'as long as he did his job' he could remain with the company until he reached retirement age. He further indicated that he had been told by Bell that if he came to EcoCare he would never have to look for another job because she didn't know of anyone ever being discharged. Wayne also told us that a copy of the Supervisory Manual was handed to him during his interview with Bell. He said he specifically recalled at that time reading through the sections of the manual that pertained to discipline and termination procedures [see Appendix for relevant sections]. The manual is given to all management employees as an aid in supervising persons in their charge and not as a record of the contract terms of an employee's hiring.

"At the end of the pre-employment interview Bell made Wayne a job offer, which he accepted. Our policy has always been to discharge for 'just cause only' pursuant to the procedures described in the manual. These procedures apply to all EcoCare employees who have completed their probationary period.

"During his five years as assistant to the treasurer, Wayne received above-average performance ratings. Last year, he was given the responsibility of administering the company's employee car program. In April of this year, other employees began complaining to Bell and Findlay about Wayne's handling of the program. Wayne indicated that he had had only a brief conversation with Bell about these complaints before the meeting of May 6.

"I also spoke with Bell and Findlay about Wayne's employment and subsequent termination. According to Bell, she did tell Wayne during the interview that he would have a job as long as his performance was satisfactory. Bell told us that she made that statement based on her understanding of our company's policies, and did not intend her statement to represent a promise of a permanent job.

"Bell and Findlay report that Wayne was fired because of continued personality conflicts with other employees. They report that he was unable to work with other employees and that good interpersonal skills were an important job requirement for anyone managing the employee car program. After receiving numerous complaints about Wayne's handling of the program, they finally requested various reports and documents from him concerning the odometer discrepancies. Ultimately, they called a meeting with Wayne in an attempt to resolve the problems. During the May 6 meeting, Wayne was reported to have been defensive and insubordinate and was unable to provide satisfactory answers to their questions. At the conclusion of the meeting, they both felt that it would be in the best interest of the company if Wayne were asked to resign. Bell called Wayne into her office the next day and asked for his resignation."

APPENDIX

Excerpts from Supervisory Manual

Section IV. Disciplinary Procedures

(Note: If the unacceptable behaviour is repeated between six months and one year after the last incident of such behaviour, the last disciplinary action will be applied. If the behaviour is repeated after one year has passed without further incidents, it will be treated as a new occurrence for disciplinary purposes.)

A. All discipline shall be administered in a fair, consistent, and reasonable manner within EcoCare.

B. Whenever the work performance or personal behaviour of an employee is below departmental standards, a series of progressive, corrective steps will be taken. Before any of these steps are undertaken, however, the employee shall be counselled about his or her performance discrepancy, what he or she must do to improve the performance, and the action the supervisor will take if the performance is not corrected.

C. Within our discipline system, discipline will be given only for cause. Furthermore, the disciplinary action should fit the problem it is intended to correct.

D. All disciplinary action should be duly documented and reported by the supervisor on Form 29B. The form also requires the employee's signature.

E. The following series of steps shall be followed in administering discipline within EcoCare:

1. Oral Warning: Supervisor should discuss the unacceptable behaviour with the employee and document the discussion by completing Section A of Form 29B and obtaining the employee's signature.

2. Written Warning: A written warning should be issued if the unacceptable behaviour continues. The supervisor completes Section B of Form 29B and gives the employee the blue copy. The Human Resource Department receives the canary copy.

3. Suspension: If the employee's behaviour continues uncorrected, the employee shall be suspended for a given time without pay. Normally, suspension should not exceed five working days. Supervisors should consult with their immediate supervisor and the Human Resource Department before implementing this action. The supervisor shall complete Section C of Form 29B and also include the date the employee should return to work.

4. Discharge: If the employee's behaviour is not corrected, the employee shall be terminated. Due to the serious nature of termination, it is recommended that the supervisor review the case with both his or her immediate supervisor and the Human Resource Department before discharging the employee. Examples of reasons for termination without prior corrective discipline are covered in Section V. Note, however, that in such cases the employee should first be suspended according to the following procedures:

Suspension Pending Discharge: (This paragraph applies to all proposed discharges except those that are a result of application of the normal disciplinary procedures.)

   a. When an employee's misconduct warrants immediate discharge under Section V, the employee should be first suspended without pay.
   b. At the time of suspension, the employee should be informed by the supervisor to leave the premises and that he or she will be notified if and when he or she is to return to work.
   c. The supervisor should document the suspension by completing an Employee Discipline Report. The supervisor should consult with the Human Resource Department to determine the appropriate course of action.

Section V. Termination

(Reasons for immediate termination.)

1. Misconduct, such as fighting, gambling, or use of profane or abusive language toward others.
2. Furnishing proprietary company information to unauthorized agents or persons.
3. Refusal to obey direct orders from the immediate supervisor (insubordination).
4. Willful damage of company property.
5. Failure to contact supervisor or manager during three successive working days of absence.
6. Engaging in a business likely to conflict with the business of the company, without prior permission.
7. Dishonesty, including falsification of employee's own or others' time cards, company records, or employment applications.
8. Illegal use or possession of alcohol and/or drugs.
9. Reporting to work or engaging in company business under the influence of alcohol or drugs.

Questions

1. Did Wayne have an employment contract, either oral or written, with EcoCare? Why or why not?
2. What problems, if any, do you see with EcoCare's pre-employment process?
3. Can an employer's written human resource policies ever be construed as a contract between an employer and an employee?
4. Was Wayne terminated for "just cause"? Why or why not?
5. How can companies protect themselves against lawsuits alleging wrongful dismissal?

The Broken Employment Contract? **Case 81**

The Drug Testing Problem at Standard Chemical

Standard Chemical Company's Processing Division processes volatile, toxic chemicals that are sold for commercial use. The division has 500 employees. Approximately half are unionized, represented by a local of the International Association of Machinists and Aerospace Workers. Safety is a critical issue at the plant because of the potential for environmental hazards resulting from accidents.

Vicky Jacobson, Human Resource Manager, had attended a seminar on drug abuse in the work force and was concerned that some of the job-related accidents in the Processing Division might be drug-related. As a result of Jacobson's concerns and the concerns of management at the other plants, the company decided to implement an Alcohol and Drug Abuse Prevention Program.

Notification of the new program was sent to the president of the union local. When Jacobson met with union representatives at the plant, she found little opposition to the policy. However, there was concern about how the policy would be enforced. Bob James, the union's business agent, was concerned that the policy would be used by supervisors as a witch hunt to get rid of people they did not like. Jacobson assured him that there would be checks and balances so that the program would be administered even-handedly. She further assured the union that the emphasis would be on rehabilitation, not termination.

Employees' Notification about the Program

The program was presented to employees during a series of group meetings. Jacobson read the following prepared statement at each meeting to be certain that the policy was presented uniformly to all employees:

> Standard Chemical is implementing a company-wide Alcohol and Drug Abuse Prevention Program effective January 1, 2005. We do not believe we have a serious problem with drug or alcohol abuse at Standard. However, we are committed to maintaining high standards of job performance and to protecting the safety of our employees, our community, and our environment. Therefore, we have implemented a policy that will significantly reduce the possibility that our employees or our environment might be harmed through alcohol or drug use by any individual employed at Standard Chemical. Please familiarize yourself with the policy as described to you in the brochure.

Brochures were distributed to each employee at the group meetings (see Exhibit 5.1 for a description of the brochure's contents).

Suspension under the Program

While the policy has been in effect, Jacobson has, in practice, enforced the policy by suspending employees when there was reasonable suspicion of drug use. Suspended employees were given three options regarding drug testing:

1. Refusing to undergo a drug test, which resulted in immediate termination.

2. Taking the drug test. If the drug test was negative, back pay was awarded for the time on suspension. If the drug test was positive, the employee was given the opportunity to participate in the Employee Assistance Program (EAP).

3. Enrolling directly in the EAP's drug and alcohol program in lieu of submitting to a drug test.

On March 7, Jacobson was in her office when John Martin, the company's security guard, asked to speak to her. "Ms. Jacobson, I thought I better report this to you. The forklift driver on the last shift must have been out of it when he parked that machine. The blade was driven through the crack between the concrete floor and the outer steel wall. The next shift driver is out there and he's having a heck of a time getting it out." The guard also told Jacobson that other employees had commented, "It was probably that 'pothead' Peter Carpenter."

When Jacobson and the guard walked over to where the forklift was parked, she noticed that the lower portion of the steel wall had buckled. During that day, she talked to several employees who had information about the accident. She discovered that Peter Carpenter was the driver of the forklift and that he had been seen driving the lift too fast around the corner at the end of his shift. Carpenter had worked for Standard Chemical for five and a half years.

Jacobson met with Carpenter, his supervisors, and union representatives and questioned him about the forklift accident. According to Jacobson, the following conversation took place:

"Look, Ms. Jacobson, I admit that I parked that forklift there, but I had no idea I had parked so close to the wall."

Jacobson responded, "Mr. Carpenter, I have worked in this plant for 23 years and have seen my share of accidents. The blade of the forklift was wedged in the crack between the wall and the floor with enough force to buckle the steel wall. In my opinion, this accident is evidence enough for reasonable suspicion of drug or alcohol abuse."

After talking to Carpenter's supervisors and conferring with the plant manager, Jacobson met again with Carpenter and told him, "Mr. Carpenter, you are suspended effective immediately, based on reasonable suspicion of drug or alcohol use on the job. Company policy requires that you submit to a drug test or be terminated, effective immediately. If your drug test is negative, you will be paid for the time of your suspension. If it is positive, then you must enroll in the Employee Assistance Program and demonstrate a sincere commitment to the treatment program. You do have the option of enrolling directly into the EAP's alcohol and drug program. If you choose that option, you can forego the drug test at this time."

"Ms. Jacobson, I'd like to go ahead and get some help. I'll go on and get started with the EAP," replied Carpenter.

The Drug Testing Problem at Standard Chemical **Case 82**

In Jacobson's presence, Carpenter then signed the company's EAP consent form, which included the following statement:

> If I fail to meet my obligation to the EAP program, I will be subject to disciplinary action, including termination of employment.

After he signed the form, Jacobson telephoned the EAP (conducted by a local treatment facility for individuals with substance abuse problems). Carpenter was given an appointment to meet with a counsellor the next evening, March 8.

Carpenter kept his scheduled appointment. During that first meeting with the counsellor at the facility, he signed a Release of Information form authorizing the EAP to release information about his participation in the program, including keeping appointments, following EAP suggestions, and reporting to the designated lab for drug testing. He refused to give the EAP counsellor permission to release the results of his drug tests to Standard Chemical.

Report from the Counsellor

Robert Johnson, the EAP counsellor, telephoned Jacobson to confirm that Carpenter had kept his appointment and explained that he had not given permission for the EAP to disclose results of the drug testing. Johnson also recommended that Carpenter be allowed to return to work while attending counselling sessions on an outpatient basis.

On March 13, Jacobson sent Carpenter a letter stating that his discharge was "held in abeyance" while he received counselling sessions. The letter further stated that Carpenter must attend counselling sessions, follow the guidelines of the program, and submit to urine testing if instructed to do so by his EAP counsellor. The letter also included the following statement:

> Any incident in the future that would indicate failure to comply with the EAP program will result in disciplinary action up to and including termination of employment.

Carpenter attended EAP sessions regularly for the next eight weeks. Reports to Jacobson from his supervisors during that time period were extremely positive. His job performance was excellent and he had no safety violations.

On May 9, Johnson, the EAP counsellor, called Sarah Green, the plant nurse, to discuss several EAP-related matters. They specifically discussed Carpenter's case because of the counsellor's concerns about Carpenter. He noted that while Carpenter had attended every session and his supervisors reported that he had been an exemplary employee, his lab tests showed ascending levels of cannabinoids (marijuana metabolites). Johnson intimated that he was not sure that the EAP counselling sessions would be successful.

Green called Jacobson and reported that Carpenter's lab reports were positive. Jacobson telephoned Johnson and confirmed what had been said to Green, the plant nurse. She also telephoned the company's medical department and was told that cannabinoids normally stay in a person's system for 35–45 days.

Later that same day, Jacobson met with Carpenter and the union representatives and confronted him with the information she had received about his drug tests. Carpenter argued with Jacobson and said that he did not understand why she was questioning him. He told her that he had attended every counselling session and felt like the sessions were helping him. Carpenter told her that his performance and his safety record had been great since he started the program. Carpenter further told her that he knew that his supervisors had reported his excellent work record to her. He also told her that he had stopped smoking marijuana. Jacobson then asked him to submit to a urine sample test. She told him that if he refused he would be terminated in compliance with company policy. Carpenter agreed to take the drug tests.*

On May 17, the lab reported that the results of both drug tests were positive. Later that same day, Jacobson met with Carpenter and informed him that he was fired. Carpenter immediately filed a grievance.

On May 26, the union recommended that Carpenter take another drug test. Standard Chemical agreed to take the results into consideration. Later that same day, Carpenter took the drug test.

On May 30, Standard Chemical received the lab report. Carpenter had tested negative for cannabinoids.

On June 21 and July 12, Carpenter's drug tests were again negative for cannabinoids. Ten months later, Carpenter took another drug test that was also negative.

Questions

1. Was Carpenter's suspension justified?
2. Was Carpenter's termination justified?
3. Evaluate the adequacy of the company's drug and alcohol abuse policy. Are there any components that need improvement?
4. Were Carpenter's privacy rights protected?

*The company uses two tests: the enzyme multiplied immunoassay technique (EMIT) and gas chromatography/mass spectrometry.

Original case contributed by Dr. Susan Corriher.

Exhibit 5.1 *Excerpt from the Brochure Given to Employees during the Group Meetings*

Standard Chemical Alcohol and Drug Abuse Prevention Policy
1. Use or abuse of any substance that may have an adverse effect on job performance or safety is a violation of Company policy.
2. Reporting to work or working while under the influence of alcohol or unauthorized drugs is a violation of Company policy.
3. Unauthorized drugs are any drugs that cannot be obtained legally or have been illegally obtained. Prescription drugs obtained without a prescription, or over-the-counter drugs used other than as instructed, are considered to be unauthorized drugs.
4. Drug testing is required as a condition of employment when there is reasonable suspicion of drug or alcohol use.
5. Reasonable suspicion is a basis for drug testing when, in the opinion of management, a job-related accident may have been caused by human error that may be drug- or alcohol-related.
6. Employees who test positive may, if circumstances warrant, be permitted to continue employment provided they agree to undergo periodic drug/alcohol screening and participate in the Company-approved Employee Assistance Program (EAP).

The Drug Testing Problem at Standard Chemical **Case 82**

Violence at Work: Westside Clinic

Maryanne Walker arrived at work relaxed and refreshed from her two-week vacation in Florida. Maryanne was director of pharmacy services at Westside Clinic, and the first item on her calendar was a regularly scheduled total quality management meeting with the four supervisors who reported directly to her. The meeting covered routine business matters, and normal progress reports on projects were presented. However, Maryanne was very disturbed by what was discussed at the close of the meeting.

Rhonda Carter reported that one pharmacy technician, Susan Miller, had allegedly assaulted another, Brenda Lawson, in the receiving area of the clinic pharmacy. Neither of the technicians reported the incident, and there were no witnesses; Rhonda only learned of the altercation from another employee. Maryanne stressed her desire to be kept informed on all matters and her complete confidence in an open communication system on which total quality management was based. Maryanne asked Rhonda why she did not view the event as important enough to contact her during her vacation. Rhonda reported that the episode had not occurred during her vacation but six weeks earlier. Maryanne was perplexed to find out that something that had happened six weeks ago was just being brought to her attention.

Maryanne had dealt with problems of job performance but had never faced staff problems unrelated to performance. It never occurred to her that physical fighting would be a problem in a pharmacy whose work force was predominately women. Upon returning to her office, Maryanne received the following memo from her supervisor, Nancy Smith:

"While you were away, I was made aware that Susan Miller grabbed Brenda Lawson by the shoulders, shoved her against a partition, and perhaps drew her fist back as if to hit her. I suggest that you do further research into this matter. Dependent upon the outcome of the investigation, the appropriate responses could range from ignoring the incident as hearsay or gossip to termination. This is not the way I would wish for your week to start but I really need to talk to you as soon as possible."

As Maryanne's boss had already learned of the incident, some action must be taken.

Background

Westside Clinic was a primary-care facility with a roster of 25 full-time doctors serving approximately 800 patients, including "walk-ins". Many of the patients, after being seen by a doctor, would be referred to specialists or to other practitioners for further diagnosis or treatment. Most of the "walk-in" patients had immediate and relatively minor problems that could be treated either in the clinic itself or with a round of prescription medication.

Maryanne directed the clinic's pharmacy services. There were 15 employees in pharmacy services (9 pharmacists [5 full-time and 4 part-time],

4 technicians, 1 secretary, and 1 records clerk). All of the employees except for one pharmacist were female.

Both of the employees (Susan and Brenda) involved in the altercation were pharmacy technicians. While licensed pharmacists were required by law to fill prescriptions, pharmacy technicians did most of the routine work. Pharmacists checked the orders to ensure there would be no harmful drug interactions and then passed the prescriptions to the technicians to fill. The technicians printed out a label, filled the prescription, and returned the orders to the pharmacist to check for accuracy such as the correct drug or dosage. The technicians then delivered the medication to the prescribing doctor or directly to the patient in the clinic reception area. The work was continuous and very fast-paced. However, pharmacy technician jobs were seen as very desirable since the starting pay was over $10 per hour and did not require extensive education. Due to the unrelenting work pace and stress, and perhaps due to the unfulfilling nature of the job, the annual turnover rate among technicians was 50 percent.

Rhonda was the supervising technician to whom Brenda and Susan directly reported. Part of Brenda's job was to handle receiving in the pharmacy. In receiving, deliveries were accepted, orders were processed after receipt from the manufacturers, shipping documents were checked for accuracy, and drugs were placed in storage for inventory and tracked in inventory for expiration dates. Drugs were delivered in bulk from manufacturers, and technicians re-packed them into unit doses. The work pace in receiving was much less hectic than in the main pharmacy.

Maryanne had been the director of the Pharmacy Services department for two years, and this was her first management position. She was trained as a clinical pharmacist, and her educational background included a two-year diploma in liberal arts, a B.A. in Sociology, a Bachelor of Pharmacy, and a Pharmacy doctorate. In addition, Maryanne had been a clinical pharmacist and associate director of a Pharmacy Services department at a major hospital for two years before joining Westside. Maryanne had earned the reputation throughout Westside as "a good boss." However, none of her pharmacy education or training had prepared her to face this dilemma.

The Incident

Following the total quality management meeting, Maryanne initiated an investigation of the incident between Susan and Brenda. Maryanne interviewed the supervisor, Rhonda, and both Susan and Brenda. Maryanne also gathered all the pertinent policies from human resources management such as the Standards of Behaviour and Corrective Action (see Exhibits 5.2 and 5.3). Maryanne kept copious notes and recorded the following interviews.

Interview with Rhonda, Inventory Supervisor

"On October 20, the day of the altercation, Susan and Brenda were working alone in the receiving department of the pharmacy. Brenda was training Susan to operate the packing equipment that re-packed bulk drugs into unit doses.

"Susan is 28 years old, has been at Westside for one year, and is somewhat of a 'misfit.' Although her job performance is fine, her attitude has caused problems. Susan works hard to complete her assignments on time and is extremely organized. Although Susan is articulate and her written communication skills are excellent, she seems to have difficulty dealing with ambiguity. For example, two technicians showed Susan two different ways to do a task. Susan did not seem to understand how the same job could be done two different ways. She voiced her aggravation by calling both the job and the people doing it 'stupid.' She huffed, puffed, and shoved things around, and she always seemed to be mad. As a result, she was not as careful as she should have been and injured herself twice.

"Susan seemed obsessed with organization. If things were not organized just the way she thought they should be, she became frustrated. There were a few times when she returned to work a few hours after her scheduled shift to work on organizing things such as our filing system, emergency boxes, or narcotic forms. Sometimes she came in on her days off to reorganize the work area. I finally stopped her from coming in at unauthorized times. As she caused problems for the other employees, I formally warned her about working unauthorized overtime. One Sunday afternoon, Susan made some changes to the inventory control computer program. She thought that she was making it better, but it took the Management Information Systems Department three days to fix the program.

"Last year, there was an incident when Susan lost her temper, yelled at another employee, threw a pencil across the room, and then ran out of the pharmacy. Later, her supervisor found her curled up in a ball on the couch in the hallway leading to the main entrance of the pharmacy. Susan blamed her actions on the stress of the job and said that she had been diagnosed as suffering from clinical depression. She took both Prozac and Klonopin, and she was in counselling for her depression. Those antidepressant drugs have side effects such as erratic behaviour. Some of the other employees were really afraid of Susan because of her severe mood swings.

"Actually, Susan was overqualified for this job. The mental challenges of the pharmacy technician job under-utilized her abilities. No wonder she was frustrated. I recall that Susan was hired during a period of high turnover and turmoil in the pharmacy. Her boyfriend worked here as a computer programmer in Management Information Systems. He talked to me incessantly about Susan and her qualifications. Every day, he asked me if there were any openings. He told me that Susan was a displaced worker who had been re-engineered out of her job as an assistant curator at a museum. Susan had a B.A. in Archeology and had done some graduate work. She had also completed the three-month pharmacy technician certification program at the local community college. Perhaps we did not do as thorough a background check on Susan as we normally do. Quite frankly, we have not had many college graduates apply for these positions. Because of Susan's education and background, we thought she would have no problems handling the job. Later, there were rumours that reengineering was not the real cause of Susan's job loss at the museum. Some speculated that Susan was asked to leave the museum after a series of threatening confrontations with other employees on a dinosaur dig in Alberta.

"Brenda is a pharmacy technician employed at Westside for 18 months and trained on the job. She is a 25-year-old high school graduate. Her previous work experience consists of clerical jobs such as store sales clerk and cashier, and she is married to an assembly-line worker at a manufacturing plant.

"Brenda is a good employee. I would call her a steady and consistent performer and not a problem employee at all. However, Brenda had a habit of frequently checking to ask if her performance was satisfactory. Although I found this habit a little annoying, I shrugged it off as a need for approval. Brenda had a baby who died suddenly a few months ago. The baby had not been sick and died while Brenda held her in her arms. Brenda accepted the death as a sign that she was not destined to be a mother. This seemed to be a fatalistic attitude, and perhaps Brenda did not report the argument with Susan for similar reasons. I heard about the incident through the grapevine from another pharmacy technician who was unsure about exactly what happened. Only after making several inquiries did Brenda tell the story."

Interview with Brenda

"On October 20, I started work at 11:30 a.m. Susan mentioned that she was going to be off the week of Halloween (October 26 to November 2). She taunted me that she had switched her work schedule easily, with little notice. She knew that I had asked for the Friday after Halloween off six weeks in advance and I was refused. I was upset and said, 'You can do anything, you punch in when you want, you leave when you want, and you make personal phone calls when you want.' I suppose Susan losing that good job at the museum and not being able to find a similar job was difficult. In fact, I know she was seeing a psychiatrist. Susan then said, 'I'm sick and tired of everyone treating me like an alcoholic, like I'm incompetent.' I said, 'Susan, watch your mouth.' Susan pushed me against a partition wall, held my left shoulder against the wall, and drew back her right fist in a posture to strike me. Then I said, 'Susan, if it's going to make you feel better, go ahead and hit me.' Susan ran out the back door of the pharmacy and came back about 20 minutes later. Susan said, 'Don't worry, I'd never hit you.'

"Three weeks later, a pharmacist reprimanded Susan about some pills that she had packed incorrectly and also questioned the higher-than-average inventory count of crushed and unusable pills (Prozac). Susan grew angry and glared at me and said, 'Why didn't you tell me about the problem with the pills? Are you afraid of me?' I said, 'No Susan, I'm not afraid of you, but I am afraid to say anything to you because you take everything too personally and are too easily upset.' I also knew that Prozac was the same drug that Susan kept popping in her mouth at work.

"Susan told me she had spoken with Rhonda, our supervisor, about our argument over work schedules. I said, 'Did you tell her that you shoved me and were going to hit me?' Susan said, 'No, I told her you were upset about scheduling time off.' I asked her, 'Why not tell Rhonda about the shove?' and Susan said, 'Because I really need this job.' I looked at her and said, 'I guess if I shoved someone and was going to hit them, I wouldn't tell either.'

"About a week later, Rhonda and I were leaving work. I could sense that Rhonda had heard of my trouble with Susan. Rhonda asked me if I was tired. I said, 'No, I'm just disgusted with Susan,' and then told her about the assault. Rhonda asked me why I hadn't said anything earlier, and I said, 'I was willing to accept the situation and give Susan the benefit of the doubt. I was taught to handle my own problems and never to tell on others. However, Susan tried to intimidate me by asking if I was afraid of her! After that, I figure the situation is going to degenerate, so I've decided to report the incident.' Rhonda thanked me and said she would take care of the situation."

Interview with Susan

"Because of personal reasons, I had requested four days off between October 26 and November 2. When my request was approved, I told Brenda about it. It was not out of the ordinary for us to discuss scheduling changes since our working schedules could almost be described as a time-sharing situation. As part-time employees, we split a 40-hour work week. Upon hearing of my scheduling change, Brenda became very agitated over the possibility that my schedule change might interfere with her plans to be off on one of the days I would be gone. I told her that I had talked to our supervisor, Rhonda Carter, and had been assured that both of our absences on that day would not pose any problems for the receiving department. My assurances did not satisfy Brenda. She became very agitated, and suggested that special favours were granted to me. Brenda contended that I was a 'favoured employee' while she was being singled out for unfair treatment.

"After several attempts to calm her and defend myself against charges of favouritism, I grasped Brenda by the shoulders, looked her in the eyes, and asked her to calm down and be reasonable. Brenda was unresponsive to this gesture and her agitation was not abated. I certainly do not think my gesture was threatening. My intent was to calm Brenda and to reassure her. As friends, I did not view this act as inappropriate. I decided that the best thing for me to do was to leave the pharmacy and go on to lunch. So that's what I did.

"On the days we worked together following this incident, our relationship returned to normal, and I was unaware of any problem between the two of us. In fact, Brenda told Rhonda that she did not report the incident because 'it didn't seem like a big deal.' I really don't know what all the fuss is about; Brenda and I are friends!"

Conclusions

Following the interviews and the collection of relevant policies, Maryanne must decide on a course of action (see Exhibits 5.2 and 5.3). She scheduled a meeting with her supervisor, Nancy, for the next morning. Maryanne continued to be perplexed that the total quality management and open communication had not prevented this altercation. In addition, Maryanne was burdened with knowledge, which had not been publicly released, that Westside was planning a downsizing because of decreases in patient numbers. Maryanne thought about the workers who would be displaced by the downsizing. She wondered whether the employees would be able to find suitable employment or whether they would become "misfits."

Questions

1. If you were Maryanne, what actions would you take and why?
2. In light of this incident, should Westside change any of its "Standards of Behaviour" policies or "Corrective Action" policies? Explain.
3. How can Westside prevent future incidents of workplace violence?

Original case contributed by I.E. Jernigan and Joyce M. Beggs, University of North Carolina at Charlotte.

Exhibit 5.2 *Standards of Behaviour Policies at Westside Clinic*

The following are types of behaviour that could result in disciplinary action up to and including dismissal. This list is not all-inclusive.

1. Falsification or omission of facts on application for employment or any Westside Clinic records.
2. Giving out information of a confidential nature to unauthorized persons.
3. Altering work records or time cards.
4. Falsifying work records or time cards of another employee.
5. Insubordination or refusal to perform a work shift or assigned job.
6. Failure to perform work or assigned jobs.
7. Reporting to work unfit to assume assigned duties.
8. The sale, purchase, transfer, use, or possession of illegal drugs, or the misuse of prescription, over-the-counter drugs, or alcohol, and/or working under the influence of such.
9. Possession or use of firearms, weapons, or explosives on the premises without authorization.
10. Unauthorized removal of Clinic property, property of other employees, patients, or visitors from the premises.
11. Theft of services (e.g., telephone, parking).
12. Abuse, mistreatment, or improper care of patients.
13. Fighting or attempting to injure another person on the premises.
14. Conducting or participating in unlawful games of chance on the premises.
15. Making statements of a defamatory nature about other employees, patients, or the company.
16. Violation of the solicitation policy.
17. Sleeping on the job.
18. Excessive absenteeism.
19. Altering scheduled work shift without authorization.
20. Failure to report absences in accordance with established procedure.
21. Unsatisfactory job performance.
22. Use of threatening or abusive language toward patients, visitors, or other employees.
23. Violation of policies and procedures.

Exhibit 5.3 *Corrective Action Policies at Westside Clinic*

In order to provide continuous and efficient operation and to maintain acceptable employee behaviour, the Clinic has developed a system of corrective action. The system provides the employee with the opportunity to correct behaviour when minor violations have occurred. Minor violations may result in a verbal or written reprimand. Serious or repeated violations may result in written reprimand or suspension. Repeated violations that were not corrected previously, or more serious violations, may result in termination.

The system of corrective action is not necessarily a progressive one. The corrective action may vary depending on the nature, frequency, and gravity of the offence and on the employee's past record. The Clinic reserves the right to discharge an employee without prior warning when such action is considered to be in the best interest of the Clinic.

The corrective actions consist of: verbal counselling, written counselling, written reprimand, special review, suspension, and dismissal.

Verbal Counselling

Verbal counselling is an initial discussion between the employee and department management to address a performance deficiency or disciplinary problem of a minor degree of seriousness.

Written Counselling

Written counselling is a written record of a discussion between an employee and department management to address minor performance or disciplinary offences that have persisted despite verbal counselling, or as an initial corrective measure for more serious offences. The written counselling is also used to raise an employee's awareness of performance deficiencies.

Written Reprimand

A written reprimand is a strong, written expression of management's disapproval concerning an employee's conduct or performance. It is intended to address serious disciplinary problems or repeated minor offences.

Special Review

A special review is a period of time, usually 60 days, for close monitoring of an employee's conduct and performance, with opportunities for interaction with management to discuss problems and assist the employee to overcome deficiencies. Repeated sub-standard performance, violations of rules and regulations, or a return to work following a disciplinary suspension are situations that warrant special review. During this period, the employee is ineligible to bid on open positions or receive a wage or salary increase. At the end of the special review period, an employee may be returned to regular status if the problem is corrected, have the special review extended, or be dismissed if the deficiencies have not been corrected.

Suspension

Suspension is a management-imposed absence from work without pay following a serious or repeated violation. Suspended employees are ineligible to apply for vacant positions or to receive wage or salary increases.

Dismissal

Dismissal is a management-imposed and authorized separation from employment at the Clinic.

All forms of written corrective action are placed in the employee's personnel file. The signing of the approved Record of Employee Conference Form indicates only that the document has been read. An employee has the right to place written comments on the form. An eligible employee who disagrees with a written corrective action may employ the formal grievance procedure.

Surfing the Internet on Company Time

Helen Barnett was shocked by what she was seeing on the computer screen at the desk of James Erskine: a picture depicting a sexual act! The picture appeared on a porn website that James had evidently visited. Helen supervises 15 customer service representatives for Standard Insurance, a company specializing in home insurance. The job of a customer service representative is to assist clients with claims, insurance quotes, and other queries. Each customer service representative works in a cubicle furnished with a computer, a desk, and a phone headset. Only Helen has a personal office. Standard Insurance prides itself on its efforts to make greater use of electronic technology in servicing its clients. Quotes for insurance and even samples of policies are often sent to clients via computer. Most of the information representatives need to answer customer queries is easily found on the company's intranet.

James had been employed with Standard Insurance for the last six months. His 90-day performance review had been satisfactory. Lorraine Smalls, a coworker who sat in a cubicle close to James, had inadvertently discovered the pornographic picture. When Lorraine's computer malfunctioned, Lorraine had gone to James's cubicle to quickly retrieve some data to respond to a customer's query. It was not unusual for representatives to use each other's computers. James was out to lunch and his computer was in standby mode. When Lorraine hit the Enter key, the picture appeared and its graphic nature disturbed her. She immediately called Helen over to the workstation. When Helen checked James's browser, it seemed that James had visited the website more than a dozen times that morning. She felt that she needed to confront him about using company time in such an unproductive manner.

When James returned from lunch, Helen confronted him and told him about her discovery. James was irate. He told her that he had visited the site on his "break time," not company time. Furthermore, he felt that it was an invasion of his privacy for a coworker and Helen to gain access to his computer. Helen told James she had no recourse but to report his behaviour to the human resource manager. After he left Helen's office, James himself went to the human resource manager, Dale Gibbons. James believed that the supervisor's actions violated his constitutional right to privacy. Gibbons told James, "Even though the company does not have a written policy prohibiting visiting websites, all employees are expected to use their computers for work-related purposes. Unnecessary surfing ties up our ISDN line capacity and could affect the speed of service delivery. In addition, you exposed two of your fellow employees to pornography." He then went on to say, "Standard Insurance operates on a trust basis in all its relationships with employees."

Two days later, James was suspended for using the company's computer system for non-productive, personal purposes. When he received his suspension notification, James told Gibbons that he "would sue Standard Insurance" for violating his right to privacy. He also told Gibbons that he knew of many other employees who "surfed" the Internet and used company e-mail for personal purposes.

Questions

1. Did Helen's actions invade James's right to privacy?
2. Was the company justified in suspending James?
3. What should be the key elements of an employee computer and web use policy?

85. INCIDENT

Can He Wear an Earring at Work?

Peter Wood was hired as a personal services representative at a branch of South Town Bank, a small bank branch of a financial institution that had served South Town for over 30 years. The branch had a reputation for being one of the more conservative places of employment in town. Because it offered good wages and benefits, the branch had no problems finding employees.

Personal service representatives sit at desks in the wood-panelled bank lobby to assist customers with account queries and other problems. All bank personnel were required to dress according to company rules. Men were expected to wear dress shirts and ties, while women were required to wear dresses or skirts. It was only recently that the bank had instituted "Casual Friday" on the last Friday of each month. On that Friday, employees could wear business casual clothes. Men could wear golf shirts or other shirts with collars. Women could wear slacks with appropriate blouses and/or sweaters. No jeans, shorts, halter tops, or T-shirts were allowed. Employees with tattoos were required to wear clothes that covered their tattoos.

When Peter reported for his first day of work at the branch, he came dressed appropriately in a shirt and tie. However, he also had a discreet but noticeable gold loop earring in his left earlobe. When the branch manager saw Peter wearing the earring, he told Peter to remove the earring since it was not consistent with the bank's employee dress policy. Peter became upset and pointed out that no one had told him during the employment interview that he could not wear an earring to work. The branch manager pointed out that if Peter had worn the earring during the job interview, he probably would not have been hired. He further stated that because of the earring, Peter did not present the professional image the bank desired for its personal service representatives. Peter pointed out that female personal service representatives were allowed to wear earrings at work. The branch manager said it was customary in society for women to wear earrings but not men. He again asked Peter to remove the earring. When Peter refused, he was fired.

Peter felt that he had been wrongfully dismissed and vowed that he would take legal action. In the employee handbook, there was the following reference to the wearing of earrings: "Visible jewellery must be small and tasteful as determined by management. Jewellery must not interfere with job performance."

Questions

1. Is Peter a victim of discrimination?
2. Evaluate the branch manager's comment that Peter would not have been hired had he worn the earring during the employment interview.
3. Evaluate South Town's dress policy. Is it clear? Is it appropriate? Is it legal?

Spiked Milk

A reputable construction company employs six experienced construction supervisors for its various construction jobs. These supervisors have the overall responsibility of hiring and firing employees and seeing that the construction proceeds as close to time and cost schedules as possible. They also have the responsibility for overall quality control of the construction job.

Larry Werst, age 55, has been a supervisor for this company for many years. He is never absent and has established a reputation for getting the job done right and close to schedule. He has supervised the construction of several prominent buildings and is now supervising the construction of a condominium development. Larry's approach to handling his employees is firm and sometimes harsh. He doesn't take any back talk, and everyone who works for him usually earns his or her pay or isn't on the job for very long.

The owner and manager of the company had become concerned about Larry, because rumours implied that he was an alcoholic and that he drank on the job. The owner knew that Larry drank a lot and had a stormy home life, but he didn't know whether Larry was drinking on the job.

One day, the manager was talking with Larry and noticed a definite bad breath odour that smelled quite alcoholic. This happened again on several occasions. Office and storeroom employees also noticed the odour when they talked to Larry. Also, the storeroom clerk noticed that almost every day Larry would come in, buy two soft drinks at a time, and then take off in his company truck, presumably back to his job site.

The manager decided to talk to Larry about this subject. When he confronted Larry with the rumours, the bad breath, and the continued purchases of two soft drinks at a time, Larry denied that he was drinking. He said that the rumours were just that, and that the two soft drinks were for himself and his carpenter supervisor. The manager told him that he would have to let him go if he were ever caught drinking on the job. He reminded Larry that the firm's progressive discipline system included a rule that states: "No employee is permitted to go on duty or remain on duty if he or she possesses, is under the influence of, or is consuming an alcoholic beverage. Violation of this policy will result in dismissal."

About a year later, when the construction season was again in full swing, stories began floating around about Larry's drinking. The employees on his job talked about the quart of milk he drank every day. They wondered why he had started drinking so much of it lately, and wondered if he "spiked" it and used it to combat his odorous breath. Sometimes his speech seemed definitely slurred, but Larry was gravel-voiced and had sloppy speech habits anyway. The workers also were amused by the stories he'd tell about things that had happened to him. They were just stories, of course, but lately they were getting pathetically farfetched and made no sense at all.

The manager couldn't help finding out some of the things that were being said about Larry, and he wondered what he should do. Larry had never actually been caught drinking. The construction job he was supervising was proceeding satisfactorily, but it was a little behind schedule due to the inability to get good carpenters and labourers at the beginning of the construction season. Worker turnover was perhaps a little higher on this job than on average.

Questions

1. What course of action should the manager follow? Why?
2. To what extent should the manager go to try to catch Larry drinking on the job?
3. What action, if any, should the manager take if Larry confesses to being an alcoholic?
4. Does the manager presently have sufficient proof that Larry is working under the influence of alcohol?
5. Critique the firm's alcoholism rule.

Original case contributed by Arno F. Knapper, School of Business, The University of Kansas.

Motivating and Maintaining Morale during Downsizing

The Rutledge Company is an organization involved in the retail industry, operating more than 100 retail stores. The company's headquarters is going through what is termed "modernization." A new management information system is being implemented that will completely alter the way the firm does business. It will also affect the amount of staffing required by the company. The rollout of the new system began last year, and it is projected that at least another year will be required before the rollout is complete. All employees within the corporate office, including the large clerical staff, attended a four-day, comprehensive hands-on training program and were told to incorporate the new system into their daily tasks.

The new way business will be conducted after the completion of the rollout will primarily affect the jobs of the clerical staff. It is the company's objective to eliminate most of the jobs held by these individuals. The company anticipates that the new system will enable all management-level personnel to perform their jobs efficiently without significant amounts of clerical support. The Rutledge Company has informed its large clerical staff that most, but not all, of their jobs will disappear once the rollout is complete. The prospect of future unemployment, along with the uncertainty about when jobs will be terminated, has greatly affected staff morale. Complacency, lack of initiative, and complaining have accompanied the loss of morale.

The firm has one additional problem. Some of the clerical staff are long-term employees who are accustomed to the way the company operated 20 years ago. These employees have not adapted to the new system or the other computerized functions that have been implemented. Thus, these employees do not provide the full clerical support needed by management. Rather, they perform only those aspects of their jobs that existed prior to the introduction of computerized systems, plus other menial jobs sufficient to keep them busy.

Individual managers must determine how to motivate all of the clerical support staff for the remaining time that they will be employed, and must also determine how to motivate some employees to use the new system. Someone must also determine which clerical help should be retained once "modernization" is complete. The firm wants to keep all of its clerical staff until then.

Questions

1. What actions should be taken in order to increase the morale and motivation level of the clerical staff?
2. What actions can be taken to motivate those employees who are not using the new technology on the job?
3. What criteria should be used to determine which clerical employees should be retained?
4. Should the firm attempt to solve its motivational problems by conducting further training?

The Awards Meeting

Radio, Inc., is a holding company that owns 20 radio stations located throughout the western provinces. It employs approximately 65 media professionals at its headquarters. The firm has recently been frequently mentioned in the news, with speculations about a buyout. Market analysts' reports and news broadcasts indicate that "the company is for sale." These statements have been circulating for a month now, and insiders know that they are not unfounded. Radio, Inc., is viewed as a cash cow and has been coveted by many outsiders for years because of its large listening audiences.

Earlier this week, the headquarters of Radio, Inc., were visited by the president of a large firm. As he toured the facility, everyone recognized him, and rumours reached a feverish pace. Accountants were asked to prepare current financial statements; that request added fuel to the buyout rumours. Officially, this has all been "hush-hush," but headquarters' staff members have worked many overtime hours to provide the needed information, so there is widespread speculation about the company's intentions. Employee morale is at an all-time low and most employees at headquarters are fearful about their jobs and their future.

Meanwhile, the company's Performance Improvement and Awards Committee is finalizing plans for this year's second-quarter meeting. This committee was created several years ago to promote continuous improvement, to reward individuals for performance excellence, and to plan an off-site meeting each quarter to celebrate employee accomplishments. The first-quarter meeting was a huge success. Awards were presented with great fanfare, and the specific accomplishments of every recipient were cited. Photos of employees at work and play, gathered over the previous six months, were shown. The meeting boosted employee morale and provided incentives for employees to improve performance with hopes of gaining recognition at the next quarterly meeting. Over the years, the committee has created numerous awards that employees cherish. These include:

- People's Choice Award—given to the employee who has an infectiously positive influence on the company and on coworkers. Nominations for the award are made by peers and voted on by management; the recipient is ultimately selected by the Performance Improvement and Awards Committee.
- Fiscal Responsibility Award—given to the employee who implements the program that saved the company the most money. Nominations for the award are made by department heads or middle senior management; the recipient is ultimately selected by the Performance Improvement and Awards Committee.
- Winning Attitude Award—given to the employee who performs both routine and special job tasks with a cheerful "can do" attitude.
- Extra Effort Award—given to the employee who gives extra effort, goes the extra mile, and contributes more than 100 percent to accomplish his or her job.

- Technological Achievement Award—given to the employee who invents and implements a new program or process that uses technology and results in improvements for internal or external customers.
- Out-of-the-Box Award—given to the employee who thinks of innovative, new ways of accomplishing his/her job, or contributes fresh ideas that focus on continuous improvement, or coordinates department efforts that enhance the change process.

Since March, the committee has been preparing for this year's second-quarter event. They rented space in the "Shark Room" at the Marine Science Aquarium for the afternoon, put together a great photo display, ordered a tasty lunch from a well-known catering firm, solicited award nominations, and purchased gifts for the award recipients.

The second-quarter event is scheduled to be held on a Friday. However, on the preceding Wednesday, the president of Radio, Inc., received an attractive buyout offer that she knew the firm's Board of Directors would accept. The details of the sale were expected to be finalized and announced on the same day as the awards banquet. The announcement could not be postponed due to the risk of having confidential information leak out to the public. The president is now faced with the issue of whether the awards meeting should be held.

Questions

1. Should the awards banquet be held as scheduled, or should it be cancelled or postponed?
2. Assuming that the firm is bought out, what can the firm do to retain desirable employees and to enhance employee motivation and morale?

89. INCIDENT

"She's Just a Temp"

A consumer products manufacturing company with 800 employees had more than 100 posted job vacancies, and the facility's Human Resources Department was overrun with applications. In order to process the new applications, the department hired three temporary employees (JoAnn, Jack, and Jill). All three were hired on the same day, and all had adequate job experience to help the human resources staff get through the very intensive 10-week project of handling the applications.

JoAnn was performing her job duties like a real professional. Several members of the permanent staff were impressed by her performance. It was recommended that she be considered for a potential opening created by the promotion of a permanent member of the human resources staff.

Jack also was doing well in his job assignment. However, two weeks into the project, he accepted an offer for a permanent position at another firm. The human resources supervisor called the temporary agency and was sent a qualified replacement the next day.

Jill's performance, in the view of the supervisor, was another story. Halfway through the project, the supervisor felt that Jill's deliberate style was slowing down the process and that a change needed to be made. The supervisor had two options. First, he could counsel Jill on improving her performance. Jill seemed to be well-liked by her coworkers and to fit well in the department. However, the counselling option would take time, and the department had only five weeks to finish processing and sorting the applications. The supervisor's second option was much simpler: to get a replacement from the temporary agency. The supervisor decided on the second option and called the temporary agency with his request. On Friday, the agency called Jill after work and informed her that her assignment ended immediately. On Monday, the agency sent a qualified replacement to finish the project. Other members of the human resources staff were surprised at Jill's termination, since they personally liked her. Staff members questioned Jill's abrupt termination and wanted to know why they had not been informed of it. Some said they would have at least appreciated the chance to say goodbye. The supervisor responded, "She was just a temp."

Questions

1. Were any employee's rights violated in this case? Why or why not?
2. What employee relations fallout might the supervisor have to deal with as a result of Jill's termination?
3. If you were the supervisor, what would you do? How and why?

Original case contributed by Gerald E. Calvasina, Southern Utah University, and Joyce M. Beggs, University of North Carolina at Charlotte.

Alan Garfield

You are the director of the METRO Division of a large manufacturing organization. You have just received the following memo:

Memorandum

To: Director, METRO Division
From: Sales Manager
Subject: Customer Complaints

I am sure that you are well aware that, when you appointed me as sales manager, you emphasized that this was a sales-oriented, customer-oriented business, and you advised me to come straight to you whenever I felt that other departments were not giving sufficient support to our sales staff. We now have such a situation. It seems to be centred on one individual, Alan Garfield, supervisor of our Shipping Department.

The situation is that our customers cannot get their inquiries about shipments answered satisfactorily. We have followed the practice of establishing a direct link between customers and the Shipping Department so that customers can get the fastest and most accurate information possible on the status of their shipments. But when anybody calls with a question or a complaint about a shipment, the people on Garfield's staff always switch the call to him, after which there is an annoyingly long wait. Then Garfield finally gets on the line and gives a complex, detailed explanation of Shipping Department problems, ending with a lecture on customer patience.

As you know, Garfield is an older employee with many years of service in the company, but only three months' experience in the Shipping Department. His previous experience was in the Credit Department, Purchasing, and Mailroom.

When we promoted him to the job last fall, I tried to impress on him the importance of being tactful with complaining customers, but it doesn't seem to have done any good. I would appreciate it if you would remedy this situation as soon as possible, to ensure that our customers get satisfactory service from the Shipping Department.

Questions

1. How difficult do you anticipate it will be to change Garfield's behaviour? Why?
2. What action would you recommend in this situation?
3. What are the advantages and disadvantages of assigning someone else to handle the calls?

Original case contributed by the American Association of Retired Persons (AARP).

91. INCIDENT

Caught in the Act

It was about 1:30 in the morning in the offices of HITEC Corporation, a manufacturer of computer software. Mike Morrison, night supervisor, finally returned to his office to finish up a report. As he began writing, he heard a strange noise coming from the Quality Control Lab down the hall. He knew that no one was assigned to work in the lab at that time, so he walked down to the lab door to see what was happening. After knocking, he opened the door and was stunned to see two of his employees. Jim, a lead supervisor in Maintenance, had his back turned and was pulling up his underpants and pants. Mary, a lead supervisor on one of the production lines, was next to an inspection bench and was likewise pulling up her pants. Mike quickly shut the door and returned to his office, aghast at what had happened. Given the embarrassing nature of the situation, he decided to take no action.

Two weeks later, Teya Simpson, the Human Resource Director, was talking to another lead supervisor when she heard about the incident. Apparently, everyone in the plant knew the story, except top management, because both Jim and Mary had spread the word that they had been "caught in the act."

Teya immediately called Wayne Purdy, plant manager, to see what action, if any, should be taken. Both recognized that the firm had no work rule that specifically covered sexual relationships on the job and that the offence had occurred two weeks ago. On the other hand, both believed that the employees' behaviour was highly unprofessional and noted that both supervisors had left their work areas unattended. Furthermore, they were concerned about the effect that this incident might have on future employee behaviour if no disciplinary action was forthcoming.

Questions

1. What action should the firm take, if any, with regard to Jim and Mary? Justify your answer.
2. What action should the firm take, if any, with respect to Mike? Why?

Writing/Developing Employee Discipline Policies

I. *Objectives:*
   A. To familiarize you with how organizations resolve employee discipline problems.
   B. To allow you practice in writing a model discipline policy statement.
II. *Time required to Complete:* 2 to 3 hours
III. *Instructions:* Go to the library and read four articles that deal directly with one of the topics below, and write a brief summary of the articles. Look for articles that explain how companies handle or should handle these employee problems. (Make sure you include a full bibliography.) When your research is complete, develop a written "model" policy statement for a medium-sized manufacturing company for the topic you selected. Be sure that your statement specifies the rules and disciplinary procedures that apply.

Topics

1. Stealing/Theft/Dishonesty
2. Absenteeism
3. Insubordination
4. Tardiness
5. Alcohol/Drug Abuse
6. Safety Rule Violation
7. Harassment

LABOUR RELATIONS, COLLECTIVE BARGAINING, AND CONTRACT ADMINISTRATION

93. CASE

Union-Organizing at SGA Industries

Introduction

President Ted White sat in his office at SGA Industries thinking about the union representation vote taking place in the plant auditorium. He felt that the company had waged a successful campaign to persuade workers that their best interests would be served only if the company remained non-unionized. As he awaited the results, his mind began to wander back to the events leading up to today's vote.

Background

SGA Industries is best known as a producer of women's hosiery and employs approximately 6,500 people in 10 plants. The company's headquarters is located in Anderson, Ontario. The company's sales subsidiary, SGA, Inc., has 12 offices in major market areas throughout North America and sells its products directly to distributors around the world. The company's strategy of strong identification with the customer has made the SGA name one of the most recognized in the entire hosiery industry.

SGA was founded in 1907 by Sam Gerome Anderson. Anderson built the company and the community was named after him in 1910. Ever since, the fortunes of Anderson residents have been interwoven with those of SGA. Over the years the company has supported the community, donating land and money for churches, schools, and hospitals, and providing jobs for nearly a third of the town's residents. As the years passed, further expansion and product diversification occurred, and the company has gained a reputation as an industry leader in the design, production, and marketing of women's and men's hosiery and undergarments.

After the death of the last Anderson family member, SGA was managed by no fewer than four chief executive officers in less than a dozen years. Then the company was purchased for $250 million by Jack Phillips, a well-known entrepreneur and business leader. Soon after the purchase, Phillips appointed Ted White as president of SGA.

Labour-Management Relations

Over the years, SGA enjoyed a reputation as a steady job provider in an unstable industry. The company provided for its workers and treated them like family members. Many believe that the company's generosity to its employees and the town of Anderson helped to defeat an earlier union-organizing attempt by the International Ladies Garment Workers Union (ILGWU). By a vote of 3,937 to 1,782, the SGA work force decided to remain non-unionized. At the time of the vote, the chairman called it "an expression of confidence by employees." The outcome of the SGA vote was viewed as a severe blow to union organizing efforts.

When Phillips purchased SGA, he announced that his major goals would be to improve the community and to improve the quality of life for SGA employees and their families. Phillips invested over $100 million to reach these goals. The investments included funds for pay increases; new job benefits; capital improvements in factories, including the introduction of robots in the production process; community improvements; and other contributions. These improvements were also accompanied by a shift in management philosophy. The theme of the new management approach was self-sufficiency, and it signalled an end to the benevolent paternalism that had so long characterized employee relations at SGA. Greater emphasis was placed on employee performance and productivity.

During the mid-1980s, the entire hosiery industry had experienced major problems. Growing foreign competition and imports had a negative impact on the profitability of domestic hosiery manufacturers. Many manufacturers attempted to reverse the downturn by making intensive capital investments in new technology, reorganizing company structures, downsizing plants, and instituting programs to improve employee productivity and efficiency. SGA was also affected by these trends. Its international sales fell dramatically from $26 million to $10 million. Faced with increasing imports and weak consumer sales, the company was forced to lay off 1,500 employees, to reduce wage rates, and to rescind many of the perks that the workers had enjoyed under the ownership of the Anderson family. Many of these changes drew worker protests and created a good deal of tension between workers and management.

Wages in the industry had been rising steadily but were still lower than wages in the manufacturing sector in general. In addition, as technology advanced, more skilled workers were required, thus increasing the cost of employee turnover to companies as less skilled workers were laid off or terminated and companies competed to hire skilled workers, who were more difficult to find. Employers in the industry also were becoming increasingly more dependent on women and minorities for employees. At SGA, 40 percent of the employees were women and 35 percent of the total work force were minorities. However, minorities and women made up less than 2 percent of the management staff.

The Election Campaign

Despite the earlier unsuccessful attempt to unionize, the Union of Needletrades, Industrial, and Textile Employees (UNITE), the ILGWU's successor, was back in

Anderson, armed and ready for an organizing effort that would divert the attention of SGA management for several long and tense months.

While many employers learn of union-organizing efforts by their employees only after the Labour Relations Board informs them that an application for certification has been filed, UNITE's efforts to organize SGA employees were clearly out in the open well before then. With a union office in downtown Anderson and a healthy budget, the UNITE organizing team, led by Chris Balog, engaged in one of the most sophisticated union-organizing efforts ever seen in the area. Using computerized direct mailing to stay in touch with workers, as well as extensive radio and television advertising, the unionization campaign at SGA attracted wide attention. Many observers felt that the outcome of UNITE's organizing campaign would have significant implications for the ability of labour unions to gain membership in large companies whose work forces had traditionally been non-unionized.

The Union's Campaign

The campaign issues developed and communicated to workers were, for the most part, predictable. Job security was brought to the front early and was easily introduced to the campaign in the wake of SGA management laying off over 1,500 workers. In addition, increased workloads and reduced wage rates, implemented by SGA in attempting to become more economically efficient in the face of increasing foreign competition, were key issues raised by the union. The union repeatedly accused Phillips of engaging in unfair labour practices by threatening to sell or close the company if the union were to win the right to bargain on behalf of SGA workers. To a certain extent, the UNITE campaign did expand on the traditional wages, hours, and working conditions issues typically raised in organizing efforts. As the campaign progressed, Phillips became a focal point of union rhetoric, and the union attempted to portray Phillips as a greedy and ruthless businessman who was not interested in the long-term survival of SGA and its employees.

Management's Campaign

While Phillips became a focal point of union criticism as the campaign wore on, his role in management's response to the organizing efforts was critical throughout the months preceding the certification vote. With President White leading the anti-union campaign, backed by a sophisticated strategy developed by a law firm specializing in anti-union campaigns, SGA was able to respond quickly to every issue raised by the union.

The SGA strategy to defeat the union-organizing effort included extensive meetings with community, business, and religious leaders in an attempt to influence workers' views about the union. Letters sent to workers' homes, signed by Phillips and White, emphasized the need for team spirit, not only to keep the union out, but to overcome the threat to SGA's business created by imports of foreign-made hosiery. President White put it this way: "We intend to do everything that is proper and legal in this campaign to defeat the union. This is essential if we are to remain competitive in the hosiery business. Every day, we are facing more foreign competition. Not only do our workers understand this, but I think the public does also. We have been able to communicate with our workers in the past, and we don't need a third-party voice. We all must work together as a team. The only way SGA can beat the encroaching foreign competition is to streamline and consolidate our operations."

White and Phillips made repeated visits to the plant to shake hands and listen to workers' concerns. The weekly employee newsletter was filled with anti-union letters written by workers and community members. Late in the campaign, a letter from Phillips was sent to SGA workers explaining why they should vote against the union (see Exhibit 5.4). In response to the union claim that Phillips was attempting to sell the company, Phillips told the workers, "SGA is not for sale, but if I determine that the company cannot operate competitively, I can and I will cease to operate SGA. This is entirely up to me and nobody can stop me—including this union."

Employees' Views

The employees were divided over the union-organizing campaign. Several employees formed an Anti-Union Committee that organized an SGA Loyalty Day. A statement by Terry Floyd, a shift leader, summed up the view expressed by some employees: "We, as employees of SGA, do not feel that it is in the best interest of our company and its employees to be represented by UNITE. Many generations of the same families have worked at this plant; part of our strength is family heritage. A union will destroy that strength. We feel that a union is not needed and that we can work with management as a team." At one rally sponsored by the Anti-Union Committee, "No Union" badges, "Be Wise—Don't Unionize" T-shirts, and "Vote No" hats were worn by several hundred employees.

Others workers expressed support for the union. One worker stated, "We need a union for protection. At least it would give us a voice. Supervisors can be too arbitrary." Others pointed to pay increases and bonuses being awarded to top management while plant workers faced wage cuts and layoffs. Many older employees, who remembered the generosity of the Anderson family, also expressed bitterness toward SGA and worried about their pensions.

Questions

1. What was the impetus for the union-organizing effort at SGA Industries?
2. Discuss SGA's strategy in managing the representation campaign.
3. Look at the definition of "unfair labour practices" in your region's labour relations legislation. Would any of SGA management's actions during the campaign qualify as unfair labour practices under this definition? If there are any, what would be an appropriate response by the Labour Relations Board?

Original case contributed by Dr. Gerald Calvasina, Southern Utah University.

Exhibit 5.4 *Letter to SGA Employees*

To All SGA Employees:

It is only fair for you to know SGA's policy on unions. Our policy is quite simple. We are absolutely opposed to a union at any of our plants. We intend to use every legal and proper means to stay non-union.

As you know, the hosiery industry has been under great pressure and competition from foreign firms. Sales in the industry have dwindled over the past few years, and we are in a poor profit position. Our government has done little to protect your jobs and stop the imports from eroding our sales. Only you and I can save this company and your jobs.

Our whole industry has been forced to modernize our production process to make it more efficient. In fact, you know that many firms have merged together to strengthen their market position. Our company, too, will have to explore the possible advantages of pooling resources and products. In the long run, such a strategy can only benefit employees and management alike. I know bringing in UNITE at this time will only drive up our operating expenses and jeopardize our chances of making such arrangements. Only management has the right to decide how to operate this company. If we find we cannot operate this company profitably, we may be forced to consider other options.

We are convinced that unions have the tendency to create an adversarial relationship between employees and management. Cooperation and teamwork cannot exist in such a hostile environment. It is only through cooperation and teamwork that we will get through the crisis.

No SGA employee is ever going to need a union to keep his or her job. We know that UNITE cannot help this company or you, and it will probably cause us to lose even more of our market and threaten your job security. I urge you—do not vote for the union. Let's all pull together and remember the goodwill of the Anderson family and how it has stood behind you all of these years.

Sincerely,

Jack Phillips

Jack Phillips
Chief Executive Officer

The Frustrated Quality Circle Team

Background

Pearl Press, a large printing firm based in Eastern Canada, operates a number of industrial plants. Ten years ago, the company's human resource manager initiated an innovation in labour-management relations labelled the "Quality of Work Life" program (QWL). The purpose of the innovation was not to replace collective bargaining but to supplement it with a program of employee participation. Therefore, the mission of the program was to improve working conditions in any areas that did not contradict the collective agreement negotiated between Pearl Press and the locals of the Communication, Energy and Paperworkers Union of Canada that represented its workers.

The program was structured around the creation of a "quality team" in each plant. The plant team always included a member of management, a union representative, and two to five union members (depending on the size of the facility). The team met once a week for one hour during the workday to discuss ways of improving working conditions in their own facility. Only those suggestions on which there was total consensus could be put forward as proposals.

Once a consensus on a proposal was achieved, the team wrote up a document detailing the need and/or problem, reasons for the problem, the proposed solution, and the benefits to the plant of implementing the solution. This proposal was then sent to the company's head office. The regional manager in charge of the plant had to approve or disapprove the proposal within seven days. If the proposal was rejected, reasons had to be given and the team could appeal to the company's vice president in charge of operations.

The QWL Program

The newest Pearl Press plant began a QWL program two years ago. The team consisted of a supervisor, a union shop steward, and three union members who had volunteered for the program. Among the proposals on which the team achieved consensus and made recommendations to the regional manager were ceiling fans to improve air circulation, fatigue mats for workers to stand on while operating presses, and a photocopying machine on the shop floor for all workers to use instead of having to take photocopying jobs to the plant's administrative office.

All of these proposals were accepted in writing by the regional manager within the required seven-day period. The team leader was told that the work orders for these three items had been issued. Other proposals such as eliminating time clocks were also considered, but consensus was not achieved on them.

After 10 weeks, the team was becoming frustrated because none of the items that were "on order" had arrived. Team members who had shared their approved recommendations with other workers began to hear complaints that the process was a "farce," "nothing is going to change," and "you guys are wasting your time." Again, the team leader checked with the regional manager and was told everything was "on order."

After four more weeks without results, the team decided to check with the operations vice president, since copies of all paperwork connected with the QWL program were automatically sent to him. The team was told that, as far as the operations vice president was aware, none of the items had been ordered. Other than the initial approval by the regional manager, there was no other paperwork. The team then decided to ask the regional manager for copies of the work orders. They were told that none of the work orders had been kept (even though the company's internal control systems required retention of work orders until the item is received).

The Decisions

By then, the team was extremely frustrated. Two team members suggested simply not meeting again until the approved items were received. Several teams at other Pearl Press plants had done just that as a result of similar frustrations. However, the team eventually decided to use the system rather than abandon it. This meant they would bring the problem to the attention of the operations vice president and hope that the vice president would put pressure on the regional manager to implement the recommendations.

The team spent two weeks discussing how to go about implementing this approach. All members of the team agreed on a course of action, except for the supervisor. The supervisor acknowledged that a problem existed, but he was concerned about the impact a complaint might have on him, as he reported directly to the regional manager and the regional manager evaluated him for the purpose of salary increases and promotions. The supervisor feared that his own promotion prospects and salary increases would be threatened if he signed any statement indicating the regional manager was the cause of the problem. However, since all proposals had to be made by consensus, the supervisor reluctantly agreed to sign the document that accused the regional manager of approving all proposals but not implementing any. It took a lot of pressure from other team members before the supervisor agreed to sign. The team leader then gave the regional manager a copy of this document and sent the original to the operations vice president.

Questions

1. Describe the nature and causes of the problem in this case.
2. How would you explain the regional manager's behaviour? What is his management style? What were his goals and objectives? Why?
3. Given the total situation, how would you evaluate the actions of the local team? Did they handle the situation properly? Did the supervisor make the right decision? Why or why not?
4. If you were the operations vice president, what would you do now? How would you ensure that this type of problem did not recur in this or any other plant?
5. Are innovations in labour-management relations such as QWL programs a passing fad or a permanent part of the labour-management structure?

The Give Back: A Case of Union Busting

Several years ago, Local 974 of the Canadian Auto Workers made significant contract concessions in their negotiations for a collective agreement covering the workers in the North American Tire plant in Mississauga, Ontario. The concessions were made to assist in the company's economic survival and to help the plant to remain open. Now, following a period of great economic prosperity, North American Tire and the union were back at the bargaining table. This time, though, the union was not looking to give back but to receive. The union wanted not only to get back what had been given up in previous negotiations, but also to get their share of the economic prosperity pie that past contract concessions had made possible. However, the company had other goals for negotiations.

The company's initial proposals did not satisfy the union's negotiating team, a strike resulted, and both sides indicated their resolve was strong. While picket lines and demonstrations at the plant were rather uneventful, a war of words was fought in the media. On the one hand, full-page ads appeared in the local papers condemning the company for going back on their word to make up for the "give backs" of the past. On the other hand, the company claimed it needed to maintain its competitive position in an industry undergoing a shakeout of underperforming competitors. North American's parent company Swiss Financial (based in Europe) reported that operating profit rose 20 percent, to $68 million on sales of $1.1 billion, in the most recent quarter. North American's non-unionized plants were operating at capacity, and Swiss Financial had recently announced its purchase of Mexico's largest tire maker.

Negotiations broke down when the union rejected what the company called its best offer. The company stated that the wage rates in its contract proposal were well above average for the geographic area in which the plant was located. However, the union countered that the rates were well below industry standards. In addition, the union filed unfair labour practice charges with the Ontario Labour Relations Board. The union complained that the company was engaging in unfair labour practices, including the company's alleged refusal to bargain over improved medical insurance coverage or to bring its decision-makers to the bargaining table.

Supervisors and clerical employees kept the Mississauga tire plant operating at less than 30 percent of capacity. The company increased production capacity at its other plants, and the union alleged that work usually carried out at the Mississauga plant was being transferred to other plants, which had never happened in the past. The Labour Relations Board appointed a mediator in an attempt to get both sides back to the bargaining table to resume negotiations.

Questions

1. What are the pros and cons of the firm's strategy of continuing production during the strike?
2. Assuming that the firm's goal is to break the union, what are the advantages and disadvantages of this strategy?
3. What standard (industry or geographic) should be used in establishing comparative wage rates?

Original case contributed by Gerald E. Calvasina, Southern Utah University, and Joyce M. Beggs, University of North Carolina at Charlotte.

Collective Bargaining Role Play—Bush Corporation

I. *Objectives:*
   A. To allow you to experience the collective bargaining process.
   B. To help you to understand the skills necessary to successfully nego-
      tiate a union contract.
II. *Out-of-Class Preparation Time:* 2 hours
III. *In-Class Time Suggested:* 45 minutes
IV. *Procedures:*
   A. The instructor will divide the class in half. Each half will be desig-
      nated either as a union team or a management team. There will be
      two simultaneous bargaining sessions (A and B).
   B. Read the description of the situation at Bush Corporation before
      class and familiarize yourself with the current contract and bar-
      gaining issues. Also read the role sheets (union or management)
      provided by the instructor.
   C. Each negotiation team should meet to develop a strategy for
      achieving a favourable agreement. Each team should consider three
      items: (1) degree of flexibility on each provision, (2) issues that are
      most critical, and (3) willingness to take a strike. Teams may meet
      prior to class to develop their strategy.
   D. Your instructor will designate the amount of time for the actual
      bargaining session.
   E. Each team should appoint a chief negotiator and a secretary who
      will complete Form 1, indicating all the issues agreed upon in each
      of the areas under negotiation.

Negotiating Rules

1. At the beginning of the bargaining session, each team's chief negotiator
   should present an opening statement (one minute or less) outlining the
   team's objectives.

2. Each team is allowed two three-minute caucuses during the bargaining session.

3. Each team is required to bargain in good faith and make every effort to
   reach an agreement. Failure to reach an agreement will lead to a strike.

4. Once a settlement is reached on a contract provision, that issue cannot be
   re-opened.

Situation

Bush Corporation is a general aviation and business aircraft firm located in a large
city. The company manufactures aircraft, aircraft parts, avionics, and other aircraft accessories, in addition to providing aircraft maintenance and overhaul
services. The company's major aircraft models—fanjets and propjets—are generally used for business and recreational flying. The company's products have fared
well in a highly competitive market. However, in the first half of the last decade,

there has been a slump in the market for new general aviation aircraft. Industry experts attribute this slump to high aircraft costs and overcapacity in corporate flight departments. Many large corporations are increasingly turning to on-demand charter flights to meet their business flying needs. A combination of weak market demand and high product liability insurance rates have plagued the industry and have forced many companies to cut back production and lay off workers. Economic forecasts indicate that demand may pick up in the latter half of the decade as international sales increase. Top management at Bush is very concerned about keeping labour costs down in order to remain competitive. Last year, the company had to close down one production line and lay off 450 workers for six weeks. The aerospace industry is becoming increasingly automated, and Bush is planning to increase its use of robots in the production process.

Most of Bush's 2,500 production employees are members of the Aerospace, Transportation and General Workers Union of Canada. Historically, the company and the union have had a relatively good relationship, but recently their interactions have become somewhat strained because of the large-scale layoffs last year. While the union is aware of the company's economic situation, it is most concerned with employment security and a better position in terms of benefits. The present three-year contract (see Exhibit 5.5) is set to expire, and contract negotiations are to begin. Union and company bargaining proposals are shown in Exhibit 5.6.

Exhibit 5.5 *Major Provisions of Present Three-Year Contract between Bush Corporation and the Aerospace, Transportation and General Workers Union of Canada*

1. Wages	Average hourly wage	= $21.48
2. Cost-of-living adjustment	Pre-paid increase of 2 percent and 1 cent for each 0.3 point adjustment rise in consumer price index; adjustments made annually	
3. Shift differential	Additional 25 cents/hour for third shift	
4. Overtime	Overtime paid at time and one-half	
5. Layoff notice	Minimum of two weeks notice	
6. Paid sick leave	2 but less than 4 years of service	= 1 day
	4 but less than 6 years of service	= 2 days
	6 but less than 8 years of service	= 3 days
	8 but less than 10 years of service	= 4 days
	10 but less than 25 years of service	= 5 days
7. Vacations	1 but less than 3 years of service	= 1 week
	3 but less than 10 years of service	= 2 weeks
	10 but less than 17 years of service	= 3 weeks
	17 but less than 25 years of service	= 4 weeks
	25 years or more	= 5 weeks
8. Holidays	8 (Christmas Day, Boxing Day, New Year's Day, Good Friday, Victoria Day, Canada Day, Labour Day, and Thanksgiving Day)	
9. Life insurance	$15,000 group life plan; $10,500 accidental death and dismemberment (AD&D)	
10. Health insurance	$250,000 lifetime; company pays 75 percent of extended individual medical coverage	
11. Pensions	The company and the employee will share the cost of Canada Pension Plan contributions; the company will also contribute $30 per month per year of credited service	
12. Union security	All employed by the company who fall under the jurisdiction of the union shall, as a condition of employment, become members of the union at the expiration of the sixty (60) day probationary period	

Exhibit 5.6 *Union and Company Proposals*

Issue	Union Proposal	Company Proposal	Industry Average
1. Wages	$2.00 general wage increase per hour	$1.00 per hour	Average hourly rate $24.00 in aerospace industry (local labour market $20.00 for skilled workers)
2. Cost-of-living adjustment	1 cent increase for each 0.175% rise in inflation rate; adjustments made quarterly	Keep current provisions	1 cent increase for each 0.3% increase in inflation rate; adjustments made quarterly
3. Shift differential	30 cents/hour second shift; 35 cents/hour third shift	Keep current provisions	40 cents/hour for third shift only
4. Overtime	Double time for all hours worked outside of normal assigned shift; time and one-half for Sunday and holiday work	Keep current provisions	All overtime paid at time and one-half
5. Layoff notice	Minimum of four weeks	Keep current provisions	Three weeks
6. Paid sick leave	7 days per year after 10 years of service	Keep current provisions	5 days per year after 10 years of service
7. Vacations	1 year but less than 3 years = 2 weeks 3 years but less than 10 years = 3 weeks 10 years but less than 17 years = 4 weeks Over 17 years = 5 weeks	1 year but less than 3 years = 1 week 3 years but less than 10 years = 2 weeks 10 years but less than 17 years = 3 weeks Over 17 years = 4 weeks	1 year but less than 5 years = 2 weeks 5 years but less than 10 years = 3 weeks Over 10 years = 4 weeks
8. Holidays	Additional 3: Christmas Eve, New Year's Eve, first Friday after Thanksgiving Sunday	Keep current provision	11 holidays
9. Life insurance	$25,000 group life insurance; $12,000 AD&D	Increase AD&D coverage to $11,000	$25,000 Life Insurance; $10,000 AD&D
10. Health insurance	$750,000; company pays 85% of extended individual medical coverage	$500,000; company pays 75% of extended individual medical coverage	$500,000; company pays 90% of extended individual medical coverage
11. Pensions	$34 per month per year of credited service; increase service retirees' monthly benefits by 50 cents for each service year	$30 per year for past service; $32 per year for service after new collective agreement is in effect	$32 per month per year of credited service
12. Union security	Union membership required after 30 days	Keep current provisions	60-day requirement

Other Bargaining Issues Not Covered by Present Three-Year Contract

Management would like to:

A. Include a contract clause to establish a lower-wage structure for new employees beginning in the first year of the new contract. These new employees would have an average hourly rate of $13.50 versus the present average entry rate of $15.50.

B. Establish a joint committee to work toward containment of benefit costs.

The union would like to:

A. Include a contract provision to protect workers affected by new technology. This provision would require Bush to:

   1. Notify the union six months in advance of the purchase or projected introduction of any technological change that would affect employees' jobs or job content.

   2. Provide the union with full information about this new technology and its anticipated effects.

   3. Handle any reduction in work force caused by use of the new technology through normal attrition and turnover.

   4. Not reduce the pay of any employee who is transferred or displaced because of the new technology.

   5. Provide workers with cross-training and retraining for jobs created by the new technology.

   6. Provide employees who cannot be retrained with training for jobs outside of the company and outplacement assistance.

B. Include a contract provision providing for an employee savings plan with a Registered Retirement Savings Plan feature.

Form 1 *Issues Agreed Upon in Each Area*

1. Wages

2. Cost-of-living adjustment

3. Shift differential

4. Overtime

5. Layoff notice

6. Paid sick leave

7. Vacations

8. Holidays

9. Life insurance

10. Health insurance

11. Pensions

12. Union security

13. Other issues

97. EXERCISE

Applying the Canada Labour Code: How Do You Respond?

I. *Objectives:*
    A. To help you understand the application of the Canada Labour Code.
    B. To help you understand rulings associated with complaints made under the Canada Labour Code.

II. *Out-of-Class Preparation Time:* 60 minutes

III. *In-Class Time Suggested:* 45 minutes

IV. *Procedures:*
    A. Read the exercise, review the Canada Labour Code, and complete any additional reading assigned by the instructor.
    B. The class should be divided into groups of four.
    C. Each group should read each of the case incidents that follow and develop responses to each situation.
    D. The instructor may also assign you to review the relevant provincial or territorial labour relations legislation. After doing so, read the case incidents again and develop alternate responses to each situation if your response would be different under the provisions of this legislation.

1. You are the supervisor in a workplace where a union-organizing campaign is being conducted. The application for certification was filed at the start of last month. The manager you report to has told you that, effective immediately, the company will no longer pay overtime to employees involved in travel outside the city on company business, and that, contrary to previous practice, any employees involved in traffic accidents while on company business will now be held liable for the cost of damage to company-owned vehicles.

2. A supervisor in a unionized workplace asks an employee to perform a task. The employee responds that she has not received training for the task, that she has never performed the task in more than 10 years' employment with the company, and that the task is usually performed by individuals in another job classification. She refuses to carry out the task. The supervisor accepts this decision, and informs you, the human resource manager, of these events. As required by company policy, an investigation of the situation automatically commences, and eventually you decide to place demerit points on the employee's record for her refusal to follow the supervisor's directions. The employee then files a grievance stating that she refused the task because of safety concerns and asks for the demerit points to be removed.

3. You are a first-line supervisor in a unionized workplace, where a collective agreement is currently in effect. The collective agreement states that employees who quit are required to give two weeks' notice and will receive any outstanding pay "as soon as possible but in any event no later than on the next regular payday." An employee who quits on a payday is entitled to receive their pay up to the end of that pay period and any remaining pay

on the next scheduled payday. In the last few months, you have been contacted by several former employees who report that the money they are owed after quitting is being paid late (in some cases, three months after quitting), or that unauthorized or unexplained deductions are being taken from their final cheques.

4. As your company's human resource manager, you have been made aware that Mr. Smith, a former employee who was recently terminated, has filed a Labour Relations Board complaint. The complaint alleges that the termination was in retaliation for the employee's refusal to do work that he considered to be unsafe. Smith's employee record shows the following incidents, listed in chronological order:

- Smith wrote rude comments about fellow employees on a record sheet when he was forced to wait to make a delivery; Smith was verbally warned by his supervisor that this was not professional behaviour, and Smith agreed to act more appropriately in the future. Smith now claims that this was not a formal disciplinary meeting as defined in the company's progressive discipline policy.

- Smith argued with his supervisor over the weight of a shipment he was assigned to deliver; Smith contended that the shipment's weight was in excess of the labelled amount and that handling the shipment without mechanical aid would pose a threat to his personal safety. Because of the alleged safety threat, he refused to carry out the assignment. The argument included profane language from Smith directed at the supervisor and a human resource department representative. The supervisor did not request that Smith complete the delivery of the shipment, but instead assigned responsibility for the shipment to another employee. Two days later, Smith was called to a meeting with the supervisor and the human resource department representative and was told that his inappropriate language would not be tolerated and he would be disciplined for this incident. He was given a written warning of a second offence of using "profanities and slanderous words" and an unpaid suspension of two days. A note in Smith's handwriting on the record of the meeting states that Smith does not acknowledge this as a second offence.

- After Smith returned from his suspension, a company mechanic saw Smith park his own vehicle in the company parking lot and then leave the same parking lot five minutes later in a company truck. The mechanic concluded that because of the length of time between these two events, Smith could not have conducted the safety inspection required prior to using a company truck, which usually takes 15 to 30 minutes. The mechanic reported these events to the supervisor and the human resource manager, and Smith was dismissed three days later based on this evidence. The employer stated that the truck had stickers inside the hood indicating that a regular mechanical service was overdue, and Smith had not asked for this service to be performed. The employer took this as evidence that Smith had not inspected the vehicle as required.

Source: Canada Industrial Relations Board cases.

Labour Arbitration

I. *Objectives:*
- A. To familiarize you with the arbitration process.
- B. To give you practice in presenting a case before others.
- C. To examine issues relating to contract administration.

II. *Out-of-Class Preparation Time:* 40–50 minutes

III. *Procedures:* Either at the beginning of or before class, each student should read the exercise. To start the exercise, the instructor will divide the class into the following three groups:
- A. Union representatives (approximately five individuals)
- B. Company representatives (approximately five individuals)
- C. Arbitrators (all remaining participants, divided into groups of three to five members)

The union representatives should meet together and carefully examine "The Union Position" and prepare to argue and defend this position. The company representatives should do the same with reference to "The Company Position." Meanwhile, the arbitrators should read both the union position and the company position and discuss among themselves the arguments for and against each position.

After both the union and company representatives have prepared their position statements, each should present their case to the arbitrators. Each group will be allowed five minutes for their presentation, then an additional five minutes to counter the other group's position.

After all presentations are complete, each group of arbitrators will be given 10 minutes to discuss the case and reach a decision. These decisions should be presented, along with the reasoning behind them, to all participants.

Finally, the instructor may (optionally) present the arbitrator's actual decision in this case.

The Issue

Was the grievant discharged for just cause? The company claimed the employee's negligence of duty resulted in the discharge, and the union claimed poor performance was the issue. If the union is right, what is the appropriate remedy?

Relevant Provisions of the Collective Agreement

Article 1. Purpose of the Agreement.

1.3 The management of the company retains the right to administer the direction of the working force, including the right to plan, direct, and control operations; the right to hire, suspend, transfer, or discharge for just and sufficient cause; the right to relieve employees from duties because of lack of work or for other legitimate business reasons; and the right to introduce new or improved methods or facilities of production; provided, however, that such rights shall not be exercised for the purpose of discriminating against any employee, and that the application of such rights shall not conflict with the provisions of this agreement.

Article 33. Discipline and Discharge.

33.1 In cases of poor job performance, the following procedure dealing with discipline will be accomplished with written notification to the Union:

a. Formal written warning in the first instance with copy to the employee.

b. In subsequent instances, formal written warning and/or suspension without pay for a period not to exceed five working days.

c. After three or more instances, any one of which results in a suspension within any two-year period, discharge for just cause will be accomplished.

33.1.1 For purposes of this article, evaluation of job performance shall include consideration of the following factors:

a. Attendance record, including absenteeism, tardiness, and proven abuse of sick leave.

b. Adherence to industrial safety rules.

c. Adherence to Company house rules.

d. Ability to perform assigned tasks satisfactorily.

33.2 In cases of personal misconduct, the disciplinary action taken, including discharge, will be consistent with the gravity of the offence.

Background

The individual in question was employed as a service technician for the ABC Petroleum/Gas Company from August 1999 to April 2003. On January 26, 2003, this employee was dispatched to the residence of a customer who reported a strong gas odour. The service report completed by this employee showed that he spent 26 minutes on the call, that no leaks were found, and that no repairs were made. The employee did not perform a pressure/manometer test.

Later that same day, in response to a second call, another technician was sent to the customer's home. The second technician checked the gas tank and gauge readings, added some gas, used the track, and did the pressure/manometer test. He tested the lines and identified the source of the gas odour as a leak in the heater connector of the shutoff valve on the heater. The leak was located less than 60 cm (2 ft.) from the pilot light on the water heater; the pilot light was lit. The second technician replaced the heater connector and put the old one in the back of his truck. Subsequently, the employee's immediate supervisor talked with the second technician and examined the damaged heater connector. On January 28, 2003, the supervisor met with the first technician and informed him that he was being suspended, pending an investigation. The reason for the suspension was "Negligent in responding to report of gas odour on January 26, failure to perform leak investigation according to company procedures, leaving party with hazardous condition." The employee was notified by letter on April 16, 2003, that he was being terminated based on the company's findings indicating that "the incident was of such a serious nature that we would be remiss in continuing your employment as a technician."

The Company's Position

The company contends that the employee failed to follow normal procedures necessary to determine whether there was a gas leak, and that leaving the customer in a hazardous condition constituted just cause for discharge. The employee's failure to find or repair the gas leak was not poor performance but negligence of duty. The company defined "poor performance" as involving a lack of skills or intelligence, and contended that the employee's behaviour was not caused by a lack of skills or innate inability. The company specifically refers to Article 1.3 of the collective agreement, which permits the company to discharge an employee for "just cause," and states that under Article 1.3 no prior warnings are required. The company also noted in its presentation that the employee had been previously suspended for five days in 2000, and that he has been reprimanded on numerous occasions for various infractions.

The Union's Position

The union contends that the employee should have been disciplined under Section 33.1 for poor job performance. The union contends that the employee performed three of the four tests usually performed and that, at worst, used poor judgment in not pressure-testing the system. Further, the union contends that the company failed to give the employee adequate notice of the rule or the consequences of his action. The employee did not know that he could be discharged for negligence in performance of his duties. Further, the union claimed that the company did not conduct a proper investigation and relied solely on the evidence in the report written by the second technician sent to the customer's home. The company made no attempt to visit the job site to determine firsthand if the employee had followed company rules.

Original case contributed by Dr. Gerald Calvasina, Southern Utah University.

99. SKILL BUILDER

Communications with Employees during Certification Campaigns

I. *Objectives:*
  A. To give you practice in preparing an effective and legal company communication to employees during a certification campaign.
  B. To help you understand the practical application of the relevant labour legislation.

II. *Time Required to Complete:* 1 hour

III. *Instructions:* Your company, Fruit Canners, Inc., has recently become aware that the United Food and Commercial Workers Union is attempting to convince employees in your plant to sign a petition supporting an application for certification. Management is somewhat surprised by the campaign because employee relations have generally been good. Prepare a one-page letter to be sent to all plant employees stating the company's position on the union drive and the company's desire to remain non-union. Be certain that the content of your letter does not violate the provisions of the relevant provincial or territorial labour legislation.

Original case contributed by Dr. Gerald Calvasina, Southern Utah University.

Human Resource Audits/
Term Assignments

Part 6

Human Resource System Evaluation

I. *Objective:* To help you critically analyze a human resource management system, identify problems, and recommend constructive improvements.
II. *Out-of-Class Preparation Time:* 30–40 hours per group
III. *In-Class Time Suggested:* none, unless an oral report is required by the instructor
IV. *Procedures:* In groups of two to three people, you should identify a real organization and receive permission from management to study the organization. Once permission is received, your group should arrange to interview as many of the following as possible: the executive in charge of human resource management; employees performing human resource management functions; employees performing different functions at different levels in the organization; and labour union officials (if any). Optionally, instead of completing the entire Human Resource System Evaluation outlined here, the instructor could assign only specific sections to a given student group.
V. *General Purpose:* The study will focus on the selected organization's human resources and employee relations objectives, structures, policies, practices, and selected administrative problems. It will give you the opportunity to learn firsthand about the management of human resource systems in actual organizations. It will also provide you with the opportunity to develop field research methodologies and evaluation skills that should prove beneficial in future academic and professional assignments. Finally, for the organization cooperating with each of the student projects, the results of these studies should be helpful in future efforts to improve the efficiency and effectiveness of its human resource systems.

The final product of this study will be a comprehensive written report to be submitted no later than one week before the end of the term. Each of you should assume the stance of an outside consultant who has been called in to evaluate the human resource system of the particular organization. At a minimum, the paper should reflect the items contained in the Evaluation Guide that follows. Alternatively, your instructor may permit each group to focus on one or a few selected parts of the organization's human resource system.

Evaluation Guide

I. **The Organization and Its Mission**
   A. When and why was this organization established?
      1. Under what statutory or legal authority was it created?
      2. What are the principal needs and objectives that the organization is designed to fulfill?
   B. What are the structural components of the organization?
      1. How is the organization structured to carry out its objectives?

2. Where is the focus of decision-making authority for carrying out these objectives?
   a. How centralized or decentralized is the decision-making process with respect to
      i. organizational planning?
      ii. operational management?
   b. What is the relationship between the leadership of this organization and
      i. elected public officials?
      ii. other public officials?
      iii. leaders in the private sector?
      iv. representatives of employee organizations or associations, if any?
      v. professional and technical staff?
3. What budgetary constraints confront the organization?
   a. What are the sources of revenue for this company?
      i. for capital expenditures?
      ii. for operating expenditures?
   b. What changes have occurred in the organization's budget in recent years?
      i. Have there been any noticeable increases or decreases in revenues or profits?
      ii. Have there been any new sources of funding?
      iii. Have any old sources of funding been reduced or eliminated?
      iv. How have these trends affected management of the organization?
4. What is the total number of employees in the organization?
   a. How are these employees distributed throughout the organization?
      i. by department or operational function?
      ii. by skill, e.g., managerial, professional, technical, clerical, skilled craftsperson, semiskilled operatives, unskilled labourers?
      iii. by location, if there are multiple places of business?
   b. What have been some of the noticeable employment trends in recent years?
5. Does the organization operate overseas? If so, where?
C. What are the major problems and opportunities confronting this organization? Up to this point, how has the organization responded to these challenges?
D. Does the organization have a strategic management plan, including goals, objectives, and timetables?
E. What recommendations do you have for the organization (if any) for any problems you have identified in this area, and what effect do you believe these recommendations will have if implemented?

II. **The Role of the Human Resource Function**
   A. Does this organization have a formal and identifiable human resource function (department)?

1. When was this department or function formally established, and why was it established?
2. How is the human resource function or department organized to carry out the objectives of the organization?
3. How many individuals are directly associated with the human resource function or department?
4. What are the academic and employment backgrounds of those involved in the function or department?
5. If there is no formal and identifiable human resource function (department), why, and how are human resource functions carried out?

B. Where is the decision-making authority for human resource matters located within the company?
   1. Who establishes the objectives and policies related to human resource matters?
   2. What is the relationship between those responsible for the human resource functions and those responsible for other operations of the organization in the administration of human resource policies and practices?

C. To what degree has the human resource function used information technology to manage information?

D. To what degree is the Internet used in the human resource function? How is it used?

E. What is the perceived importance within the organization of the human resource function, in comparison to other organizational functions?

F. Does the human resource function provide support for operations in foreign countries? What problems or challenges does this present?

G. What recommendations do you have for the organization (if any) for any problems you have identified in this area, and what effect do you believe these recommendations will have if implemented?

III. Employment Decisions
   A. To what degree is human resource management integrated into the strategic management of the organization? How is it integrated?
   B. Who is responsible for human resource planning and forecasting for the organization?
      1. What methods are used to determine staffing needs?
      2. Does the organization focus primarily upon short-run or long-run human resource needs, or both?
      3. Are job analyses conducted and job descriptions developed for each position in the organization? How often are they updated, and how extensively?
      4. What specific problems have been encountered in the human resource planning process, and what are their causes?
      5. If no human resource planning is done:
         a. Why not?
         b. Has the lack of human resource planning had any negative impact on the organization?

6. Does the organization provide career planning and career counselling for employees? Why or why not?

C. Once staffing needs are established, what procedures are utilized for filling job vacancies?

1. Who is responsible for staffing the organization—the human resource department or the respective functional departments?
2. What methods are used to recruit new employees?
3. What methods and criteria are used for evaluating and selecting job applicants? Have these methods been validated, and, if so, how?
4. To what extent are new employee recruitment, evaluation, and selection procedures aided or restricted by
   a. established policies or practices of the organization?
   b. provisions of employment legislation?
   c. factors associated with local labour markets?
5. Does the organization seek to fill existing job vacancies from among present employees or by recruiting new employees? If a preference exists, why?
6. To what degree do staffing practices address the acquisition of employees with the skills, knowledge, and abilities necessary to successfully implement the strategic goals of the organization?
7. To what degree does the organization support a goal of diversity in the workplace? How does it demonstrate this support?
8. What does the organization do to enhance work-family balance for its employees?

D. What recommendations do you have for the organization (if any) for any problems you have identified in this area, and what effect do you believe these recommendations will have if implemented?

IV. Determination of Working Conditions and Rewards

A. Is an occupational classification system utilized by the organization?

1. Who is responsible for determining the classification system?
2. What are the basic features of this system?
   a. Does the classification system appropriately reflect variations in job skills?
   b. Is it used as a mechanism for identifying career paths, and, if so, how?
   c. Have there been any recent reviews and evaluations of the performance of the classification system in relation to organizational and staffing goals? If so, what has been the outcome of the review or evaluation?

B. How are wage and salary levels and annual improvements determined?

1. Does the organization conduct periodic internal and external wage surveys?
2. Are salary levels adequate to enable the organization to attract and maintain an effective work force? Why or why not?
3. Do differentials in salary grades appropriately reflect differentials in skills and responsibilities?
4. Are large proportions of employees grouped into particular salary grade levels?

5. How do salary levels compare with those of similar organizations for comparable occupational or experience groupings?
6. Does the current reward system adequately reward employees with the requisite knowledge, skills, and abilities to successfully implement the goals of the strategic plan?
7. What trends have taken place in salary levels over the past few years?
8. To what degree is incentive compensation used, and, if used, in what areas?

C. What methods are used for evaluating employees for the purpose of determining their effectiveness and/or awarding any salary increases?
1. Do employee performance appraisal systems actually reflect job performance? Why or why not?
2. How adequate or inadequate are the performance appraisal methods currently being used? Why?
3. Do these systems or methods incorporate the knowledge, skills, and abilities needed to successfully implement the department's or organization's strategic goals?

D. What non-wage benefits are available?
1. How are these benefits determined?
2. Are these benefits available to all employees? If not, how is eligibility determined?
3. How do these benefits compare with those offered at similar organizations?
4. Have they changed in recent years? Will they change in the future, and, if so, how?

E. Has the organization introduced any special programs or activities to improve health and safety conditions on the job?

F. What does the organization do to maintain or improve employee morale and job satisfaction?

G. Does the organization provide for flexible work options such as telecommuting or job sharing? Please provide details.

H. To what degree is outsourcing used? If it is used, in what functional areas is it used, and why? Does the organization have any plans to change its use of outsourcing, and, if so, why?

I. What retirement options are currently offered? Are they expected to change in the future, and, if so, how?

J. What recommendations do you have for the organization (if any) for any problems you have identified in this area, and what effect do you believe these recommendations will have if implemented?

V. Employee Training and Development
A. Has the organization supported programs for employee training and development? Why or why not?
1. If programs exist, what kinds of programs have been established? Have they been oriented toward
   a. job skills?
   b. supervisory and leadership skills?
   c. basic educational skills?

       d. knowledge, skills, and abilities necessary for strategic goal attainment?

       e. any other goals or outcomes?

    2. How do these programs relate to the organization's strategic and operational objectives?

    3. Does the organization maintain its own training staff, or are outside organizations, individuals, or programs used for training purposes?

    4. What proportion of employees have participated in training and development programs supported by the organization?

    5. Does the organization provide any incentives for employees to undertake job-related training and development activities not supported by the organization?

B. To what extent has an employee's participation in the organization's training and development programs been used in making decisions related to promotions and transfers within the organization?

    1. Are promotion decisions based primarily upon the measured and observed abilities of employees, upon their seniority in the job, or upon other criteria? What is the rationale for using these decision criteria?

    2. Are promotion decisions based partly on an employee's willingness to take advantage of development opportunities?

C. What recommendations do you have for the organization (if any) for any problems you have identified in this area, and what effect do you believe these recommendations will have if implemented?

VI. Employee Frictions

A. What methods and procedures are available for resolving employee complaints and grievances?

    1. How many of these grievances are filed on average (on a yearly, quarterly, or monthly basis)? Are there any factors that affect the number of grievances?

    2. What types of complaints are reflected in these grievances? What is the most common type of complaint?

    3. Has the number of grievances been growing or declining in the past few years? If so, why? Has there been any noticeable change in the types of complaints?

B. Have there been many employee discipline problems?

    1. Are there clearly spelled-out formal procedures within the organization for handling discipline cases? If so, what are they?

    2. How often are employees disciplined or discharged?

       a. What are the most common reasons for this action being taken by the organization?

       b. Does the organization have a procedure that must be followed prior to the decision to dismiss an employee? If so, what is it?

C. To what extent have employee tardiness, absenteeism, and turnover been problems?

    1. What are the most common reasons for these problems occurring? Has the organization conducted any research to determine the causes?

2. What steps have been taken to resolve these problems, if they exist?

D. Have any of the employees sought to unionize for the purpose of engaging in collective bargaining over such issues as wages, hours, and working conditions?

    1. Why have, or have not, such organizing activities taken place?

    2. What is the official position of the organization toward acceptance or rejection of unionism for its employees?

    3. If a labour union is certified as the bargaining agent for employees of this organization, what effect has the presence of the union had upon

        a. overall decision-making within the organization?

        b. the efficiency and productivity of the organization?

        c. the administration of the human resource function?

        d. the relations between the managers of the organization and its non-managerial or unionized employees?

        e. the interpersonal relationships among non-managerial employees?

E. How would the relationship between management and the union be characterized (e.g., cooperative; neutral; cold; hostile)?

    1. Have there been any noticeable recent changes in the nature of this relationship? Why or why not?

    2. Have there been any work stoppages among employees in order to pressure management into agreeing to union demands?

        a. What were the issue(s) leading to the stoppages?

        b. Why did the issue(s) develop?

        c. How was the dispute resolved?

        d. What has been its subsequent impact upon

            i. the operation of the company?

            ii. employee performance?

            iii. the work environment?

            iv. the organization's decision-making process?

F. What recommendations do you have for the organization (if any) for any problems you have identified in this area, and what effect do you believe these recommendations will have if implemented?

VII. Summary and Evaluation

A. Is the human resource function of this organization contributing to the fulfillment of the organization's mission, objectives, and strategic plan? Is it making an effective contribution? Why or why not?

B. What human resource management problems have been adequately solved or are now in the process of being solved by the organization?

C. Are there major human resource problems that remain to be confronted and solved? If so, what are they?

D. What would appear to be among the most desirable solutions to these problems? Provide specific detail and justification for your recommendations.

101. TERM PROJECT

Human Resource Manager Interview

I. *Objectives:*
  A. To analyze the role of human resource managers in organizations.
  B. To allow you to gain a better understanding of the nature of a human resource manager's job.
  C. To help you understand the interface between human resource and line managers.
II. *Out-of-Class Preparation Time:* 8–10 hours
III. *In-Class Time Suggested:* none, unless instructor wants an oral report
IV. *Procedures:*
  A. This assignment is to be done individually by each student.
  B. Locate a human resource manager to interview. You may select a human resource generalist or a human resource specialist. After the manager understands the research project and agrees to cooperate, conduct the interview. The interview should take about 45 minutes to one hour.
  C. If possible, also interview a line manager or supervisor in the same organization to gain his or her views of the human resource management function.
  D. A suggested interview outline is given (Exhibit 6.1) for the questions to be asked. You are expected to prepare additional questions. Your instructor may ask you to submit the final interview questions, along with the name of the organization and manager you will interview, for approval prior to your conducting the actual interview. Additionally, you should gather research information on the company before the interview.
  E. Prepare a written report (8–10 pages) summarizing the results of the interviews, including:
    1. a description of the overall operations and role of the human resource department;
    2. a description of the human resource function you explored in depth;
    3. the type of interaction between human resource and line managers or supervisors;
    4. the extent to which the organization's human resource management practices conform to theoretical prescriptions. If differences between theory and practice are found, discuss why they exist.

Exhibit 6.1   *Interview Outline*

Part I: Organization Information

  a. Type of business/industry/organization
  b. General description of company's products/services/operations
  c. Brief company history

d. Overall number of employees and number of employees in each general occupational classification (e.g., managerial, clerical, skilled trades)
   e. Organizational structure
   f. Size and structure of the human resources department

Part II: Background of the Human Resource Manager

   a. Title
   b. Academic qualification (highest degree earned and field of study)
   c. Years with organization
   d. Years of human resource management experience
   e. Other work experience
   f. Current membership in professional associations/organizations

Part III: Human Resource Management Functions

Ask the human resource manager to check off and rate the human resource activities listed in Form 1.

Part IV: Role of Human Resources Department

Ask the human resource manager the following general questions:
   a. What is the role of the human resource department in your organization?
   b. To what extent is the human resource department involved in strategic business planning? Explain the nature of the involvement.
   c. In your opinion, what are some of the most pressing human resource issues faced by organizations today? Why?
   d. What was the most difficult organizational problem faced by your human resource department in the last five years? How was it resolved? In retrospect, would you have addressed the problem differently, and, if so, how?

Part V: In-Depth Review of Human Resource Management (HRM) Function

Explore one of the HRM functions in depth with the human resource manager (for example: recruiting, selection/staffing, compensation, training and development, performance evaluation). You should first review the material in the text on the human resource function you choose, and then prepare a set of questions for the manager relating to how that function is carried out in the organization. During the interview, be sure to obtain enough information on how the function is developed and administered so you can describe the function in detail in your written report. Ask the manager to comment on the effectiveness of the function and of his or her interaction with line managers or supervisors in carrying out the function. Try to obtain examples of any forms and/or materials used in developing or administering the function.

Part VI: Interaction with Line Managers or Supervisors

Once you have interviewed the human resource manager, also interview one of the line managers or supervisors in the organization. The purpose of this interview is to understand the way in which the human resource function interacts with other functions in the organization. Ask the manager or supervisor:
   a. To rate the activities listed in Form 2.
   b. To explain what is done by the human resources department to support them in their position.
   c. To explain what they "ideally" expect from the human resources department to help them in performing their job.

Form 1 *Form for Ranking of Human Resource Activities by Human Resource Manager*

Instructions: Place a check mark next to those human resource activities that are part of your responsibility, and indicate the importance of these responsibilities in your position, using a scale of 1 (very important) to 5 (not very important).

Human Resource Activities   **Importance**

____ 1. Ensure fair and consistent implementation of human resource policies and procedures.   _____

____ 2. Advise and counsel managers and/or supervisors on employee problems.   _____

____ 3. Design appropriate staffing and recruiting policies and programs.   _____

____ 4. Assist in interviewing, selecting, and hiring of employees.   _____

____ 5. Design and implement performance evaluation system(s).   _____

____ 6. Administer compensation and benefit programs.   _____

____ 7. Ensure compliance with legislation governing employment practices.   _____

____ 8. Counsel employees on job-related and/or personal problems.   _____

____ 9. Develop and maintain employee records and record-keeping systems.   _____

____10. Develop employment equity or diversity policy and communicate policy to all managers.   _____

____11. Ensure compliance with safety and health standards.   _____

____12. Oversee administration of employee grievance procedures.   _____

____13. Provide state-of-the-art solutions to employee relations problems.   _____

____14. Plan for future human resource needs.   _____

____15. Work with top management on human resource implications of business plans and strategies.   _____

____16. Design and implement employee training and career development programs.   _____

____17. Negotiate the collective agreement.   _____

____18. Administer and enforce provisions of the collective agreement.   _____

____19. Manage work-life programs.   _____

____20. Other (write in).   _____

Form 2 *Form for Ranking of Human Resource Activities by Line Manager or Supervisor*

Instructions: Here is a list of typical activities performed by human resources departments. Please indicate the importance to you of the activities performed by the human resources department in your organization, using a scale of 1 (very important) to 5 (not very important).

Human Resource Activities	**Importance**
1. Ensure fair and consistent implementation of human resource policies and procedures.	_____
2. Advise and counsel managers and/or supervisors on employee problems.	_____
3. Design appropriate staffing and recruiting policies and programs.	_____
4. Assist in interviewing, selecting, and hiring of employees.	_____
5. Design and implement performance evaluation system(s).	_____
6. Administer compensation and benefit programs.	_____
7. Ensure compliance with legislation governing employment practices.	_____
8. Counsel employees on job-related and/or personal problems.	_____
9. Develop and maintain employee records and record-keeping systems.	_____
10. Develop employment equity or diversity policy and communicate policy to all managers.	_____
11. Ensure compliance with safety and health standards.	_____
12. Oversee administration of employee grievance procedures.	_____
13. Provide state-of-the-art solutions to employee relations problems.	_____
14. Plan for future human resource needs.	_____
15. Work with top management on human resource implications of business plans and strategies.	_____
16. Design and implement employee training and career development programs.	_____
17. Negotiate the collective agreement.	_____
18. Administer and enforce provisions of the collective agreement.	_____
19. Manage work-life programs.	_____
20. Other (write in).	_____